# Acknowledgements

Additional text: Wayne Van Dien, Chris Halla

Art Direction, Design and Production: Frank Seiy

Printing and Separations: Graphic Associates

First published in 1989 by Harley-Davidson Motor Company, P.O. Box 653, 3700 W. Juneau Avenue, Milwaukee, Wisconsin 53208 U.S.A. Revised and updated 1991 and 2002.

The information in this book is true and complete to the best of our knowledge. All recommendations are made without any guarantee on the part of the author or the publisher, who also disclaim any liability incurred in connection with the use of this data or specific details.

Library of Congress Cataloging-in Publication Data available.
Bolfert, Thomas C.
     The Big Book of Harley-Davidson: Official Publication by Harley-Davidson Motor Company;
     Thomas C. Bolfert - Centennial Edition
     ISBN 0-7603-1446-2

Book Trade Distribution by Motorbooks Intl.
St. Paul, MN  55082
To order: 1-800-458-0454

# THE BIG BOOK
# OF HARLEY-DAVIDSON.

Official Publication by
Harley-Davidson Motor Company

— **Centennial Edition** —

# THE BIG BOOK OF

# HARLEY-DAVIDSON®

## — Centennial Edition —

Official Publication by
Harley-Davidson
Motor Company

Thomas C. Bolfert

# TABLE OF CONTENTS

**Introduction**......................Page 10

**Preface**.................................Page 14

Part I
**Chapter 1 - The 1900'S**........Page 17
An Idea Becomes Reality.

**Chapter 2 - The 1910'S**........Page 45
Harley Goes To War.

**Chapter 3 - The 1920'S**........Page 81
Roaring Into The Twenties.

# TABLE OF CONTENTS

# INTRODUCTION

The Building looms behind a tiny shopping center, a towering monument to the great manufacturing might of Milwaukee. Rising six stories high, this massive red brick structure, surrounded by a residential area, is the main headquarters of an internationally known success story called Harley-Davidson, Inc.

While many of the area's great corporate names of the past have either closed their doors or moved to gentler climates, Harley-Davidson has stayed in this industrial center of the Midwest and has not only weathered the ravages of Wisconsin winters and economic downturns, but has emerged stronger and healthier than ever before.

At first glance, the building—in fact, the entire complex—looks old; and it is. Harley-Davidson has been headquartered at this Juneau Avenue site since 1906, only a block away from its 1903 birthplace. Having gone through numerous expansion programs, the main building attained its current configuration in 1918. An adjacent building, erected a short time later, currently houses Harley-Davidson University and the corporate Archives.

The image the building portrays, like that of the company itself, is deceptive. Instead of being a decaying symbol of America's declining industrial strength, it is rock solid, the end result of years of updating and modernizing. No dingy, grime-encrusted bricks here. The walls of Harley-Davidson are deep red with gleaming white mortar joints. Brand new, steel-sash windows have replaced the earlier wooden-framed windows with blacked-out glass dating back to World War II.

The main lobby also denies the age of the building. Replaced are the institutional metal walls and tile floors of years past. The lobby of Harley-Davidson exudes warmth and welcome. A black slate floor and gray carpet leads to the reception area, where visitors are greeted by both the past and present of America's sole remaining domestic motorcycle manufacturer. Under muted lighting and raised on pedestals are a current production-year motorcycle, and an impeccably restored original from the very first years of the company's existence. Adorning the walls are tastefully-framed portraits of the four founders, one Harley and a trio of Davidsons, plus early photos of the plant.

Inside, the offices of Harley-Davidson are simple and functional. Even those of the corporate officers are small and comfortable, decorated with personal momentos and keepsakes, rather than sprawling penthouses decorated with power trophies. Everywhere throughout the company, employees' offices and work areas are liberally decorated with articles closest to their hearts, or funnybones. Each area has its own personality, reflecting the interests and humor of each employee.

And, of course, Harley-Davidson memorabilia is everywhere. Mountains of it. Employees wear shirts, jackets, belts, buckles, sunglasses, and sweaters with Harley-Davidson logos to work everyday. Walls, doors and file cabinets

# THE 1900'S

## An Idea Becomes Reality.

# THE 1900'S

While the motorcycle is generally regarded as a product of the Twentieth Century, its origins actually go back all the way to the late 1700s, when the steam engine was being developed as a source of power. As early as 1785, William Murdock—a pupil of James Watt, inventor of the steam engine—built what was called a steam tricycle. In 1868, an early pioneering effort called the Austin velocipede marked the mating of a steam engine to a two-wheeled vehicle. This was also attempted later in 1884 by two Californians, L.D. and W.E. Copeland. Like Murdock's tricycle, these proved unsuccessful. Over the decades, many other inventors experimented with steam-powered vehicles with little success.

By the late 1800s, when the gasoline engine was going through the same formative period as the steam engine did a century earlier, a Frenchman by the name of Delamare-Deboutteville produced what is generally regarded as the first motor-driven tricycle, utilizing a carburetor which he patented in 1884. While it marked the first successful mating of a gasoline engine to a tricycle chassis, the contraption apparently was never produced on any scale and slipped into obscurity.

Carl Benz of Mannheim, Germany, later of Mercedes-Benz fame, developed a gasoline tricycle about the same time and actually patented it in 1885. His invention was not a commercial success, either.

Gottlieb Daimler, a German contemporary of Deboutteville and Benz, was also developing a gasoline-powered machine at this time, but his was two-wheeled. Propelled by a half-horsepower motor, Daimler's wooden-wheeled invention was successfully ridden for the first time on November 10, 1885 and marked the inauspicious beginning of the true motor bicycle or motorcycle, as it was later called.

Whether unable to see the practical application of his remarkable invention, despite earning a U. S. patent for it in 1885, or perhaps occupied with other interests, Gottlieb Daimler produced that one and only machine. He died in 1899, unaware of the future of the sport he had pioneered.

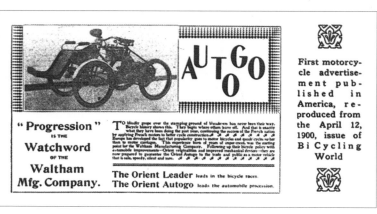

First motorcycle advertisement published in America, reproduced from the April 12, 1900, issue of BiCycling World

# THE FIRST MOTORCYCLE

Gottlieb Daimler, of Wurtemberg, Germany, is generally regarded as the inventor of the first gasoline powered motorcycle, taking his inaugural ride on November 10, 1885. From that humble beginning over a century ago, a sport and industry sprang into being. Hundreds of makers worldwide began producing well over a thousand different models of motorcycles, capturing the minds, hearts and imagination of tens of millions of devotees and enthusiasts.

Daimler's invention bore little resemblance to the motorcycles of today, other than it was a two-wheeled vehicle and even that was subject of interpretation. Evidently harboring some doubts regarding the stability of his creation, Daimler outfitted it with rather large outrigger or trundle wheels to keep it from falling side ways.

This grandfather of motorcycles sported a springless wooden frame with a vertical fork and iron-tired wooden wheels, topped by a padded saddle. The motor was a half-horsepower, single-cylinder affair with a thin metal jacket surrounding the cylinder. Air was forced around the cylinder by a fan on the crankshaft to provide cooling for the tiny powerplant. Final drive was achieved by means of a flat leather belt, tensioned by an idler pulley.

Gottlieb Daimler's motorized velocipede was crude by today's standards, and few, if any, of his concepts are still in use in their original form. However, many of his ideas formed the basics of early motorcycles and were used throughout the first decades of motorcycle building. Of course, from those humble beginnings grew the motorcycles we're all familiar with today.

Interestingly, while motorcycles have progressed so far since Daimler's invention, they really haven't changed all that much; they've just become more sophisticated. Today's motorcycle still has two wheels, a front fork with handlebars, and a frame cradling an engine with a seat above it. The basic concepts are still sound. It is the execution that makes the modern motorcycle what it is.

Popular music and advertising provided evidence of the interest in motorized transportation

You have only to say

## Warwick

and the riding public know what you mean.

THE BUILT-ON-HONOR WARWICK QUALITY IS ALWAYS THERE.

VERMILION.   Weight, 98½ Lbs.

## Warwick Motor Cycle

Cannot be beaten climbing hills or wading through sand.

PLENTY OF ENERGY ALL THE TIME.

MODEL 95.   PRICE, $50.

## Warwick Bicycles

A FULL LINE.

$25.00 Buys a Good Men's Wheel.
$35.00 Buys a Better Men's Wheel.
$50.00 Buys the Best Men's Wheel.
$30.00 Buys our Women's Wheel.

SEND FOR CATALOGUE.

WARWICK CYCLE & AUTOMOBILE CO.,

**I**nterestingly, there was little advancement in the development of the motorcycle prior to 1900, despite the efforts of Daimler and the others. Instead, it was paced bicycle racing that was the rage in the closing years of the Nineteenth Century. As speed records for human-powered bicycles inched higher and higher, it was felt that men simply could not go much faster under their own power. Gradually, bicycle builders began thinking again of combining the rapidly developing gasoline engine with the bicycle frame to reduce effort and increase speed. Toward that end, by 1900 about a dozen companies were building motor bicycles in the United States, and the sport was born.

While motorcycling was still in its infancy, another sport was too: major league baseball

England's Queen Victoria was featured on cigar bands, along with other notables of the time.

City Hall, Milwaukee, as seen from East Water Street and what is now Wisconsin Avenue.

WILLIAM S. HARLEY                    ARTHUR DAVIDSON, SR.

Enter 21-year-old William S. Harley and his next door neighbor and friend since boyhood, 20-year-old Arthur Davidson. The two young men worked at the same Milwaukee manufacturing company, Harley as an apprentice draftsman and Davidson as a pattern maker. Like many of their contemporaries--the great automotive pioneers— they were hobby designers, ever tinkering to put their designs to practical use, while people around them just shrugged their shoulders. One idea they had was to produce a motor-driven bicycle for their own personal use, since a motor obviously removed much of the work from cycling. Fortunately, a German draftsman who knew something of early European motorcycles and the DeDion gasoline engine also worked at the same firm.

Using the German's special knowledge, Harley's earlier experience in building bicycles and Davidson's patterns for a small air-cooled gasoline engine, they spent their evenings experimenting in a basement workshop. Finances were modest, and the tools they worked with were unsophisticated. The friends built their first motorcycle in 1902, an under-powered affair that was essentially a bicycle with a small motor to propel. They weren't satisfied with their creation and began work on an improved version with a more powerful motor designed by Bill Harley. Work progressed into the next year. That is, it progressed as far as it could without the help of a skilled mechanic.

Arthur Davidson's brother, Walter, was just such a skilled mechanic, then working as a railroad machinist in Parsons, Kansas and soon due in Milwaukee for the wedding of a third Davidson brother, William. So Arthur Davidson wrote to Walter, offering him a ride on their new motorcycle when he arrived and painting a glorious picture of how great the event would be.

As Walter later said, "Imagine my chargrin to find that the motor bicycle in question had reached the stage of blueprints, and before I could have the promised ride, I had to help finish the mechine." Infected by their enthusiasm, Walter stayed in Milwaukee to help.

An early motor bicycle shortly after the turn of the century.

25

It wasn't long before William Davidson also joined in the project, lending his skills as an experienced toolmaker. Every spare minute that Bill Harley and the Davidson brothers could find was devoted to putting their idea in motion. Assistance in overcoming various mechanical problems came from the German draftsman. Another friend and neighbor lent them the use of his small shop, lathe and drill press for completing the machine, in return for a complete set of the engine castings they were building. Evenings and weekends ran together as parts were machined by hand, and the first Harley-Davidson motorcycle began taking shape.

To truly appreciate the kinds of problems the young men from Milwaukee encountered, we have to put ourselves in a turn-of-the-century state of mind. Problems that would seem simple to solve today were major roadblocks during the early years of the 20th Century. There were few books or engineering manuals on the subject and no ready-made parts. All parts had to be fabricated from limited existing materials with plenty of good old American ingenuity. And you didn't go to the local filling station for five gallons of gas. You bought it at the corner drugstore, a pint at a time.

The first Harley-Davidson carburetor was allegedly made from a tomato can. "The first spark plugs were as big as doorknobs," Bill Harley remarked later, "and they cost us $3 each."

The first completed engine was an extremely primitive affair, with a 2-1/8 x 2-7/8 inch bore and stroke for a 25 cubic inch displacement. With its tiny five-inch diameter flywheel, the engine was designed to fit into a bicycle frame. Realizing it would be too underpowered to take all of the work out of cycling, they went back and redesigned a larger engine using the same proportions.

The next task for the young inventors was developing a new frame to hold the more powerful motor. The diamond-shaped bicycle frame used on motor bicycles of that time would simply not be strong enough. Eventually, they settled on a loop frame design. It proved to be so ideal, it was used for decades to follow.

WALTER DAVIDSON, SR.

WILLIAM A. DAVIDSON

Finally, in 1902, Harley and the Davidson brothers completed the first true Harley-Davidson engine. Bore and stroke on the new engine was increased to 3 x 3-1/2 inches to produce three horsepower. The flywheel more than doubled in size, growing to 11-1/2 inches. It also had side pocket valves, and featured one-inch radiating fins to dissipate heat. With help from Ole Evinrude, who was later to make his mark in the outboard motor field, several months were spent finding a satisfactory carburetor design. At last, Bill Harley and the Davidson brothers were ready to put their idea into production.

The year was 1903, and Teddy Roosevelt was running for his first full term, having become president following McKinley's assassination. In Milwaukee, the first production Harley-Davidson motorcycle—a single-cylinder, belt-driven machine painted a lustrous gloss black—was ready to take its place alongside the 15 or so other makes which served an eager, growing group of enthusiasts. However, motorcycle production meant the need for more space; a friend's shop was no longer suitable. With the help of Davidson's cabinetmaker father, William C., a 10- x 15-foot "factory" was erected in the family's backyard, just a block away from the current site of Harley-Davidson's main offices. They painted Harley-Davidson's Motor Co. on the door, and a legend was born.

The fact that there were three Davidsons and only one Harley suggests the name should have been "Davidson-Harley Motor Co." However, the brothers felt Bill Harley's name should take key billing because he had engineered the first cycle. It's interesting to speculate whether, had the names been reversed, we would now abbreviate the name by referring to it as a "Davidson" rather than a "Harley."

During 1903, Harley-Davidson Motor Company reportedly turned out a grand total of three motorcycles. A fellow named Meyer took delivery of the first production cycle and rode it for 6,000 miles before selling it to George Lyon, who put another 15,000 miles on it. It was then owned by a Dr. Webster, Louis Fluke and Stephen Sparough, in that order, who collectively accumulated another 62,000 miles of dependable travel. In 1913, Harley-Davidson advertised that their first motorcycle had covered 100,000 miles, was still in operation with its original bearings and had no major components replaced. Durability was the byword, right from the start.

In 1900, Americans enjoyed life under President McKinley enough to re-elect him, with "Rough Rider" Teddy Roosevelt as Vice President. The next year, McKinley would be assassinated.

1904 saw the size of the original Harley-Davidson factory, in the backyard of the Davidson family's Milwaukee home double to 10 x 30 feet.

**1904**
Vacuum electron tube for
radio telephony invented
by Fleming in England.

Christian Hulsmeyer of
Germany introduces radar
with one-mile range.

**1905:**
John McGraw's Giants
beat Connie Mack's
Athletics in World Series.

Gyrocompass invented
by Elmer A. Sperry.

General strike in Russia;
first workers' soviet is
set up.

First Rotary Club founded
in Chicago.

**1906:**
San Francisco earthquake
and three-day fire kills
over 500.

Norwegian explorer
Amundsen fixes magnetic
North Pole.

Pure Food and Drug Act
and Meat Inspection Act
are passed.

**1907:**
Financial panic and
economic depression
in U.S.

First world cruise of U.S.
Navy's "Great White Fleet."

Second Hague Peace
Conference.

Spangler introduces
electric vacuum
cleaner in U.S.

# INSIDE SERIAL NUMBER ONE

Reverently displayed in a glass case for several years in the lobby of the Harley-Davidson corporate headquarters in Milwaukee is a pristine, all-black motorcycle acknowledged as the oldest Harley-Davidson in existence. Previously called a 1903 model or a 1903/04 model, it is now simply referred to as Serial Number One and holds a special place within the history of the Motor Company.

Like so much of the early history of the Motor Company, the origins of Serial Number One are clouded by rumor, conjecture, speculation and time itself. For decades it existed within the halls of Harley-Davidson as a pinstriped street model with fenders. When somewhat restored in the mid-Seventies it was to once again take on the look of the 1906 and later Singles. Company lore and legend until recently had determined that it had indeed been built to look the way it did and, for decades, that look was accepted as fact.

In 1996, Harley-Davidson historian, Marty Rosenblum, and Ray Schlee, motorcycle restorer, asked Willie G. Davidson, Vice President of Styling and grandson of one of the founders, if they could take a detailed look at the motorcycle to see if they could discover its true origins. They were eager to learn once and for all if it really was as old as legend proclaimed. A committee of knowledgeable internal and external people was established to judge the worth of the project and its ongoing accuracy. Ray disassembled the motor and a full restoration began.

Ray immediately discovered that the engine had brass main bearings instead of bronze, and a six bolt crankcase, which made the engine date to pre-1905. Further inspection showed the bore to be 3 1/8 inches instead of the accepted 3 inch and the compression to be that normally found in competition engines of the time. Speculation is the cylinder was replaced at some later time, perhaps as part of a rebuild. Most interesting, perhaps, was the discovery that some of the major engine components, like the flywheels, had a "1" stamped on them, as well as the front forks and some carburetor parts.

Next, Ray and Marty learned the frame was not a 1903 but was probably a mid-1905 frame, giving rise to the probability that the early frame had failed and was replaced by a later one. Investigation and research showed that the bike originally had no fenders, lower handlebars and a different seat than had been shown for so long. Also, the prominent gold pinstriping and "Harley-Davidson" did not appear on both sides of the gas tank. The company name, hand-lettered instead of a decal, should appear only on the left side of the tank.

Marty Rosenblum, left, and Ray Schlee spearheaded the restoration process.

Now knowing how the bike should look, the restoration process was one of painstaking devotion by a group of dedicated enthusiasts. Ray Schlee performed all the engine work and some of the body work, even fabricating missing components as necessary. Milwaukee motorcycle restoration expert, John Rank, did the sheet metal repairs and painting while Ray Drea, from Harley-Davidson's Styling Department, hand lettered the name on the gas tank. The finished product debuted at Harley-Davidson's annual show during the 1997 Daytona Bike Week to universal acclaim. As one member of the motorcycle press stated, "Serial Number One was the most photographed motorcycle at Bike Week!"

Based on Marty and Ray's extensive research, Serial Number One was probably one of three bikes built during 1903, two of which were sold. This one was retained as a competition machine and, over the first decade, was partially partsed out as things broke. In 1915 the Motor Company entered a display in an exposition in California and sought to present a bike from every year. Using various later parts, the bike was rebuilt to look more like a contemporary street machine with fenders, higher handlebars and pinstriping. They even went so far as to add a Bar & Shield logo on the fork head, a logo that wouldn't officially appear until 1910.

Below, Serial Number One as it appeared before its most recent restoration, complete with fenders and striping.

The motorcycle existed in that configuration until the mid-Seventies when a rather hurried restoration made it cosmetically more attractive but retained the "street" look from 1915. For decades, it was accepted as fact that the bike was originally built to look like that. It wasn't until Marty and Ray and others unearthed the truth and Serial Number One was restored to what Harley-Davidson scholars now believe is its correct look. Has it been fired up? According to Ray Schlee, it has compression, spark and a good carburetor so would run if started. Because it is a rare and precious part of Harley-Davidson history it has not been fired up since its restoration.

Why is it now called Serial Number One instead of a 1903? The engine is the oldest, and perhaps even the first, of the engines the founders developed for their early bikes. The frame is clearly of 1905 vintage. And many of the major engine components and even some of the other parts are clearly stamped with a "1". Is Serial Number One the very first successful Harley-Davidson motorcycle? Very possibly, yes. Is it the oldest Harley-Davidson motorcycle in the world? Absolutely yes! Consequently, it is only fitting that it be called Serial Number One.

**E**arly Harley-Davidsons soon earned the nickname of "Silent Gray Fellow," for several reasons. "Silent" came from the company's campaign to keep motorcycling a quiet activity by installing large, quiet mufflers and by condemning the practice of opening muffler cutouts to increase exhaust noise. "Gray" became the standard color following the first few years' basic black machines, although black was still available as an option. And, Harley-Davidson's efforts to promote their motorcycle as a companion on the lonesome road gave it human traits, which led to the "Fellow."

Three more machines were built in 1904, and the next year the size of the original factory doubled, delivering seven machines. In 1905, the company also hired its first employee outside the small group of founders. By year-end, the company was selling not only motorcycles, but motorcycle motors, marine motors, reversible propellers and float feed carburetors. A sales brochure of the time stated: "In making our motorcycle, we have not endeavored to see how cheap we could make it, but how good." The price was $200.

Harley-Davidson Motor Company was definitely headed in the right direction on the road to success. When the calendar turned to 1906, the first building on Harley-Davidson's current Juneau Avenue site was erected, although then it was called Chesnut Street. It was a whopping 28- x 80-foot structure, financed by a loan from the Davidson's uncle, James McLay in Madison, Wisconsin.  Since Uncle James was a beekeeper, this first loan was always referred to as coming from the "honey uncle."

The first Harley-Davidson plant was built a block away from the original, at 38th and Chestnut (now Juneau Avenue).

Following the incorporation of Harley-Davidson Motor Company in 1907, the proud founders and their employees lined up outside the 2,380-square-foot factory. On the far right is Arthur Davidson,while William Davidson—sporting the mustache he wore at the time—is fifth from the right. Seventh from the right is Walter Davidson, wearing a light-colored jacket and black cap. William Harley had just graduated from the University of Wisconsin and was not present for this photograph.

"After we had the framework up," Walter Davidson later recalled, "the railroad surveyors notified us that we were encroaching on the right-of-way of the adjacent railroad. So we got about eight or ten fellows, picked up the entire shop and moved it back about a foot and a half, so that we were safe."

1906 saw Harley-Davidson production leap to 50 motorcycles, and five extra workers were hired to meet the demand. The next year the bikes got their first spring front end, as constant improvement became a design philosophy from the very beginning. By then, Bill Harley and Arthur, Walter and William Davidson had given up their regular jobs to devote their full time and energies to the new, rapidly growing company.

As Walter Davidson recalled those early days, "We worked every day, Sunday included, until 10 o'clock at night. I remember it was an event when we quit work on Christmas night at 8 o'clock to attend a family reunion."

It was now becoming obvious that Harley and the Davidsons had a going—and growing—business venture. They could foresee nothing that might hinder production of their machines but their own limitations as technicians. So while the Davidsons stayed in Milwaukee to tend the store, Bill Harley packed his bags and headed for the University of Wisconsin at Madison. At UW, he majored in engineering, specializing in internal combustion engines, and worked his way through school by waiting on tables at a fraternity house.

# AN AGE OF INVENTION

Perhaps through a coincidence of factors, 1903 stands out as a hallmark year in transportation history. American enterprise and creativity in adapting the internal combustion engine for a variety of uses was gaining momentum. In Dearborn, Michigan, a couple of hundred miles east of the site where the Davidsons and Harley were putting their motorized bicycle into production, an automotive pioneer named Henry Ford revolutionized the automobile industry by mass producing his Model A car.

Meanwhile, another motorized marvel of transportation was born at Kitty Hawk, North Carolina, when the Wright brothers soared over a sandy beach in man's first powered flight.

Both events were part of an era of inventive genius in American history. Within a few years, Albert Einstein would announce his General Theory of Relativity. Thomas Edison, whose inventions included incandescent lighting, the phonograph, the concept behind motion pictures and countless others (his patents totalled 1,033), was currently developing the storage battery. Perhaps not as well known is that Edison's invention of the carbon transmitter was a major factor in bringing Alexander Graham Bell's telephone into practical use. Such inventions would play dramatic roles in America's transition from an agrarian to an industrial society.

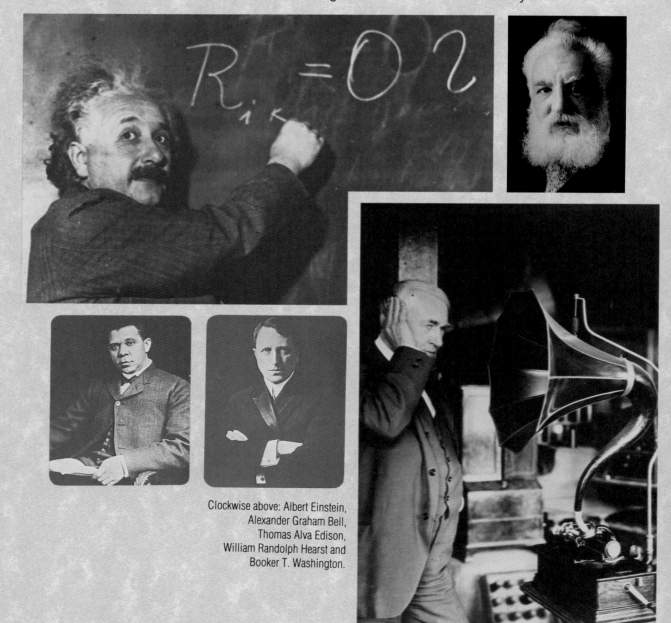

Clockwise above: Albert Einstein,
Alexander Graham Bell,
Thomas Alva Edison,
William Randolph Hearst and
Booker T. Washington.

# The Real Test of a Machine Is in the Private Owners' Hands

—AND THAT IS WHERE THE—

# Harley-Davidson
## MAKE GOOD EVERY TIME

Observe the showing made by Mr. Delevan in Aurora, Ill.

MR. DEALER, if you let our 1909 proposition get away from you, you will regret it the rest of your life.

## Harley-Davidson Motor Co.
### MILWAUKEE, WISCONSIN

There was
## ONLY ONE HARLEY-DAVIDSON
in the LOS ANGELES (CAL.) MOTORCYCLE CLUB'S ENDURANCE CONTEST
May 30 and 31

which trying contest was run right up to the strict requirements of the F. A. M.

That solitary entry was, however, quite enough to

### Uphold the Harley-Davidson Reputation

This is more than can be said of any other of the other brands represented. There were only four perfect scores; the Harley-Davidson's was one of the four.

The Harley-Davidson Earned its Reputation by "Making Good" in this Fashion

Are you interested in a machine of the sort?

**HARLEY-DAVIDSON MOTOR CO., Milwaukee, Wis.**

---

## DID YOU NOTICE?

When the REAL results were announced the

## HARLEY-DAVIDSON

made much the best showing in the Chicago Motorcycle Club's Third Annual Endurance Run.

### WINS PRIVATE OWNER'S CUP!

The ONLY machine that finished in this class. A stock machine not ridden by a factory expert. This was a REAL test of reliability.

1104 MILES IN 5 DAYS

But the HARLEY-DAVIDSON showed just as consistent a performance in the trade rider's class also. Only ONE HARLEY-DAVIDSON entered in this class. Other makes entered teams of two and three men, but the ONE HARLEY-DAVIDSON survived ALL the teams; and when the Eliminating Test was declared off at the end of five days, it had covered **1,104** miles with an absolutely perfect score.

**The HARLEY-DAVIDSON is made for just that kind of work.**

## HARLEY-DAVIDSON MOTOR CO.
### MILWAUKEE, WISCONSIN

---

## Men who ride Harley-Davidsons

have good reason to be not only satisfied, but congratulated. The various motorcycles exhibited at the New York show bore witness to a plentitude of that imitation which is said to be the sincerest form of flattery. Of necessity radical changes in the H-D were not possible, but there are a sufficient number of improvements to keep it well in advance of the "flatterers." It would be impolite to call them counterfeiters. If you have not yet "tied up," our proposition merits your inquiry.

**Harley-Davidson Motor Co.** Milwaukee Wisconsin

---

## THE DESIGN OF THE HARLEY-DAVIDSON

was correct. That is why it has been so freely copied and why there was no necessity for our tearing it down and offering an experimental new model for 1909.

That's the only "Plus 5" Diamond Medal Winner

That's the Machine that made the World's Economy Record

## The Performance of the Harley-Davidson

proved the correctness of the design and quickly placed it in the enviable position it occupies today. In every public competition which makes instructive comparison possible, the Harley-Davidson has acquitted itself handsomely and with high honors. It won the highest honors of 1908—the ONLY diamond medal and the ONLY "plus 5" perfect score in the F. A. M. national endurance contest, likewise first prize and a world's record in the national economy contest. A motorcycle of that sort ought to merit YOUR inquiry and consideration.

## HARLEY-DAVIDSON MOTOR COMPANY, Milwaukee, Wis.

FPG

# A DIAMOND FOR DAVIDSON

At precisely six a.m. on June 29, 1908, the first motorcycle rider left the starting line, heralding the beginning of the seventh annual Federation of American Motorcyclist (FAM) endurance and reliability contest held in the scenic Catskill Mountains of New York. Of the 65 entrants in the gruelling two-day, 365-mile event, only 61 actually started that morning. Five were mounted on Harley-Davidson motorcycles. One of the five, riding a stock single-cylinder machine, was the president of Harley-Davidson Motor Company, Walter Davidson. In all, 17 brands of motorcycles were represented.

Following a complaint that previous events had been too easy, the 1908 contest was the most rugged to date. The first day's course,175 miles long, followed a meandering route over gravel and dirt roads, up mountains and down through valleys, from Catskill, south to New York City. Following an inspection by FAM officials, each machine was sealed, numbered and dispatched in the order of their numbering, at four minute intervals. Walter Davidson was number 35.

According to the FAM, the purpose of the contest was "to test the endurance, skill and judgment of the competitors, and the capability, endurance and reliability of the motorcycles they use, and the consistent performance of both."

The event certainly lived up to its credo as competitors braved primitive roads, demanding mountain passes, punctured tires, collisions with livestock, heat, dust and mechanical break-downs. They raced against the clock from checkpoint to checkpoint, ever mindful of the man who might jump out of the bushes waving a green flag, the signal for an emergency braking test. To attain the coveted perfect score of 1,000 points—or even to simply finish the event—a rider had to possess both the skill to traverse the rugged course and the confidence in his mount.

Walter Davidson knew his company built a reliable motorcycle. "So strong was my confidence," he later said, "that I carried with me no additional parts or repairs, which was quite in contrast with many of the manufacturers' riders who had automobiles with complete duplicate parts following them." Indeed, he finished the first day's ride without a mishap, passing through every checkpoint perfectly.

At the next morning's start of the second phase of the event, only 43 competitors were able to leave the starting line. It was obvious that the previous day's demanding route had levied a heavy toll on motorcycle and rider alike. Fortunately for both, the 190-mile route circumnavigating Long Island was comparatively mild. Just the same, accumulated wear and tear, as well as wandering cows, plagued the entrants. Davidson's only incident was a punctured tire, as he and his motor-cycle again performed flawlessly the entire way.

When the results were tallied, Walter Davidson had earned the perfect score of 1,000 points, plus an additional five points and the diamond medal—the only one awarded for consistency of both rider and machine.

The FAM declared, "Davidson's title to the medal is beyond question. During the two days of the contest, he varied by eight minutes from the exact schedule, which places him so far in advance of all others as to leave his qualification for the award beyond dispute."

William Harley, left, and Walter Davidson giving a 1909 model a little assistance over a rocky stretch of shoreline.

The year 1910 started in a big way for Harley-Davidson, with the completion of the company's first reinforced concrete building. Production space was boosted to 9,520 square feet and the number of employees to 149. But the new decade also saw a major disappointment for the company.

The new V-twin engine, announced at the end of the previous decade, was developed to compete with the many foreign and domestic twins and multi-cylinder motorcycles on the market. The Harley-Davidson twin employed an automatic intake valve—a system that worked well in single-cylinder engines, but not in the V-twin configuration. The engine was a failure.

Only a few dozen twins were produced by Harley-Davidson in 1909, and none of the 3,200 motorcycles built in 1910 were twin-cylinder models. Only single-cylinder models were advertised and sold, as Harley-Davidson engineers went back to the drawing boards to redesign the engine.

This plant illustration appeared in the 1910 brochure.

Have You Been Watching the Remarkably Consistent Winning of the 1910 Single Cylinder

## HARLEY-DAVIDSON?

New York Quarterly Trials, April 3—One Entry—Perfect Score.
Linden Endurance Contest, April 17—One Entry—Perfect Score.
Minneapolis Hill Climb, May 22—One Entry—Finished First.
South Bend Endurance Contest, May 15—Five Entries—Five Perfect Scores.
Oklahoma City Racemeet, April 22—Won First, Second and Third in Every Event.
Los Angeles Annual Endurance Contest—Two Perfect Scores.
Denver Stock Machine Race, Tuilleries Track—Won First.
Denver-Greeley Road Race—Won First and Second, Defeating the Time of the Fastest Double Cylinder Entry by Nearly Ten Minutes.

The Harley-Davidson Makes Good Because It Is Made Good

HARLEY-DAVIDSON MOTOR CO., Milwaukee, Wis.

In 1911, Harley-Davidson reintroduced the V-twin model, this time with a new frame which substantially lowered the seat position without sacrificing any ground clearance. Vanadium, chrome and nickel steels and, in some places, high-carbon steel were used to produce a motorcycle renowned for its endurance and reliability. Best of all, perhaps, was the introduction of mechanical inlet valves which solved the earlier problem and made the twin-cylinder Harley-Davidson the equal of its peers.

A leading theatrical star of the time was actress Sarah Bernhardt.

Samuel Clemens, better known as Mark Twain, died in 1910.

nnovation was key in the year 1912. On a national scale, voters elected Woodrow Wilson, the first Democratic president since 1896. At Harley-Davidson, the twin-cylinder X8E featured the first commercially successful motorcycle clutch, a "free wheeling" rear wheel mechanism designed by Bill Harley. This made it possible to use a roller chain to power the motorcycle instead of the commonly used leather belt, which was prone to slip when wet. Up to that point, the company had used a left-hand-controlled belt tensioner, which made it possible to disengage power to the rear wheel when stopping. However, the chain showed great promise of being more efficient. "Separate and independent chain adjustments are provided for all three chains," said the product literature. Pedals were still connected by chain to the rear wheel to start the motorcycle. Another Bill Harley innovation that year was the introduction of the center post saddle suspension, or "Ful-floteing Seat."

All the while, Harley-Davidson machines were entering and winning races with independent owners in the saddle. The company's policy, at that time, was to build no special racing machines, and there were no "factory riders." A Harley-Davidson ad, which appeared September 21, 1911 in Motorcycle Illustrated, proclaimed: "No, we don't believe in racing and we don't make a practice of it, but when Harley-Davidson owners win races with their own stock machines hundreds of miles from the factory, we can't help crowing about it."

Early Harley-Davidson employees on Highland Avenue in Milwaukee, circa 1912. Note the Davidson house in the center of the picture, with the old wooden factory building still standing in the backyard.

The 1912 presidential election was a three-way battle, with Wilson winning over Republican William Howard Taft and Progressive Teddy Roosevelt.

**1910:**
Panama Canal opens.

Boy Scouts of America founded.

**1911:**
First transcontinental airplane flight takes 82 hours, 4 minutes — plus stops.

**1912:**
Teddy Roosevelt gives 80-minute speech in Milwaukee, despite a recent wound from assassination attempt.

Titanic sinks, drowning over 1,500.

**1913:**
First movie version of *Quo Vadis* opens in New York.

**1914:**
Ford raises basic wage rates from $2.40 for nine-hour day, to $5 for eight-hour day.

**1915:**
Alexander Graham Bell makes first transcontinental phone call—New York to San Francisco.

D. W. Griffith makes *Birth of a Nation*.

British ship, Lusitania, sunk by German submarine.

Einstein publishes *General Theory of Relativity*.

In 1912, stone stock eight-horsepower twins ridden by private owners won the Bakersfield and San Jose Road Races. At San Jose, the winning rider finished *17 miles* ahead of the number two machine. During 1913, Harley-Davidsons took the first three places in a 225 mile race from Harrisburg to Philadelphia and back.

Later that year, in what was intended to be a challenge race between Indian and Excelsior motorcycles, a dealer entered a Harley-Davidson with Curley Fredericks riding. Floyd Clymer, who became a dealer/rider for Harley-Davidson, was riding the Excelsior. He later recalled the exciting race in his Motor Scrapbook: "I got away first and Boyd on his Indian gradually drew near me. We were about nip and tuck at the end of the first mile. Then I heard a quiet hum. Not even making much noise, Fredericks went by so fast that we could not even get in his draft. He was carrying a very high gear ratio, and at the finish he must have been a quarter mile ahead of both of us."

A new single-cylinder model was added to the Harley-Davidson line for 1913. Designated as the 5-35 model, the numbers signified the engine specifications of five horsepower and 35 cubic inches. The choice of a chain or belt drive to accompany the new single was given to the customer. A two-speed rear hub was also introduced that year.

Before then, the motorcycle had been started in one of two ways: either pedaling in bicycle fashion or running alongside until the engine started. Harley-Davidson introduced a step starter in 1914, eliminating the need to put the machine on its rear stand for starting. The internal expanding rear brake and carburetor choke were offered as well, followed a year later by the revolutionary three-speed sliding gear transmission and engine clutch.

Irish immigrants at Ellis Island.

While motorcycling was generally looked upon as a purely masculine sport, a surprising number of women were also early enthusiasts. The June 18, 1910 issue of *The Bicycling World and Motorcycle Review* has this report on one of these feminine iconoclasts, Leda Leslie, who is shown in the photograph below:

"Just now, Akron, Ohio has more than tires and rubber to interest it and to test the elasticity of its inhabitants' necks. A young woman who rides a motor bicycle is the new cause for interest and neck-stretching.

"She is Miss Leda Leslie, who, astride her Harley-Davidson, is the subject of the accompanying illustration. Miss Leslie is reputed a skillful rider, even if she did 'get herself into print' by plunging through a plate glass show window."

In Miss Leslie's defense, the article continued: "That was an accident that might have happened to even a masculine rider and 'doesn't count' anyway."

One of the best-loved and most popular figures of the time was humorist Will Rogers.

Ed Wynn was one of America's favorite funny men.

**B**y 1914, the Harley-Davidson motorcycle had earned such a solid reputation that nine departments of the federal government employed its service. The U.S. Postal Service alone used over 4,800 Harleys for rural deliveries.

In 1915, a new delivery side-van was introduced for commercial use. Essentially, it was a large wooden box with a hinged top for loading. Mounted on the standard sidecar chassis, it had the added benefit of being interchangeable with the sidecar body, so the owner could use the equipped motorcycle for both business and pleasure. The side-van bodies could be ordered from the factory with their company name and information painted on it for ten cents per letter. The sidecar could be ordered with a folding top and side curtains, offering all-weather protection for its occupant. Comfort had come to motorcycling.

Just four of the 4,800 Harley-Davidson motorcycles employed by the U. S. Postal Service in 1914.

Author,
Carl Sandburg.

The side-van
proved very popluar
and useful for
companies seeking
a speedy and
economical way to
deliver their goods.

From the very beginning, there has been a deep feeling of comraderie among the employees of Harley-Davidson. This family-like atmosphere prompted a group of employees to help out a fellow employee who lived in a tarpaper shanty with his wife and two children. Using materials supplied by William Davidson, well-known for his kindness and generosity, the employees built their fellow worker's family a fine two-story home.

# WHAT HAPPENED TO MR. MOORMAN

**"Happenings" Began in Moorsville and the Young Man is Glad He's Alive—His Motorcycle "Fatally Injured."**

If only a moving picture man had been present to see it all on April 17, at Moorsville, Ind., he would have had a film that would have taken rank with the "six best renters," for what happened to Bert Moormann, an amateur motorcycle rider, and his new motorcycle on that day in that town was little short of a miracle. The whirl started with a puncture. Moormann laughed. 'Twas nothing!

A boy threw a rock at him. Moormann spoke to the boy's father, who chased Moormann with a knife.

"B-r-r-r-r" from the new motorcycle, and Moormann was out of reach. He laughed. Then things really began to happen.

Moormann bumped a traction car. Later he was forced to jump from his machine to avoid death under a C. H. & D. train. The motorcycle was struck. Moormann was bruised, but he just laughed.

Moormann then continued on his explosive way, until he hit Prosecutor Dennis O'Neil. Both hit the street. Moormann did not dare laugh, because O'Neil did not see the humor in the situation.

"Me for the country and the open road," said Moormann.

The new motorcycle sputtered gayly forth and was "going good," much to Moormann's exhilaration, when it struck an automobile. The collision was mutual, with the motorcycle underneath. Moormann was thrown many feet, but escaped with only a bruise or two. The new motorcycle was damaged beyond using and Moormann's headlong career was ended for the day.

While the popularity of motorcycling grew as a sport, there were probably few who found more excitement in it than Bert Moormann, whose one-day adventure was humorously described in this April 22, 1911 story from *The Bicycling World And Motorcycle Review.*

nable to ignore the racing success of independent Harley-Davidson riders, Bill Harley established the company's official Racing Department in 1914. Before the year was out, Harley-Davidson had captured the win at the One Hour National Championships under FAM Sanction at Birmingham, Alabama. The following year, Harley-Davidson motorcycles raced to a total of 26 major firsts.

1916 saw more of the same. There were 15 victories in all—on board tracks, flat tracks and in the FAM Nationals—and more than a couple were complete sweeps. Racing had become such an important part of the motorcycling scene that Harley-Davidson began selling stripped stock models for competition. A brochure of that year offered 11-horsepower, twin-cylinder racers that were capable of 70 to 75 miles per hour, direct from the factory. Optional equipment included different oiling systems, seats, tires and even the wheelbase. In addition, a choice of gas tanks was offered, which included the new, sleeker rounded tank introduced that year. Price was $250 F.O.B Milwaukee.

# Harley-Davidson
## 1915 Long Distance Champion

IN the three big races of the year the 1915 stock Harley-Davidson has won both first and second.

It has taken remarkable reliability, and sustained speed previously unheard of in a stock machine, to make these unparalleled performances possible.

### Venice International Grand Prize
300 Miles.  Average 68½ Miles an Hour

### Oklahoma City Road Race
150 Miles.  Average 64³⁄₁₀ Miles an Hour

### Phoenix 200-Mile Race
Average 64.07 Miles an Hour

## Ride A Winner

Harley-Davidson Motor Co., Milwaukee Wis., U.S.A.

The advertiser wants to know—Therefore mention MOTOR CYCLE ILLUSTRATED.

Leslie "Red" Parkhurst establishes new motorcycle 24-hour record at Sheepshead Bay, N.Y., of 1,452 miles.

An early example of motorcycle clothing was this suit supplied by a Chicago firm, made of English whipcord.

Otto Walker, with passenger Carl Lutgens, establishes new motorcycle-sidecar record of 1,158 miles.

Suffragist Susan B. Anthony did not live to see the proposal of the 19th Amendment, granting women the right to vote, in 1919.

**1916:**
Auto/truck production passes million mark for first time; average car price is $600.

Margaret Sanger opens first birth control clinic.

U. S. establishes military government in Dominican Republic.

**1917:**
U. S. enters WWI, sends first combat troops to France.

Congress approves Prohibition Amendment.

Balfour Declaration promises Jewish homeland in Palestine.

**1918:**
Over a million American troops in Europe before WWI ends.

First airmail service with regular flights between New York and Washington.

**1919:**
First transatlantic non-stop flight by U. S. Navy seaplane.

White Sox loss in World Series to Reds later becomes "Black Sox" scandal.

## WAR INTERRUPTS AMERICANS' TOUR OF SWEDEN

A 1915 article in *The Bicycling World and Motorcycle Review* indicates the coming war in Europe. According to the story, Carl A. Peterson of Natick, Mass., shown in the photo with his wife, had his motorcycle vacation trip through Sweden "rudely interrupted by the European war. The tourists did considerable traveling in Sweden, mostly over excellent roads, before they decided to curtail their outing.

"Swedish riders were deeply impressed by the power of Peterson's Harley-Davidson," the article continued, "and by the ease with which he whisked Mrs. Peterson about the country on the tandem seat.

"The Petersons had planned to ride through Germany before sailing on the return trip, but when war broke out, there was confusion on all sides, and it was considered advisable to get out of Europe with all possible speed. Accordingly, the motorcycle was recrated, and after much difficulty and unraveling a great deal of official red tape, the machine was taken on board the ship.

"In some respects the outing did not come up to our expectations," says Peterson, "but the machine performed perfectly, and the riding we managed to do while in Sweden amply repaid us."

## DELLA'S FAMOUS ADVENTURE

In the first few decades of the Twentieth Century, the roads made motorcycle touring a rugged sport. Before concrete interstates and blacktop secondary roads crisscrossed America, most roads were dirt or gravel trails. Venturing far outside the city required a flair for adventure, a lot of stamina and a rugged machine. The fact that American men ventured forth under those conditions was unquestioned, but for women to do the same caused a great deal of attention, because of their presumably more passive role.

Even among these exceptional female motorcycle pioneers, some stood out. . .like a Waco, Texas woman named Della Crewe. On June 24, 1915, she set out to see America by motorcycle, after rejecting both train and steamship as being not only too expensive, but also uninteresting. With only 10 days of riding experience on her 1914 Harley-Davidson V-twin, she filled her sidecar with 125 pounds of baggage, including her dog, appropriately named "Trouble," and began her tour. Despite warnings from friends that she would get held up by hobos or kill herself in an accident, she wanted the freedom and mobility offered only by a motorcycle.

Her first destination was the June 3 motorcycle races in Dodge City, Kansas. With today's modern roads, it would be a one or two day trip, but things were different in 1915. An extremely wet winter and spring had made roads across Texas and Oklahoma badly rutted mires of mud and sand. And if that weren't enough, there was the added danger of hidden stumps, logs and rocks in the so-called roads. All those miles of sand beds and rugged hills took their toll on both the rider and the motorcycle.

Despite a collision with a stump which knocked her sidecar out of line, Della made it to the paved streets of Oklahoma City without a major mishap. The 75 miles of macadam in the city were a welcome relief to the lady motorcyclist, but upon entering Kansas, heavy rains made the road such a quagmire she had to install tire chains. Finally, even chains couldn't provide enough traction and with Trouble in the sidecar, Della struck out through four miles of Kansas wheat fields before finding a usable road. She made it to Dodge City in time for the race, one of the premier motorcycle events of the time.

Deciding to head to New York and see the country along the way, the pair headed north through the beautiful scenery of Missouri. With good weather and fine roads, they made good time as they raced up one hill and down another. After a 15¢ ferry ride across the Mississippi River, they were into Illinois and more hills. The trip to Chicago and then to the Harley-Davidson factory in Milwaukee was comparatively quick and uneventful.

After leaving Milwaukee, they headed south again, through Chicago and into Indiana, where authorities stopped her twice because of the dog. There was a quarantine in Indiana because of hoof and mouth disease, and Della had to promise that her dog wouldn't leave the sidecar before they could proceed. Nevertheless, upon arriving in Goshen, Indiana, they were invited to participate in a local parade, which gave them an excellent opportunity to see the city. Traveling at a mile and a half per hour in a parade was taxing for a relatively new rider like Della, and she was glad when it was over. Resuming her journey shortly thereafter, Della and her dog encountered a considerable number of road repairs, causing numerous detours.

Having spent the summer and fall months heading north and then east, the travelers inevitably ran into cold November weather in Ohio, an indication of what was ahead for the rest of the trip. Bitter cold forced a three-day layover in Toledo, and the ride around the southern edge of Lake Erie turned into a snowy one as they approached Cleveland. Traveling northeast up the coast toward Painesville, Ohio, the drifting snow sent the motor-cycle into the ditches several times, and eventually they were forced to seek shelter at a farmhouse. The farmer refused her request at first, with the illogical excuse that she didn't belong on the road in that kind of severe weather. Fortunately, the farmer's wife was the boss of that house, and Della soon found herself drying her clothes before a warm fire.

On Thanksgiving Day, Della and her canine partner were back on the road again. Thawing snow had made the roads so bad it took them two hours to travel 2-1/2 miles to the nearest town. Several times she needed the aid of local farm boys to free the motorcycle and get it rolling again. The Texans were forced to pick their way through eighteen miles of obstacles such as rutted roads, slippery conditions, and stuck or sliding cars, riding most of the way in low gear. While a number of motorcyclists on solo machines were forced to lay over and wait for better conditions, Della was thankful that the stability of a sidecar allowed her to continue.

Crossing the corner of Pennsylvania, the pair entered New York State. Approaching Buffalo, they had to struggle through nine miles of sticky clay which clung to everything and clogged the wheels. Physically spent, Della had to hire a farmer and his horse to pull them the last mile.

Thankfully, the ride across the state was easy. However, bitter cold and heavy snow returned to haunt them as they left Albany, making the trip to their long-sought destination of New York City a rugged two-day journey.

From Waco to Milwaukee to New York City with numerous side trips, Della and Trouble logged a total of 5,378 miles as their motorcycle performed flawlessly. As Della stated after completing the journey, "I had a glorious trip. I am in perfect health, and my desire is stronger than ever to keep going."

A few days later, Della Crewe, Trouble and their 1914 Harley-Davidson twin with sidecar sailed for Jacksonville, Florida with plans to tour the South, Cuba and South America.

**W**hile racing symbolized the ultimate in exciting motorcycle challenge, international events were forcing attention on a more serious side. Much as it might protest, the United States was being brought into the international conflicts that raged around the globe.

In 1916, Harley-Davidson motorcycles saw their first military duty in border skirmishes with Pancho Villa. The Mexican revolutionary was angered at President Wilson's support of his opponents and retaliated by raiding U. S. territory along the border. General "Black Jack" Pershing was sent with his troops to quiet things down. In order to track down this elusive bandit, the use of motorcycles with mounted machine guns, which had been in the War Department's service for many years, was increased dramatically to combat the rugged southeastern terrain.

On March 16, 1916, the War Department telegraphed Harley-Davidson requesting a dozen motorcycles to be shipped immediately. They arrived at the border two days later, ready for service. A second order was received March 27, and those machines arrived 33 hours later. The motorcycles were equipped with a sidecar gun carriage, developed by William Harley, to serve as a platform for mounting a Colt machine gun.

## Uncle Sam's Choice
### Harley-Davidsons

Nine o'clock Thursday morning, March 16, the Harley-Davidson Motor Co. received a telegraphic order from Fort Sam Houston for 12 Harley-Davidson Motorcycles. All 12 machines were shipped on the afternoon of the same day. Monday morning, March 27th, at 10 o'clock a telegraphic order was received for 6 more machines. These 6 were shipped on the same afternoon. Uncle Sam now has 34 Harley-Davidsons in Mexican frontier service.

Harley-Davidson machine gun squad scouting on U.S.-Mexican border.

63

In the meantime, the black clouds of war stormed over Europe. The "war to end all wars" had started in 1914, and Harley-Davidson was ready to do its part when America was forced into the conflict.

On April 6, 1917, the United States formally declared war, and the motorcycle industry immediately swung its efforts over to military production. At an August sales meeting in Milwaukee, Arthur Davidson pointed out the need for everyone associated with Harley-Davidson to ally himself with the spirit of Americanism. He said: "The time is coming when no man can be in the middle of the road. He must be either for America or against America, and the sooner we get together on this question, the better able we will be to win the war."

And Harley-Davidson responded. During the first year of the U.S. involvement in the war, approximately half of Harley-Davidson's production went to the military. By the time the war ended, *all* new Harley-Davidson motorcycles were made for the government. All of the motorcycle manufacturers halted racing until the victory in Europe was won.

FPG

Actress Mary Pickford
was known as
"America's Sweetheart."

Just as World War I altered the lives of individuals around the world, it also made a major impact on the young Harley-Davidson Motor Co. During the period just prior to the United States' entry into the war, suspension of British civilian cycle production had forced the world's nonmilitary riders to look Stateside for new mounts. Harley-Davidson drew a good share of this business, and its reputation overseas grew accordingly.

Prior to the war, copies of Harley-Davidson service bulletins emphasized the value of civilian preparation and organization for military action. When the war came, those who knew the ins and outs of motorcycles would be ready to perform a valuable service for their country. In total, some 20,000 cycles would see dispatch and scout duty before the war ended, and most of those would come from Milwaukee.

Harley-Davidson's "now and then" publication (meaning it was published every now and then), *The Enthusiast*, was launched in 1916. It, too, stood firmly behind the war effort, keeping riders on both sides of the Atlantic informed on military motorcycle matters. *The Enthusiast* is still published today, making it America's longest continuously published motorcycle magazine.

The War was responsible for another Harley-Davidson tradition that has continued into modern times. As the Army continued to build its fleet of motorcycles, it soon became apparent that it had no program to maintain them. To meet that need, the first Harley-Davidson Service School was established in 1917 to help train military personnel to repair and maintain all of those hard working cycles abroad. Also, Harley-Davidson began sending an expert serviceman to accompany each shipment of machines to its assigned army camp. Once the motorcycles were properly set up by a designated squad of men, the serviceman would have the job of selecting and training the riders. Eventually, he would set up and train a staff for the on-camp service area.

For more comprehensive training, Harley-Davidson created a service school at its Milwaukee plant where mechanics could learn about proper repair procedures and tools in an intensive three-week course. The very first class, in July of 1917, consisted of nine corporals from Fort Sam Houston, Texas. Eventually, three classes were conducted at a time, with 45 men per class.

By the end of the war, Harley-Davidson was preparing to train 1,000 riders and mechanics per month in a special Milwaukee area service school. After the war, the regular school was continued to provide qualified mechanics for civilian motorcycles.

Public service was a way of life at Harley-Davidson from the early days. Shown in this photo is Margaret Davidson, six year old daughter of Arthur Davidson and youngest member of Milwaukee's Washington Park Division of the Red Cross.

Harley-Davidson motorcycles on patrol in a French Village in 1918.

# THE FIRST YANK ENTERING GERMANY

One of the most famous motorcycle stories to come out of World War I involved a Harley-Davidson and a Yank from Chippewa Falls, Wisconsin, named Roy Holtz.

On the night of November 8, 1918, Holtz, a corporal, and his buddies were stationed in Northern Belgium near Spa. The big drive toward the German border was on. The enemy was reeling backward and surrender was expected momentarily. On the night of November 8, a rumor circulated among the Americans that peace was declared. Late that night Cpl. Holtz was ordered to take his captain on a night mission. It had been pouring rain for days. The roads were thick with mud and well plowed up from the big shells.

The corporal started out with his captain in the sidecar of the Harley-Davidson. As they slid along in the darkness, Corporal Holtz who knew the country well remonstrated that they were going in the wrong direction and were heading for the enemy lines. The captain disagreed, first politely, then more vehemently. The corporal became more and more convinced as they skidded along that the captain was wrong.

They came to the rise of a little hill. At the foot they could see a light in an old farmhouse. When they reached the bottom, Cpl. Holtz was ordered to go in and get directions. The thoroughly disgruntled corporal plodded up to the door and pounded fiercely.

Suddenly it was opened and instinctively he stepped in out of the soaking rain. When he had wiped away the rain he glanced across the room unbelievingly. There at a long table were a dozen or more enemy officers—all eyes staring at him coldly.

Actually they were officers of the Fifth Bavarian division. Cpl. Holtz and his captain had blundered into enemy divisional headquarters. Inwardly the corporal was boiling. He had a hunch something like this might happen—but orders are orders!

**THE SATURDAY EVENING POST**

An Illustrated Weekly
Founded A.D. by Benj. Franklin

JUNE 1, 1918        5c. THE COPY

At the Front of the Front—By Irvin S. Cobb

The corporal was ordered to call in his captain which he admits was not an unpleasant duty. He went to the door and hollered: "Hey, Sam, come on in," omitting "sir" and "captain." In stamped the captain and when he saw the uniforms his jaw dropped.

"See what you and your blasted directions got us into," snapped Cpl. Holtz.

The captain never answered. They both realized then the armistice report had been a very false one. While the two Americans stood there a German general, hearing the commotion, came striding into the room.

"What have we here?" he demanded in German.

"Two Americans," the officers chorused.

Turning to an orderly, the general, still talking German, asked that an interpreter be sent in. Cpl. Holtz immediately spoke up and said in German:

"It is not necessary to call an interpreter. I can speak German."

The assembled officers were thunderstruck. Then the general took Cpl. Holtz into a side room for further questioning. He assumed a very kindly air and commanded the orderly to send in some schnapps. He poured out two schnapps—one for Holtz and one for himself.

Ah, ha, thought the corporal, he's either trying to poison me or get me canned so I'll talk. Watching the general closely, Holtz assured himself that the general was also going to drink the stuff. Then the general lifted his glass and said:

"Gesundheit." Down went the drink.

Holtz followed suit and almost choked. It burned like fire. He discovered later that it was very potent potato whisky. Three more were had at close intervals. In the meantime, the general did his darndest to pump Holtz about the American positions, their strength and so forth, but the corporal wouldn't talk. At last, in disgust, Holtz was sent back to the main room where his captain was sitting very uncomfortably. It was decided to send the Americans to German general headquarters. The general ordered a German captain to accompany Holtz and his captain on the Harley-Davidson. The German got astride the rear wheel on the hard luggage carrier. Away they went. It wasn't long until the German captain began complaining of the hard seat. The more he'd complain, the harder Holtz drove. He headed for every bump and hole he could possibly find. By the time headquarters was reached, at Spa, Belgium, the German captain was in awful shape. Spa, incidentally, was a town of several thousand near the Belgium-German border.

At headquarters, the Americans underwent another cross-examination and were then put in jail. They stayed there until November 11. One of their guards came up to them late in the morning and said: "The war is at an end."

After it had been certified that the war was actually over, the Germans returned Holtz's automatic and his Harley-Davidson and the captain got his belongings.

They had to return about fifty or sixty miles, they estimated, to reach their outfit. Naturally, the members of their company had no idea where the two were. But being reported missing was common and any one of several things could have happened to them.

On their way back, Holtz drove his Harley-Davidson as fast as he could over the terrible roads. They got off the right road and wound up in another little Belgian village. They went to the home of the village priest to ask for directions. When he saw the two Americans he was so excited and happy that he ordered the sexton to ring the church bells for an hour. Soon villagers began streaming in. Holtz and the captain were the first Americans to reach the village, the priest told them, and gave them affidavits covering this fact. The joy of the villagers knew no bounds. These were the first two Americans they had seen, the first of an army which was coming to rescue them. In a way, it was really embarrassing admits Holtz.

The happy girls and townsfolk threw their arms around them and kissed them to, show their great joy.

The kind-hearted village priest prepared a soft bed for the two in spite of the fact that they were not entirely free of dirt, the

grime of war and the inevitable cooties. They were welcome guests, indeed, in the parish house that night.

The next day after oft-repeated farewells, and with the right directions ringing in their ears, the Harley-Davidson and its

occupants started out again. Not long afterwards, the Harley-Davidson bumped to a stop in front of their own headquarters. They arrived just in time as their outfit was ready to move forward.

On November 12, Cpl. Holtz crossed into Germany. He rode his Harley-Davidson back and forth across the border many times in the days which followed. He spent a total of eight months with the Army of Occupation in Germany and a total of twenty months overseas.

Reprinted from February 1944 Euthusiast magazine

The people of Harley-Davidson served their country well during World War I, receiving several commendations from the military for their loyalty and dedication to the war effort. William Harley served as a member of the Motorcycle War Service Board and contributed to the government's decision to give motorcycles a B-4 classification, which meant the industry was deemed essential and was able to procure needed materials for production.

In all, 312 employees entered military service during the war, and all but three returned—those having paid the ultimate price for their country. Harley-Davidson invited all veterans to return to the company and resume their old jobs, or jobs of equal worth. Most did just that.

The conversion back to civilian production was relatively smooth and simple for Harley-Davidson. The only reminder of the war was the army green that had replaced the popular pre-war gray. It continued as the standard motorcycle color for some years after the war.

In an undoubted effort to acquaint youngsters with Harley-Davidson, a full line of bicycles was introduced in 1917, playing off the motorcycle's reputation for quality, dependability, balance and, of course, Americanism. Offered in the "soldier color" of olive drab, the nonmotorized Harley-Davidsons were advertised as "a true brother to the Harley-Davidson motorcycle." While attractive and well-made, the Harley-Davidson bicycles were expensive for the times—$30 to $45 retail—and disappeared from the product line a few years later. However, these bicycles began a policy of involving the rider's family in Harley-Davidson products that continues to this day.

"Most All the Fellows Have Harley-Davidsons, Dad"

WHEREVER "the bunch" gets together, you'll find most of the fellows ride the classy-looking, easy-running

## Harley-Davidson
"America's Finest Bicycle"

A Harley-Davidson is a Harley-Davidson, whether it's a bicycle or a motorcycle.

So you can't get a better built, better equipped, better looking bike. Any of the other fellows will tell you so.

Get Dad to go with you to the Harley-Davidson Dealer's.

### Come In And Look Them Over

Harley-Davidson motorcycles won the World's Championship at Marion, Indiana, September 1st, 1919

A bicycle race held in Plaza del Congress, Buenos Aires, Argentina.

## Of Course It's a Harley-Davidson

That's the bike red-blooded fellows choose—choose it because it stands the "gaff," because it's a bike they can always be proud of.

If you want a bicycle that has the sturdy build and the ruggedness to withstand all kinds of hard riding, you, too, will choose a

### Harley-Davidson Bicycle

It's a beauty, too. Classy lines and a cleancut construction. Well designed frame and "soldier" color. A fit running mate for the famcus Harley-Davidson motorcycle.

Dad knows—bring him with you when you come in to look at the new models. They're here now.

(Dealers Name)

HARLEY-DAVIDSON
MOTORCYCLES
BICYCLES

"Gee Dad! buy Me a HARLEY-DAVIDSON"

WE HAVE A COMPLETE LINE OF HARLEY-DAVIDSON BICYCLES IN STOCK

(Dealer's Name Here)

The clear-skinned, keen-eyed, athletic boy of today is fully alive to the wonderful flavor of Kellogg's Toasted Corn-Flakes. He misses this flavor in the imitations of Kellogg's. He wants the Original Toasted Corn-Flakes—with their crisp, fresh-from-the-oven taste—and you can leave it to him to get them.

W.K.Kellogg

Kellogg's TOASTED CORN FLAKES

# THE HARLEY-DAVIDSON COMMERCIAL MOTORCYCLE

During the first decade of the Motor Company the founders felt a need to expand the product line and grow the business. With motorcycles becoming more and powerful and dependable, it became apparent to William Harley and the three Davidson brothers that their vehicles could provide greater service than just inexpensive transportation.

After six years of studying the light commercial transportation industry they arrived at the conclusion that there was a need for a delivery vehicle that was both maneuverable and inexpensive to operate. In 1914, following two years of rigid testing, Harley-Davidson introduced its first commercial vehicle, which it called the Motorcycle Truck or Delivery Van. The Model 10G, later dubbed the Forecar, was unique in Harley-Davidson history in that it had a large cargo box in front of the motorcycle, where the front fork assembly would normally be. It was flanked by a pair of wheels and topped by two headlights.

The Forecar was attached to what was essentially a standard twin cylinder chassis with a 61 cubic inch V-twin engine. The transmission was a two-speed type located in the rear hub along with the clutch and brake. Tests conducted by the U.S. Government showed that in parcel post service, the Forecar, in a 14.2 mile mail route, could make 200 stops in eight hours, a sixty percent increase over horse drawn outfits, and at only one-fifth of a cent for fuel per delivery. Despite this unprecedented economy of operation, the Forecar was only produced for two years.

In 1915, concurrent with the Forecar, Harley-Davidson introduced its first commercial sidevan, or Package Truck. Initially utilizing a standard sidecar chassis, the Package Trucks were offered in a variety of sizes and shapes and were quickly adopted as delivery vehicles by both business and government. Obvious advantages over the Forecar was the capability of selecting different configurations more suited to individual needs combined with the ability to easily remove the box and install a sidecar body for passenger duty, if desired.

The early Package Truck boxes were made of 3/8-inch whitewood on a white ash frame. Most had a bowed top made of wood with a black waterproof canvas covering. There were several sizes offered in different configurations. The U.S.Postal Service generally used a small box for delivery while certain businesses, such as cleaners and milliners, took advantage of the high box capable of hanging a double row of garments. Most of the boxes, available for either right side or left side mounting, were decorated or lettered to advertise the business. Harley-Davidson even offered simple lettering at no additional charge.

The chassis had adjustable tread that could easily be widened from 44 to 56 inches in minutes for added stability or to accommodate a wider box. There was also a wider tread, which could go from 48 to 60 inches for, as the Harley-Davidson advertisements said, "the Southern roads". In later years the chassis for the Package Truck was altered so it sat lower than that of the sidecar, though it remained visually similar. The boxes, too, changed later on from all wood to being wood with a sheet metal skin.

The Package Trucks were a hugely successful venture for Harley-Davidson and were produced into the mid-Fifties when the growing use of vans and light trucks for light commercial delivery pretty much spelled their end.

**Harley-Davidson Motorcycle Truck** $425.00
Capacity, 600 pounds and driver. Gasoline consumption, 30 to 40 miles per gallon with full load. Speed, 2 to 35 miles per hour.
F. O. B. MILWAUKEE

One version of the Package Truck was a simple flat platform with three vertical bars for transporting tires.

**Model 18-QA, $105**

Attached to Motorcycle Model 19-J, $610
Attached to Motorcycle Model 18-F, $500

Hinged top parcelcar. Inside dimensions, 44 inches long by 20 inches wide by 15 inches high.

THIS single compartment hinged top parcelcar has proved to be the most popular Harley-Davidson type. A large percentage of the parcelcars made in the past have been of this style. Body built of wood throughout, of non-rattling construction.

The tall box could easily carry numerous garments on hangers for wrinkle-free delivery to happy customers

A—Interior view of the sturdy van.

B—Note the two substantial steel reinforcements and check strap.

C—Extension axles adjustable to 44 ins. or 56 ins. 48 ins. or 60 ins.

Price, $65.00
F. O. B. Milwaukee

Since British motorcycle manufacturers had been out of the civilian style business for practically all of 1914-1918, Harley-Davidson's position in the world market steadily improved. By 1919, Harley-Davidson motorcycles were sold in nearly every civilized country in the world, and some not so civilized. Some 2,000 dealers worldwide delivered machines in such diverse areas as Tasmania, Japan, Fiji Islands, Ceylon, Iceland, South Africa, all of Europe and—before the 1917 Bolshevik Revolution—even Russia. Fully one-sixth of Harley-Davidson's production was going to foreign enthusiasts, and an important part of the company's business has been in exports ever since.

A 1918 Harley
with covered
sidecar.

# THE UNIQUE MODEL W SPORT

The advertising literature for 1919 summed up the brand new Sport Model appropriately when it stated, "This latest Harley-Davidson creation is certainly something different. Indeed, it incorporates so many new features it is hard to know where to begin to describe it."   So completely new and different was the Sport that it ranks among a very select group of Harley-Davidson motorcycles that were totally unique from the ground up, a group that includes the very first Single, the 1942 XA, the 1952 Model K and the 2002 V-Rod.

A radical departure from the traditional V-twin, the Sport featured a unit power plant, which combined the engine with the transmission, something that wouldn't be seen again in a Harley-Davidson until the Fifties. Similar in design to the Indian Model O and the British Douglas, both of which preceded the Sport, the engine itself was a six horsepower opposed twin mounted fore and aft in the chassis. The three-speed, sliding gear transmission, mounted above the 37 cubic inch engine, was connected by a spiral gear system that replaced the primary drive chain of the V-twin models. The final drive chain was completely enclosed and lubricated by a breather pipe from the crankcase.

Highly unusual was the manifold, which combined both the intake and the exhaust in a single casting. The heat from the exhaust gases, which passed through the lower part of the manifold, served to both warm the intake gases for improved, more efficient combustion and helped to eliminate condensation accumulation. With the carburetor placed above the rear cylinder, intake gases had to travel over fifteen inches to the front cylinder.

Another unusual aspect of the Sport Model, which was produced from 1919 to 1923, was the use of a Keystone frame. Manufactured from high carbon steel, the double trussed frame formed a Keystone construction wherein the engine became a structural member of the chassis and provided for added rigidity. No Harley-Davidson twin cylinder model before or since has employed a Keystone frame. The trussed front cushion forks, too, never appeared on another model after the Sport. The Sport, unlike the other Harley-Davidson models, employed a single coil spring in the front suspension.

The tanks, also unlike other contemporary Harley-Davidson models, were made up as one complete unit holding both gasoline and oil and were contained within the upper and lower frame tubes rather than encompassing them. The gas tank held three gallons of fuel while the oil tank held two quarts. Fuel consumption was amazingly generous at 50 to 90 miles per gallon. The extra wide dropside fenders, previously absent on any Harley-Davidson model, were only used later on late Twenties Singles.The Sport Model, a reliable and extremely dependable motorcycle capable of speeds up to fifty miles an hour, was reportedly intended alternately for the female market or the export markets. Despite being relatively slow by the standards of its day, the Model W was nonetheless exceptionally smooth and easy to ride and virtually vibration free. With its extra quiet muffler, it was a pleasure to ride and attracted many followers. So dependable was it that the Sport set a Three-Flags record from Canada to Mexico, a distance of over 1700 miles, in just 65 hours in 1919 and was the first vehicle to conquer Pikes Peak.

Above,
A unique system of gears transferred power from the engine to the 3-speed sliding gear transmission

# THE 1920'S

## Roaring Into The Twenties

# THE 1920'S

The "war to end all wars" was over. The world was at peace. Industry had returned to peacetime pursuits, and the economy was percolating. The year was 1920 and prosperity had returned to the land. Consumers went on a buying frenzy to own those luxury items denied them while America's attention was turned towards defeating the Kaiser and his armies.

The motorcycle publications that year were filled with optimism regarding the health of the industry. Motorcycles were hard to come by and factories were working to capacity. The general consensus in the motorcycle industry was that it would take at least two years for supply to catch up with demand.

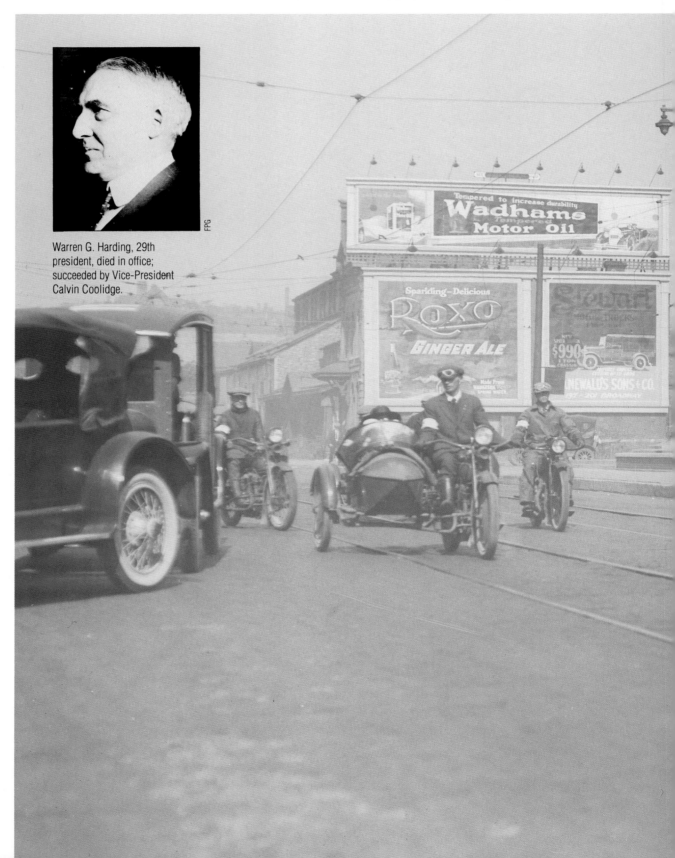

Warren G. Harding, 29th president, died in office; succeeded by Vice-President Calvin Coolidge.

In the Twenties, Harley-Davidson motorcycles were promoted for many forms of transportation, from general use to business purposes, and as "The Woman's Outdoor Companion."

In racing, Harley-Davidson was king, and the winner's circle was its throne. At Ascot Park in California, on January 4, 1920, a quartet of Harley-Davidson riders, led by the great Otto Walker, swept first through fourth in a performance that set the pace for motorcycle racing that year and the next. In February, the legendary Red Parkhurst, racing a 61 cubic inch Harley on the storm-roughened beach at Daytona, established new speed records for the one kilometer and the one mile at over 103 mph each. He also set new marks for two miles and five miles of 99 and 98 mph, respectively. Next, astride a 61 incher coupled with the brand new "Bullet" racing sidecar, Parkhurst dialed off another string of records. In all, twenty-three speed records fell to the Harley-Davidson onslaught that day. By May of the next year, Harley-Davidson also owned all the dirt track records for the one, two, five, ten, twenty-five and fifty mile races, in addition to being the first motorcycle to average over 100 miles per hour in a race.

Silent screen comic Harold Lloyd.

Red Parkhurst, with teammate Fred Ludlow in the "Bullet" sidecar, led a rampage of record-shattering wins on the beaches of Daytona in 1920, which saw 23 new records fall to Harley-Davidson in one day.

## OTTO WALKER CAPTURES ASCOT RACE

A Sunday crowd of 25,000 turned out on January 4, 1920 at Ascot Park to watch a quartet of Harley-Davidson riders clinch the first four places in the fastest race run to date at the Los Angeles track. The big event was a 100-miler that saw the best riders in the country going head-to-head for first-place honors.

While the other competitors were riding the potent eight-valve racing machines, the Harley-Davidson contingent was powered by more conventional pocket-valve machines. Smooth riding, consistent performance and superb work by the Harley-Davidson pit crew were contributing factors as Otto Walker led teammates Ralph Hepburn, Red Parkhurst and Fred Ludlow to a clean sweep of the 1920 season opener, a clear sign of things to come.

# LESLIE "RED" PARKHURST

By 1920, Harley-Davidson motorcycles were devouring the competition on race tracks all over the country as event after event fell to the machines from Milwaukee. Of all the daring young men campaigning on Harleys, undoubtedly one of the most popular was Leslie "Red" Parkhurst, a red-headed competitor with a perpetual grin.

Born in Denver, Red got the racing fever early on and began competing on the notorious motordromes of the era. Motordromes were huge oval racetracks built of pine planks, laid side-by-side like a wood floor. With their steeply-pitched sides, they were famous for high speeds and spectacular crashes that could incapacitate or kill both rider and spectator alike. Little wonder that they earned the nickname of "murderdromes."

Red heard of a new motordrome being built in Milwaukee and headed east, where he soon caught the attention of Harley-Davidson's racing department, newly formed in 1914. Recently married, Parkhurst gave up the dangers of the motordrome in favor of campaigning the new Harley racing motors on conventional tracks.

Victory after victory, and record after record fell to the amiable redhead, as he and his fellow teammates toured the country. At a track in Rockford, Illinois in 1915, he took his most serious spill. According to the doctor who attended him, Red's brain was shifted to one side in his skull, which resulted in an unbalanced mental condition for a short time. Fortunately, there were no lasting effects, and he returned to the tracks again to continue his winning ways. When America went to war, racing more or less came to a halt, and Red got a job as a superintendent at a large coal company in Milwaukee. Over the next two years, Red's oft-repeated statement was: "You'll never get me back into motorcycle racing."

But by the spring of 1919, Harley-Davidson was preparing some powerful eight-valve engines in anticipation of racing again, and after a talk with Harley racing engineer Bill Ottoway, Red was hooked one more time. At the first race of the season at Portland, Oregon, which signaled the revival of postwar motorcycle racing, it was the big grin of Red Parkhurst that was featured again in the winner's circle.

Red led a one-two-three Harley sweep in Marion, Indiana, followed by personal victories in the five, ten and twenty-five mile events in his hometown of Denver.

While many racers regularly jumped from one make of motorcycle to another, Red Parkhurst steadfastly refused all offers, regardless of how lucrative they appeared, preferring to campaign on the machines he had started on. His loyalty to Harley-Davidson earned him the respect of everyone connected with the sport.

At the height of his career, when he was probably the oldest and undoubtedly the most popular racer in the country, Red chose to retire from racing and work for Firestone Tire & Rubber Co., in Akron, Ohio. He cited a responsibility to his wife and child as his main reason for leaving professional racing. While no longer a competitor, he nonetheless retired as one of the early stars of motorcycle racing, and still frequented races on behalf of Firestone for years to come.

Red Parkhurst, right, led a 1-2-3 sweep of the Marion, Indiana race in 1919, followed by Harley-Davidson teammates Otto Walker, left, and Ralph Hepburn.

**D**espite the rosy outlook at the beginning of 1920, business took a decided downturn a few months later. The automobile industry had overproduced, companies had been paying inflated prices for goods and labor--which drove retail prices up, and banks were overloaded with loans. Consumers adopted a wait and see attitude, creating excessive inventories. To stimulate sales, Henry Ford cut prices on his cars, which put a scare into related industries, and motorcycle sales slumped.

At a national dealer convention in Milwaukee, in November 1920, company president, Walter Davidson, addressed the problem of flagging sales and pledged to make the dealers stronger than ever. A new emphasis on business management was to be the driving force behind Harley-Davidson. Dealers were educated on the need to advertise more, to provide better service, to enhance the rider's enjoyment of the sport by increasing their performance in accessory sales and to improve the somewhat negative public image of motorcyclists. These areas of improvement, as defined by Walter Davidson in 1920, are still stressed by Harley-Davidson today, some eight decades later.

The Motorcycle & Allied Trades Association, the industry's self-appointed watchdog, launched a massive campaign to both make dealers think more seriously about running their stores and improving the public image of the sport and its legion of enthusiasts. To this end, Harley-Davidson ran full page ads calling those who ride with open mufflers "boobs" and calling on concerned motorcyclists everywhere to take action "lest the entire wholesome sport of motorcycling be banished, like a leper, by legislation." The future of the sport, it was felt, was dependent on acceptance by the public at large.

Harley-Davidson Parcelcars were popular as delivery vehicles with a wide variety of service industries.

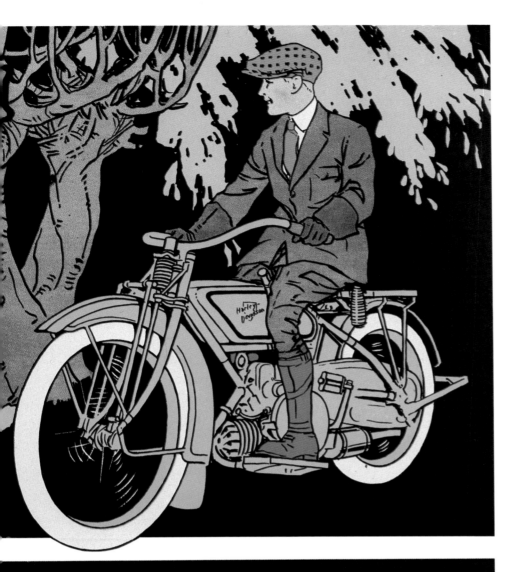

# HARLEY-DAVIDSON CHUMMY CAR

## 40 to 60 Miles per Gallon of Gasoline

**S**ales of 61 cubic inch V-twin motorcycles comprised the bulk of Harley-Davidson's sales in 1921 as production plummeted to the lowest number in almost a decade, just over 10,000 machines. Sidecars were still very popular, so, to satisfy the need for more power and give sales a needed shot in the arm, the first Harley-Davidson 74 cubic inch engine, which developed 18 horsepower, appeared in 1921. Advertised as the Superpowered Twin, it was designed for sidecar or tandem riding, while the proven 61 incher remained for solo riding. The 1922 machines were sophisticated for the times, employing 38 different types of high grade metals in their construction and undergoing a rigid test and inspection before being shipped. Gone was the army green color. Three coats of brewster green with gold striping, varnished and baked, was the new color for 1922. However, just two years later, the company returned to olive green with maroon striping.

Emphasis was placed on economy of operation, not only for the consumer but for municipal and commercial uses as well. A new model, the 21-CD, was developed for commercial use with a single-cylinder engine designed for ease of maintenance, economy and longevity. Ads soon boasted 80 miles per gallon and a penny-a-mile operating costs. Numerous ads and flyers extolled the virtues of using Harley-Davidson motorcycles for businesses and municipalities. By 1924, 1,400 police and sheriff's departments were using Harley-Davidson motorcycles, as were countless private businesses.

Illustrations from a 1921 promotional flyer titled "My Harley-Davidson with the Pal Car" promoted the "good fellowship" of the Harley-Davidson sidecar with the theme: "No matter where my trail may be, My Pal will always ride with me."

# Keep Warm!

## Articles That Add Greatly to the Comfort and Pleasure of Winter Driving

Early in the game, Harley-Davidson realized the importance of providing riders with clothing and accessories which were unique to the sport and unavailable except through Harley-Davidson dealers.

**Lamb Lined Moleskin Vest**

IX-340—Made of fine gray moleskin cloth with sleeves of genuine cowhide leather. Body is lined with lambskin 3 inches from front and bottom facing. Collar and wristlets are of knitted brown wool. Pockets are leather trimmed. Length 25 in. Sizes 36 to 44 inclusive.

$13.50

JX-285
One-Finger Style

**Mackinaw**

HX-331—Classiest Mackinaw on the market—and the warmest. Made up in a handsome plaid of a hard finish, all wool, wind resisting, heavy Mackinaw cloth. Length 34 inches. Sizes 36 to 44 inclusive.

$17.50

**Boy's Mackinaw**

HX-331 B—Just like the above in sizes 12, 14, 16 and 18 years.

$15.00

"Flexicuf"

Ideal for winter
warm lamb lining
lambskin.

Cuffs are the new
lined and extra
heavy mackinaw

Leather used is the
hide. In producing
ing is used in
strength and dur
particular stock i

Made in an extr
dom of the hand.

Fit is perfect and

# For Fall Driving

## Sweater Coats
## Sweaters
## Leather Coat
## Windproof Vests
## Leather Helmet

**Extra Heavy All Wool Sweater Coat**

IX-305—Blue heather with special storm collar of a new type. Knit in the Shaker stitch. Sizes 36 to 44 inclusive.

$26.50

**Medium Weight All Wool Sweater Coat**

IX-305—Blue heather. Knit in the Shaker stitch. Comes with a large full roll storm collar. Sizes 36 to 44 inclusive.

$13.50

**Slip-Over Sweater**

IX-303—Green heather. Knit in the Shaker stitch of pure wool worsted yarn. V neck. May be worn over a blouse or vest. Sizes 34 to 42 inclusive.

$10.00

**Sweater with Shawl Collar**

JX-304—Very snappy. Blue heather with Oxford Gray collar, wrists and bottom. All wool and knit in the Shaker stitch. Extra heavy. Sizes 36 to 44 inclusive.

$13.50

**Leather Lined Windproof Vest**

IX-338—Lined with genuine cowhide leather. Outer material is a Leathe-Suede cloth. Has leather sleeves with knitted brown wool wristlets. Collar may be buttoned. Length of vest is 25 inches. Sizes 36 to 44 inclusive.

$15.00

**Leatho-Suede Vest**

IX-337—An unlined vest made of soft, pliable Leathe-Suede cloth which looks and wears like leather. Collar and wristlets are knitted of brown wool. Three patch pockets. Sizes 36 to 44 inclusive.

$9.00

**Reversible Leather Coat**

IX-318—Fine for fall and winter use. Genuine tan grain leather with a smooth finish on one side and an olive Gabardine cloth on the other. Comes double breasted with convertible collar, slash type pockets and an all-around belt with buckle. Length 40 inches. Gives equal satisfaction whether riding or walking. Sizes 36 to 44 inclusive.

$65.00

**Leather Helmet**

IX-298—Made of soft tan grain leather insuring comfortable fit. Lined with khaki cotton serge. Has cups over the ears and strap at the top which facilitates removal from the head. Exposed edges bound with tan silk binding. Fastens with strap and elastic. Sizes 6¾ to 7½ inclusive.

$8.00

# Ask About Them

# OCTOBER I

## ACCESSORY FEATURES

### New Popular Articles For Winter Riding

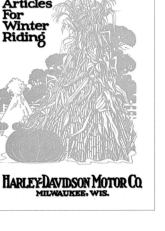

**HARLEY-DAVIDSON MOTOR CO.**
MILWAUKEE, WIS.

Taking advantage of Prohibition, Al Capone built a bootleg booze empire throughout the Twenties.

In the lean years of the early Twenties, Harley-Davidson began taking a harder line on virtually every aspect of the business. Racing was temporarily abandoned in 1923, although privateers worldwide continued to campaign on Harleys. The company not only produced large catalogs of accessories and clothing, but took an aggressive stance against the use of non-genuine parts in its motorcycles. Taking a page from an advertising tactic so popular today, Walter Davidson sent a personal message to potential buyers, via a direct mail flyer, touting the benefits of the 1924 line of Harley-Davidson motorcycles and inviting them to take advantage of a Pay-as-you-Ride Plan. No stone went unturned in the company's efforts to revitalize the sport, as dealers were given tips on how to advertise and promote their products and how to organize rallies, start clubs and sponsor competitive events. Involvement in the sport was seen as a way to not only attract new riders to motorcycling, but to also keep existing enthusiasts active and interested.

### How far did you go yesterday?

THAT'S the first question the gang will ask you when you get back on the job Monday morning. You want to be able to tell 'em right to the dot and you want to tell 'em your highest speed too. That's just what you can do if your bus is equipped with a Corbin Speedometer. If some of the fellows doubt your word just tell 'em to cast their lookers over your Corbin and the argument is settled. You're getting a real speedometer when you buy a Corbin. Total mileage, trip mileage, maximum hand, 80 or 100 mile dial, luminous dial if you like, and everything.

**Your dealer can fix you up to-day**

## Leather Togs

are now sold by your

## Harley-Davidson Dealer

Coats    Jackets
Helmets    Breeches
Belts
Sheepskin Saddle Covers

*"You'll like them"*

## Some Class!

That's what everybody will say when you step out in this Harley-Davidson racing jersey. It's the same jersey the Harley-Davidson racing stars and hill climb men have been wearing the past few years. The color is a knockout, dark green body and orange sleeves. It's also got three inch high letters that will tell 'em a mile off what motorcycle you ride. You are getting real value in this jersey. Sizes 36 to 44.

*Specify*

**No. KX 256-K**

### When you go on that big trip —

take along a can of Harley-Davidson summer oil and treat your motor right. Any old oil won't do the work in your air cooled motor. When you're miles from nowhere you'll be glad you took along a can of this good Harley-Davidson summer oil. Now supplied in flat gallon cans that fit snugly under your sidecar seat. Has a handy spout that makes it easy to pour. Before you go on that big vacation trip drop around to your dealer and get a can or two of genuine Harley-Davidson oil.

### One gallon can
## $1.65
AT FACTORY

John Barrymore's role as Hamlet was another legendary performance by a member of one of America's most famous acting families.

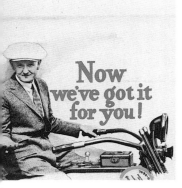

## Now we've got it for you!

## This one is Yours!

Shoot along that 1924 Harley-Davidson catalog that you're holding out for me.

Yours truly,

Street _____ City _____

My pal _____

Street _____

City _____ is another regular fellow who might be interested in the motorcycling sport.

"Flesh and the Devil" was the first of many films to pair John Gilbert and Greta Garbo as a romantic duo.

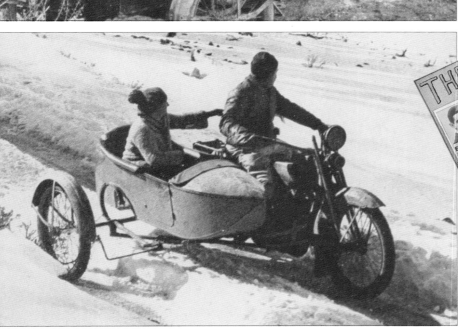

Rudolph Valentino became an all-time screen immortal when he starred as "The Sheik."

Clara Bow, the movies' "IT" girl.

**R**efinements to the Harley-Davidson motorcycle continued through-out the Twenties. An alemite lubrication system, with 12 fittings on the motorcycle, appeared in 1924, and grease guns became the rule. Drop-forged, steel-frame fittings were developed in 1925. The Tear-drop gas tank, so much a part of the unmistakable Harley-Davidson look, made its inaugural appearance that year, providing a more modern look than its boxy predecessor. Designated the "Stream-Line" models, these new offerings featured a truss-loop frame, speedster muffler, lowered riding position and a lower price. A brand new 30.50 cubic inch single, a 12-horsepower model, intended initially for foreign markets, was hailed by the press as an innovative and powerful lightweight motorcycle. Two years later, a device the motorcyclist of today generally thinks of as a "must," the front brake, came into use. At the time of its appearance, it met with some degree of rider skepticism. A carburetor air cleaner was added the same year. By 1928, production had increased to over 22,000 motorcycles.

The **New**

1925

SPEED in every line—strength in every curve —low hung for safety and easy control— better-sprung and bigger-tired for luxurious comfort—that's Harley-Davidson's latest and greatest motorcycle, the "Stream-Line"!

Never a mount like this before—so powerful, so speedy, so perfectly balanced, so roadworthy. From every standpoint of performance, good-looks and economy, the "Stream-Line" sets a new standard. *And yet the price is reduced!*

*We have a real proposition for dealers where we are not represented. Write for full particulars.*

"Stream-Line"

New

New!

New Speedster Muffler

It's Here! the Sensational "Stream-Line"

The year 1928 also welcomed the second generation of the Harley-Davidson family when William H. Davidson, son of William A. Davidson, started with the company. He was followed the next year by Walter Davidson's sons, Gordon and Walter C. Davidson, and William J. Harley.

Charles E. Lindbergh became internationally known as "Lucky Lindy" after his first solo New York-Paris nonstop flight in 1927. It took him 33.5 hours.

Now!

the 1927

HARLEY-DA

## "Stream-Lin
# HARLEY-DAVIDSON

NEWEST and finest model of the World's Greatest Motorcycle—the 1925 "Stream-Line" Harley-Davidson! How the young bloods will itch to get this handsome, speedy, peppy thoroughbred out for a trial spin!

It's the biggest news of the motorcycle business—this year or for years past. Every prospect you've talked to—every man who ever wanted a motorcycle—will BUY when he sees the new "Stream-Line".

The "Stream-Line" will make 1925 a bigger year for thousands of dealers. Why not *you*? See new features on next page. *Write—wire—phone!*

HARLEY-DAVIDSON MOTOR COMPANY, *Milwaukee, Wisconsin, U. S. A.*

*Reduced Prices:*
Model 25FE, magneto, equipped, 61" motor - - $295
Model 25JE, electric equipped, 61" motor - - 315
Model 25FDCB, magneto equipped, 74" motor - 315
Model 25JDCB, electric equipped, 74" motor - 335
Model 25QT, two passenger sidecar - - - 130
Model 25LT, single passenger sidecar - - - 100
*Above prices are at factory and do not include war tax.*

New Lower Price

1927—TWIN "74"—PRICE $320
(Electrically Equipped)

THE greatest Harley-Davidson of all — at new and lower prices! Improved — refined in many details — but no radical departures from the time-tried Harley-Davidson design. Old timers and beginners alike will recognize in these 1927 Twins the last word in engineering achievement. Powerful—speedy — built to hug the road — the most dependable and satisfactory mount that ever split the wind.

The 1927 Twin

1927—TWIN "61"—PR
(Electrically Equipp

ADDED to the greater value built into the 1927 Twins — added to improvements that every rider will welcome — prices are lower than ever before. Harley-Davidsons have always been outstanding values. Now, more than ever, the Harley-Davidson motor-cycle stands without a rival. In performance, in price, in rugged endurance, the 1927 Twins are the world's stand-ard of motorcycle comparison.

HARLEY - DAVIDSON

"The Jazz Singer," starring Al Jolson, shown in New York City in 1927, was considered the first major "talking" motion picture.

Babe Ruth hit 60 home runs in 1927.

## A New Wonderful 45 Twin

$\mathcal{H}$ERE IT IS! ... 45 twin, the motorcycle ... at the world has been ... y-Davidson to build.

...cycle!—great acceleration ... power—quiet speed that ... he parades of cars far ... Above all a motor-... y to handle, a com-... pleasure to ride.

...you would expect in ... he Harley-Davidson ... ne tanks. Features ... at stamp it the ... odern motorcycle engineering.

... put this 45 through its paces. ... 'll wonder how its price can pos-... so low . . . . $290 at the factory.

*Two Bullet Headlights* give more and better light —this means safer night riding. Handy toggle switch on right handlebar cuts out right light and depresses beam of left

RLEY

THE "45" twin —a new HARLEY-DAVIDSON 1929 sweeping ...ovements for

102

## Still Better 61 and 74 Twins

**B**ETTER equipped, better looking, always reliable, better performing than ever —the 1929 Big Twins are the finest motorcycles Harley-Davidson has ever built.

Safer night riding with two bullet type headlights, quiet exhaust with four tube muffler, instantaneous generator output control, a new electrical panel with built-in ammeter are features that keep these world famous twins far in the lead. And yet with all these advancements there is no raise in prices.

See your Harley-Davidson dealer today, look over and ride the new 1929 models. Their wonderful easy riding comfort and outstanding features will surprise you.

*New 4 Tube Muffler* changes the tone of the exhaust, blending it into a lower pitched tone that is agreeable to the ear. Muffler divides at the end of the exhaust pipe into two tubes, each carried to the rear at either side of the wheel. Each of these tubes in turn carries an additional outlet tube, providing in all four expelling tubes for the exhaust gases. This muffler is positively the most quiet muffler ever developed for motorcycles.

*New Generator Output Controller*—instantly regulates the generator output by means of an outside lever. With the always visible ammeter, this new feature should assure a fully charged battery at all times.

### ...and Prices

| | |
|---|---|
| ngle | $235.00 |
| | 290.00 |
| | 310.00 |
| pistons) | 325.00 |
| | 320.00 |
| tons) | 335.00 |
| h Two Cam | 370.00 |
| ger Sidecar | 100.00 |

re at factory.

N MOTOR CO.
Wisconsin

## The Single for 1929

**A**LL the great new features of the 1929 Twins have been built into the Single for 1929. Now more than ever, it is the outstanding value in motorcycles of its class. The ideal mount for riders who want a comfortable, dependable, so motorcycle that costs to buy and almost ing to run.

## Single Passenger Sidecar

**H**ERE is the sidecar that will appeal to the man who wants to share his motorcycling joys. Luxurious comfort for the passenger. Easy to handle. Beautiful in appearance. Richly upholstered. Lots of room for touring luggage. Inspect it and you'll find it correct in design and right in every mechanical detail.

# DAVIDSON

---

**T**he DL 45-inch side valve twin came along in 1929 and became an immediate hit. Accenting it's already sleek looks was a pair of bullet headlights, standard on the line that year. This motorcycle combined the power of the big twin and agile handling of the single. For 1929, Harley-Davidson offered V-twin engines in 45, 61 and 74 cubic inch displacements. In addition, a special twin-cam 74, powered by a version of the highly successful racing engine, was offered as "the fastest road model that Harley-Davidson has ever offered to the public."

The year 1929 was a momentous one. The American Motorcycle Association (AMA) took the reins of overseeing the industry from its predecessor, the Motorcycle & Allied Trades Association. At a January sales meeting in Milwaukee, Walter Davidson reiterated the company's pledge to help the dealer market his products. An Open House Celebration was held at Harley-Davidson dealerships all over the country that summer. The number of police departments using Harley-Davidson motorcycles swelled to more than 2,900. And, the 1930 models were announced in August amid much critical acclaim and enthusiasm.

Wyoming elects Nellie Ross as first U. S. woman governor.

John Scopes convicted of teaching the theory of evolution in public school in Tennessee "monkey trial."

First publication of *The New Yorker* magazine.

Scottish inventor, J. L. Baird, transmits human features by television.

1926

Dr. Robert Goddard demonstrates potential of rockets using liquid fuel; rocket travels 184 feet in 2.5 seconds.

Gertrude Ederle is first woman to swim English Channel.

Ford introduces 40-hour work week to check overproduction and limit unemployment.

1927

Trotsky expelled from Russian Communist Party.

1928

Alexander Fleming discovers penicillin.

Richard E. Byrd explores Antarctic.

America meets Mickey Mouse in first cartoon released by Walt Disney Productions.

1929

U. S. Stock market collapses; first phase of U. S. Depression.

St. Valentine's Day gangland massacre in Chicago.

**O**f course, 1929 also brought the start of the Great Depression, and along with it, some heavy blows for the motorcycle industry. Dozens of manufacturers dropped out of sight. A shortage of dollars for individual transportation, combined with low pricing and growth in the automobile industry, were at least partly at fault. Then, too, motorcycling had evolved into largely a recreational activity, and people were reluctant to spend money on "leisure" pursuits. Harley-Davidson suffered along with everyone else, as industry-wide sales fell sharply.

However, the company prevailed where others couldn't, and the reasons are somewhat difficult to pinpoint. Certainly a strong dealer network, long established advertising programs, quality products, an affinity for the sport and the enthusiast, police and commercial use, conservative business management, and a strong export business were all contributing factors to Harley-Davidson's survival in the decade of the Twenties, later known as the darkest in the history of America.

HARLEY-DAVIDSON for 1929

OVER the hills and far away! Up hill and down dale with the speed of the wind. The healthful fresh air on your cheek. A purring mount that responds to your every wish — always anxious to do more. Ten, twenty, thirty miles slip by before you know it. Hundreds of miles in a day. New scenes, new pleasures — life that is worth living — that's Motorcycling, Outdoors' Greatest Sport.

Can't you hear that call of the open road? Come on for a joyous week-end, a vacation trip you'll never forget, a club run or tour, a wonderful hunting or fishing trip. Swing into the saddle of your trusty Harley-Davidson and leave the long parades of cars far behind.

*Come On — Let's Go!*

MOTORCYCLING ~ Outdoors' Greatest Sport

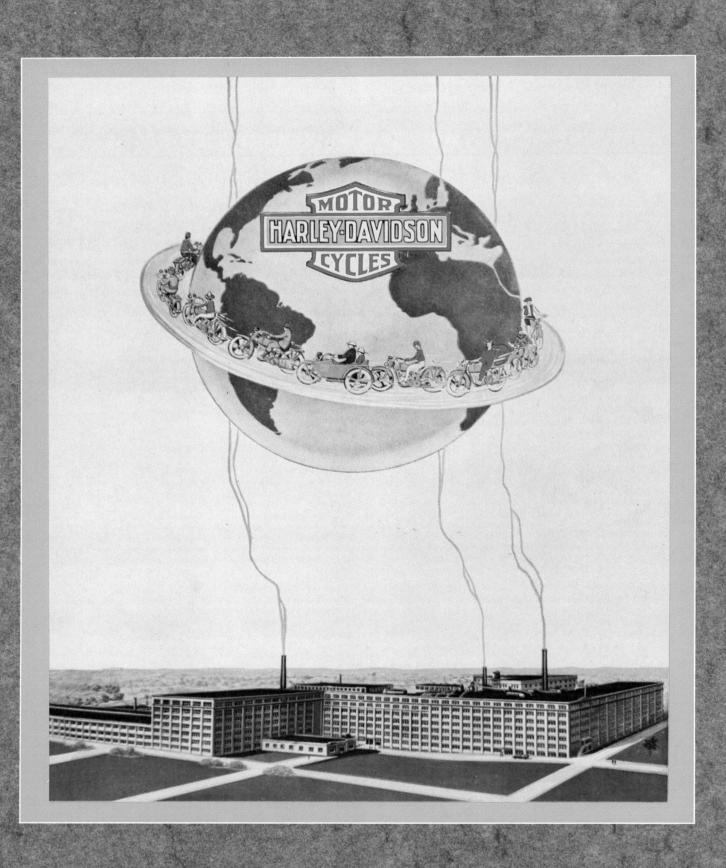

# THE 1930'S

Growing Stronger Through Hard Times

# THE 1930'S

**J**ust like the beginning of the previous decade, the Thirties started on a high note of optimism, both for the sport of motorcycling and for Harley-Davidson. Motorcycle business, in general, was up 31 percent over the prior year, reflecting a fairly steady climb over the past years. Industry experts in January of 1930, like most people, had not fully realized the overall economic impact of the stock market crash of October. In fact, they believed that quick action on the part of President Herbert Hoover had repaired any damage.

The 1930 line of Harley-Davidson motorcycles was hailed as being virtually without comparison in the industry. Referring to the fact that the company was comprised of riders—including officers and shop men alike—*American Motorcyclist and Bicycle* magazine stated: "Dealers and riders will be in accord that the 1930 Harley-Davidson motorcycles achieve a closer relation to desires of devotees of the sport, the perfect motorcycle. No new feature has been added until it has been given an exhaustive road and bench test from a staff of competent engineers."

And, the 1930 models were loaded with features. The twin-cylinder and single-cylinder models all had new Ricardo removable heads, which provided for easier maintenance, improved efficiency and dramatic horsepower increases. The high compression 74 inch model, designated the VL, delivered 15 to 20 percent more horsepower than any previous engine of its size. The 74 also sported easily detachable, interchangeable wheels.

The entire line received larger front and rear brakes, larger tires, built-in front fork lock, a lowered saddle height, increased ground clearance and dual-beam headlights. The standard color was olive green with vermillion striping, but a forthcoming special paint program was announced to fill customers' requests for something different.

"Perfect Score Award" watch fob from the 1930 A.M.A. Annual Rally & Gypsy Tour.

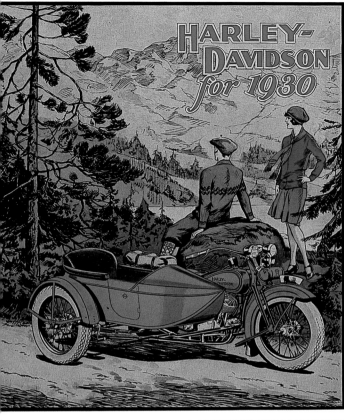

Harley-Davidson's advertising and promotion became even more aggressive in the Thirties, promoting both motorcycles and sidecars.

## Our Savings Club Plan

Pick out the model you want. You make a down deposit—as little as $2.50 is enough —and we give you your Savings Club Plan Pass Book shown above. Each week or pay day, you drop in and add to this deposit a certain amount or as much as you can. Your deposits are recorded, as made, in your book which you keep. When your deposits reach a certain total, depending on the model you select, you change over to the Pay-As-You-Ride Plan and ride out on your own mount.

**$2.50 STARTS YOU!**

## So Easy to Own One

## Pay-As-You-Ride Plan

On this plan you put down one-third the cost of the model you select and ride out. If you trade in an old motorcycle, the price we allow you counts in on the down payment. This down payment is recorded in your Pay-As-You-Ride Pass Book, which you keep. Then at regular periods you ride in to see us and make a payment as we have agreed upon. You pay as you ride and never feel the small easy payments.

**⅓ DOWN~ and you ride out**

"Garbo talks," said the publicity for Greta Garbo's first "talking" motion picture in 1930, "Anna Christie."

To launch the 1930 selling season, Harley-Davidson staged a nation-wide open house on March 1 with over 400 dealers participating. Despite bad weather in some parts of the country, an estimated 50,000 customers visited dealerships to view the new models. Because of the enthusiastic response, industry experts felt that Harley-Davidson and the industry were "heading for record-breaking sales."

Indeed, they appeared to be right, as the outlook for Harley-Davidson looked rosy. Over 3,000 police departments were on Harleys. Literature for the export market was being produced in a number of languages, including German, French and Spanish. Hillclimbs and dirt tracks became the popular events, and Harley-Davidson racked up victory after victory.

As the economy deteriorated following the stock market crash, the industry reached out to stimulate business. The American Motorcyclist Association staged a nationwide Gypsy Tour, a longtime motorcycling tradition, to keep enthusiasts involved in the sport. Most dealers in the U.S. and Canada held some kind of event—including tours, rallies, polo tournaments, races, hillclimbs, field meets, rodeos, picnics, jamborees or anything else they could think of. The turnout of motorcyclists was tremendous. Unfortunately, sales continued to decline as enthusiasm for the sport failed to be an adequate substitute for cash. As money grew more scarce, it became increasingly difficult to attract new customers.

Calling on over 27 years of engine building experience, Harley-Davidson began marketing single-cylinder commercial motors called power units.

A caption from a 1930s *Enthusiast* reads: "The Special Delivery boys in East Liberty, PA, shoot the speedys straight with Harley-Davidson horsepower. The line-up shows the clan in low gear, clutches set, throttles throbbing. . .ready to GO PLACES."

Advertising materials were printed in many languages to promote Harley-Davidson.

The 1930 HARLEY-DAVIDSON 500 c.c. Single Model—*view of right side.*

[ Page 8 ]

1930年式ハーレー・ダビッドソン 500 c.c. シングル型(右側面)

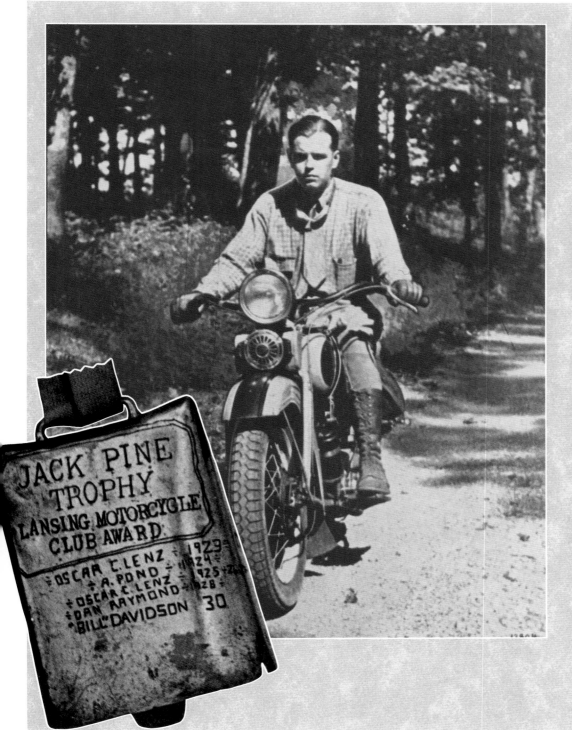

## DAVIDSON WINS "COW BELL CLASSIC"

*The New American Motorcyclist and Bicyclist* for October 1930, told how Bill Davidson was the winner in the Jack Pine Tour, nicknamed the "Cow Bell Classic." Entitled "Bill Davidson and the Cow Bell," the story read:

"Bill Davidson piled up a grand total of 997 points out of a possible 1,000 to win first honors in the annual 'Cow Bell Classic.' The individual class winners in the Jack Pine Tour were all Harley-Davidson mounted.

"Oscar Lenz, winner of the coveted bovine gong in 1923-25-26-27, gave Davidson a great battle for high honors. His score of 996 was good for second place in the Class A Solo, while his two brothers, also Harley-Davidson riders and boosters, were copping the gravy in their respective classes."

"Here we see the 1930 Jack Pine winner and his famous trophy. Bill is the son of William Davidson, vice-president and works manager of the Harley-Davidson Motor Company. In the face of the keenest competition, Bill came through to victory, putting his stock 45 through 420 miles of 'hell' in northern Michigan to win the Class A Solo event in this grueling two-day contest of brains and brawn."

A January 1931 ad promoted Harley-Davidsons as the vehicle to help reduce auto accidents with police safety patrols.

## THE NEW 1930 500 c.c. SINGLE MODEL

### 1930 年式 "500 c.c. シングル型"

小型 500 c.c. モーターも 750 c.c. 型と同様の改良を以て歐米同級車中の代表的單車乗用車として實に驚異的賞讚をうけて居ります。此の新型 500 c.c. のフレームは全く中型 750 c.c. のものと同型の低床式フレームにして新型フォークは自動的に發電出量を増加する新式ゼネレーターと共に、1930 年式 500 c.c. の主要特徴であります。尚モーターはリカルドー・ヘツド式を採用し、新型リム、大型バローン・タイヤ、獨特のハーレー・ダビツドソン・シート・ポスト、盗難防止装置、前方二聯式チェーン、自動給油装置等は何れも中型 750 c.c. 同様でありまして此等の理想的新設計によつて皆様は御愛乘に際し充分なる御滿足を御味ひになる事が出來ませう。

[ Page 9 ]

115

To stimulate sales, Harley-Davidson embarked on an aggressive marketing campaign designed to turn its legion of riders into salespersons. Riders who convinced friends to buy Harley-Davidson motorcycles received bronze, silver or gold medals, with the best "salesperson" in the country receiving a large cash prize. A later contest similarly awarded points for each sale, which were redeemable for leather luggage, radios, movie cameras and other handsome prizes.

While always an important part of the business, commercial sales of Harley-Davidson motorcycles and products took on a heightened significance as quality, economy of operation and longevity of use became ever more important to Depression-stricken companies seeking to stretch their dollars. Drawing on its reputation as an air-cooled engine builder, Harley-Davidson reintroduced an industrial motor, or power unit, for commercial uses.

In late 1931, Harley-Davidson introduced the three-wheeled Servi-Car, intended primarily for use by garages and service stations for pickup and delivery of their customers' cars. With its economical 45 cubic inch engine, large capacity rear box and automotive-type rear differential, it was offered to the major automobile franchises as the ideal vehicle to service customers who were reluctant to drive to their local garage for work on their cars. A serviceman could ride to the customer's house on the Servi-Car, attach it to the rear bumper of the customer's car with a tow bar and drive back to

Mae West's feature film career, which often ran afoul of censors, began in the 1932 production of "Night After Night."

the garage. When the work was completed, the car was delivered, and the serviceman returned to work on the Servi-Car. A task normally undertaken by two men could now be done by one.

It was soon apparent that the Servi-Car was also an ideal vehicle for police departments. Because of its stability and ease of operation, it proved to be perfect for traffic control and enforcing parking restrictions and rapidly gained widespread acceptance.

Tame by today's standards, Boris Karloff's 1931 performance as the monster in "Frankenstein" shocked movie audiences.

espite the company's best efforts, sales of new motorcycles continued to slip for the first several years of the decade. With a surplus of cars on the market, a used Ford could be purchased for as low as $50, further eroding motorcycle sales. By 1933, industry-wide sales of motorcycles reached an all-time low of 6,000 units. Harley-Davidson produced 3,700 motorcycles that year, a far cry from only a few years earlier.

But Harley-Davidson has always been a resilient company. A policy in 1920 of teaching dealers how to advertise and promote their products, plus a total involvement in the sport, ranging from rider involvement programs to an aggressive stance on the marketing of parts and accessories, provided a substantial base to help the company through the lean years. Advertising in the *Enthusiast* magazine, and dealer ad slicks, promoted an extensive line of aftermarket products, from leather riding suits to luggage racks to motorcycle lubricants. In all instances, the company stressed the importance of using genuine Harley-Davidson parts, accessories and clothing, and in seeing a dealer for service.

Racing activities continued throughout the Depression, and names like Windy Lindstrom and Joe Petrali carried Harley-Davidson to victory time and time again. Racing was an inexpensive spectator sport that helped divert people's minds from the harsh realities of a depressed economy, and it was Harley-Davidson in the winner's circle that helped keep the loyalty of motorcycle enthusiasts intact.

Even though Harley-Davidson suffered a tremendous decrease in sales by 1933, it nonetheless tried to keep as many employees working as possible. Even if they only worked two days a week, they were still working while many Americans had no income at all.

The effects of the hard times were visibly apparent in the type and volume of advertising materials the company produced. In the Twenties, Harley-Davidson created large, colorful brochures, oftentimes with original paintings as illustrations. It was not unusual for several different brochures, all elaborate, to be produced in the same model year. In addition, large ads were carried in virtually every issue of every motorcycle magazine. By the Thirties, product literature had shrunk to little more than flyers with black and white or two-color illustrations. Even the amount of materials available for dealers shrank in volume compared to the previous decade. This was a bitter pill to swallow for a company that continually exhorted its dealers to promote their sport, their business and their products. Although reduced in scope, Harley-Davidson realized the value of advertising and continued it on a scale that was probably larger than sales justified at times. Obviously, they realized they were advertising for the future.

# HARLEY-DAVIDSON
**THE WORLD'S FINEST MOTORCYCLE**

Above,
stars of the silver screen in the Thirties included Clark Gable, Gary Cooper, Cary Grant, Robert Taylor and Tyrone Power.

At left,
stars of the 1933 Harley-Davidson line were the new 74 Twin, 45 Twin, 30.50 Single, 21 Single and 74 Twin Sidecar.

119

## 1930

Ghandi's civil disobedience challenges British rulers.

More than 1,300 banks throughout U. S. shut down in economic crisis.

Oscar-winning movie "All Quiet on the Western Front" is released.

## 1931

Al Capone sentenced to 17 years for tax evasion.

U. S. unemployment estimated at four to five million.

New York's Empire State Building, world's tallest, opens.

## 1932

Amelia Earhart is first woman to fly solo across Atlantic.

Franklin D. Roosevelt elected president in Democratic landslide.

Charles Lindbergh Jr. kidnapped, later found dead.

## 1933

Prohibition recognized as a failure and repealed by 21st Amendment.

## 1934

Hitler becomes Fuhrer of Germany.

Joseph P. Kennedy named first chairman of Securities and Exchange Commission.

At the Depression's depth in 1933, Harley-Davidson made a radical departure from tradition, in both colors and tank graphics, in a further effort to stimulate sales. Gone were the block letters on an olive green background. They were replaced with Art Deco tank designs and vibrant new color options. Also available, for a $15 charge, was a chrome-plated package that included handlebars, chain guard, exhaust pipe and muffler, and several other major cosmetic pieces. Harley-Davidson had hit on the concept of factory custom parts and accessories.

By 1934, sales had climbed back to about 10,000 units, a number that would remain fairly consistent, year after year, to the end of the decade.

The Servi-Car quickly found acceptance among police departments as a practical and reliable traffic and parking enforcement tool.

Harley-Davidson motorcycles were used as emergency firefighters by the U. S. Navy at Floyd Bennett Airport in New Jersey in the early Thirties.

*Winners of first place in the Atlanta, Ga., 24-Hour Race. William Bracy, standing, and O. C. Hammond in the saddle of the stock 45 Harley-Davidson with which they piled up 1366 miles.*

# 24 Hour Race
## won by HARLEY-DAVIDSON

*Bert Baisden and his 1934 Harley-Davidson with which he and his team-mate scored second with a total of 1359 miles.*

*Third place winner, Jack Roberts, who with his relief rider, made a total of 1313 miles in the grind around the clock.*

ATLANTA, Georgia, July 15—In one of the most grueling and hardest fought races ever staged in the history of motorcycling, Harley-Davidson riders captured the first five places in the 24-Hour Race held on the historic one-mile Lakewood dirt track.

William Bracy, piloting a '33 stock 45 Harley-Davidson and relief rider, O. C. Hammond, captured first place with the stupendous total of 1366 miles — an average of nearly 57 miles per hour. A close contender most of the race, Bert Baisden, on a '34 stock 45 Harley-Davidson and relief rider, Todd Haygood, rolled up 1359 miles. Jack Roberts, on a '33 stock 45, and Harley Taylor, as relief rider, came in third with 1313 miles. Lt. Ronnie Wilson of the Augusta, Ga., Police Department came in fourth and George Gunn, Atlanta, fifth.

A furious pace was set in the race right from the start. Baisden made the first one hundred miles in eighty-eight minutes. All the time these riders handled the throttle as though they were in a twenty-five mile race instead of a twenty-four hour grind. It was a marvelous exhibition of the ability of the riders and an outstanding demonstration of the staunchness and the stamina of the Harley-Davidson motorcycles.

**HARLEY-DAVIDSON MOTOR CO.**
**MILWAUKEE, WISCONSIN, U.S.A.**

## RIDE A WINNER!

Child star, Shirley Temple, made over 25 movies in the Thirties, while sultry Jean Harlow made the cover of *Time*, captioned: "Feathers Make Fine Fans."

### SERVI-CAR for 1934

## The NEW DEAL Delivery Unit

WHY travel a ton of car or truck to deliver packages? SERVI-CAR will handle five-hundred pound loads at a fraction the cost of light trucks or autos

Ideal for druggists, merchants and delivery services Easily handled by anyone who can drive a car. Sturdy air-cooled motor and standard-differential rear axle. Speedy. rugged, distinctive.

Phone for our representative, or drop in. We are open evenings

**HARLEY-DAVIDSON**
*Motorcycles*

Sport glasses "designed and made for motorcyclists" were among the many accessories, clothing, tools and dealers' supplies in the 1933 Harley-Davidson dealer catalog.

From left: Arthur Davidson, Walter Davidson, William Harley and William Davidson inspect one of the new 61 inch OHV ELs just coming off the assembly line.

**A**s money became increasingly more scarce, people were unable to buy motorcycles, and enthusiasts kept their interest alive by going to the races. As in most sports, a star soon rose to outshine all competitors.

Joe Petrali emerged in the Thirties as the one to beat in nearly all types of motorcycle competition, but few succeeded. Symbolic of his racing dominance was his outstanding performance on the mile and half-mile dirt tracks in 1935. A perennial crowd pleaser, Petrali handily won every National Dirt Track Championship that year, a total of 13 events, to mark the first time in history that one man and one brand of motorcycle had accomplished such a feat. In the process, he set four new A.M.A. records and was crowned the 1935 Dirt Track Champion. Rarely has one person dominated a sport as thoroughly, and as long, as Joe Petrali.

Joe Petrali is shown (clockwise, from upper left): on his 30.50 cubic inch Peashooter; demonstrating classic Petrali style with the rear tire off the ground of the rough track at Union, NJ; in a posed studio photo astride the record-setting Daytona bike; hitting the timer cord with his rear wheel as he clinched the 1935 hillclimbing title.

The Marx Brothers in "A Night at the Opera."

TRANSCONTINENTAL RECORD SMASHED by HARLEY-DAVIDSON

77 hours-53 minutes (ELAPSED TIME)

HARLEY-DAVIDSON MOTOR COMPANY, MILWAUKEE, WIS., U. S. A.

# JOE PETRALI

Every sport has had its legendary heroes. Golf had Bobby Jones; boxing had Jack Dempsey; baseball had Babe Ruth; football had Red Grange; and car racing had many: Barney Oldfield, Ralph DePalma and Eddie Rickenbacker, to name a few. The sport of motorcycle racing had its own hero, as well, a star whose championship performances have never been matched and not even approached: Smokey Joe Petrali.

Joe Petrali was born in San Francisco on Washington's birthday, February 22, 1904. He first became attached to motorcycles at the early age of seven, when an adult neighbor allowed Joe to shine his early-day Flanders motorcycle. When Joe was 12, the neighbor let Joe solo on the Flanders, and Joe's love affair with motorcycles was torrid from that time on. He persuaded his father to let him acquire a used single-cylinder Indian, which Joe promptly converted and tuned for competition, and he enjoyed great success riding this machine in everything from gasoline economy runs to outlaw race meets in Northern California. Indeed, he was so good that soon he was invited to ride one of the Indian factory team's racing models on the board track at Fresno. Although Joe was only 16 years old, he finished a convincing second against the best factory riders in the sport at that time.

After this spectacular start, Joe bounced around for a time. While racing and working in cycle shops, he was always learning something new about engines and fuels. In addition, Joe had long been experimenting with alcohol and carburetion.

Then, on the 4th of July in 1925, on the board track at Altoona, Pennsylvania, it happened! Almost unknown in the east, Joe showed up a few days before the race as a member of the Indian factory team. Somehow, Petrali's Indian had gotten lost enroute, and he was without a mount. Then Ralph Hepburn, a Harley-Davidson team regular, broke his hand in a spill while practicing on his Harley-Davidson on the day before the big Independence Day race and wasn't able to ride. Petrali made a deal with Hepburn and showed up at the starting line on Hepburn's hastily repaired Harley-Davidson. The July 8, 1925 issue of *Motorcycling* magazine carried the race story under this title: "DARK HORSE WINS AT ALTOONA. PETRALI WHO CHANGED CAMPS WINS 100-MILE NATIONAL CHAMPIONSHIP. BOARD TRACK SPEED RECORDS SHATTERED."

Speed records were indeed shattered! Joe Petrali clipped an amazing 13-4/5ths seconds from the old record, and became the first rider to cover 100 miles in less than one hour in a motorcycle competition. Joe's time was 59:47-1/5, more than 100 miles per hour.

For the remainder of 1925, Petrali and his 1000cc flying Harley-Davidson continued to win and break records at super speeds, and at the year's end he was declared National Champion. However, before the year was over motorcycle racing underwent a momentous change with the introduction of a new 350cc class, which immediately became the favorite, because these tidy racers were made available to private buyers on an off-the-dealer's-floor basis. It marked the end of an era of costly super-factory teams, with a half dozen star riders on special racing machines and an army of mechanics for each team. However, it didn't end the super performances of a star like Petrali, who continued as a one-man team, briefly with a 350cc Excelsior in the late 1920s, and permanently with Harley-Davidson after 1930.

Throughout the early Thirties, Petrali successfully raced his 350cc Harley-Davidson Peashooter against other one-man teams on Indians and various British-powered 350s. Success piled on success, and in 1935 Petrali achieved the ultimate: he scored a grand slam by winning all of the 13 American Motorcycle Association National Championship dirt track races on his Harley-Davidson Peashooter, setting four new records in the process.

In 1937, on the beaches of Daytona, Florida, Petrali became the fastest man on two wheels, setting a blistering record speed of 136.183 mph on a specially streamlined Harley-Davidson powered by one of the new 61 cubic inch OHV V-twin engines. The same day he also set a similar record for 45 cubic inch motorcycles, also on a Harley-Davidson.

Always the consummate racer, Petrali was also a fierce competitor on the hillclimbing circuit, racking up national championship titles for five consecutive years, 1932 through 1936.

During 1938, motorcycle factory support of racing, which had already shrunk to almost nothing because of the continuing Depression, faded out completely. The days of the fast, reliable 350cc racing models and their crack riders came to an end, replaced by a new racing class and a new generation of riders. It was known as Class C, and provided for private owners to compete on stock 750cc road bikes.

In the years from 1925 to 1938, the swift and superb-handling 350cc Harley-Davidsons —along with similar Indians, Excelsiors and a variety of foreign-powered 350cc models —wrote thrilling motorcycle history. It was an epochal era that provided motorcycle racing fans with a great deal of pleasure and excitement.

Still at the peak of his career, Joe Petrali retired in 1938 to become the flight engineer and chief service and maintenance man for Howard Hughes. Petrali was on hand in 1947 when Hughes successfully, albeit briefly, flew his mammoth wood amphibian transport plane, dubbed the Spruce Goose. Later, he went on to become an official for the United States Auto Club and, fittingly, was the USAC timer who officially recorded Harley-Davidson's land speed record at Bonneville in October of 1970.

Following his successful record-shattering ride on the beach at Daytona, Petrali was greeted by well-wishers. William Harley is at left with the hat and glasses.

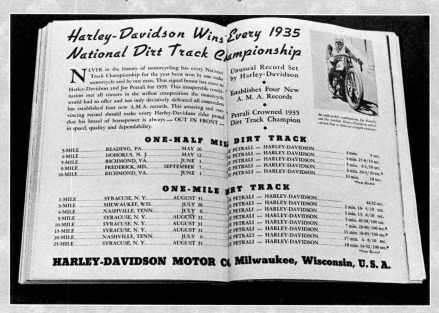

n September of 1935, Harley-Davidson announced its lineup of new models for the coming year. With the exception of the new 80 cubic inch side-valve model—including a high performance version capable of nearly 100 miles per hour—the line for 1936 reflected mainly refinements and improvements of the 1935 models, and, of course, carried new graphics.

The 1936 line did, however, have two striking new additions. In place of the long-used, speedboat-style sidecar was a redesigned sidecar body, which more accurately reflected the styling trends of the times. The side door had been eliminated and, in its place, a large step had been added for ease of entry. Richly grained black upholstery, large windshield, accent striping and stainless steel trim all served to make the 1936 sidecar a handsome complement to the new motorcycles.

The other addition to the line was the startling 61 cubic inch, overhead-valve model called the EL. It laid to rest the rumors which had circulated regarding the new engine Harley-Davidson was developing. Speculation had ranged from the downright amusing to the ridiculous, as people tried to guess what the new Harley would be.

Notorious criminal, John Dillinger, met his death while resisting arrest in 1934.

The 1936 EL model launched a
whole new generation of
Harley-Davidson motorcycles.

**I**nally, at the National Dealers' Convention in the fall of 1935, the EL was introduced with a caution to dealers that it would be a limited model, and they should concentrate on selling the rest of the line. In fact, the EL was put on the market with little promotional fanfare. At the time, the press felt that the EL was an experiment in marketing, although calculated and well-planned. Approximately 2,000 EL models were built for the 1936 model year.

In addition to the overhead-valve engine, which produced almost double the horsepower of the side-valve 61, this newest member of the Harley-Davidson family boasted a number of features not found on any of the other 1936 models. Cradling the engine was a double-loop, truss frame topped by a smoothly restyled, welded teardrop gas tank, shorter and more gracefully rounded. On top of the gas tank, a teardrop instrument cluster was mounted with an integrated speedometer and gauges. Nestled under a sleek wrap-around oil tank was a new hand-shift, four-speed transmission. The first oil circulation system also debuted on the EL. To one degree or another, all these features also found their way into most other models in the 1937 line.

The 1936 EL was a landmark motorcycle for Harley-Davidson because it proved to be the direct ancestor of the models being offered today. Many of the styling ideas and product features pioneered on the EL are used in varying forms on contemporary motorcycles. From the shape of the gas tanks to the wraparound oil tank, these are styling trends that have become synonymous with Harley-Davidson over the years and have indeed been copied extensively by competitive brands.

Marlene Dietrich, shown here in the 1936 production of "Desire," began her American film career in 1930 in "The Blue Angel."

The teardrop dashboard of the revolutionary 1936 EL model.

Florence Burnham, well-known speedboat racer, preferred a chrome and white 1936 Harley-Davidson EL when getting about on dry land.

1936 saw President Franklin Delanor Roosevelt re-elected to his second term.

FPG

Nelson Eddy and Jeanette MacDonald sang their way into the hearts of millions in "Rose Marie."

## OFFICER DOTSON GETS HIS MEN!

That was the caption of a May 1935 Harley-Davidson *Enthusiast* article, telling how "Courageous motorcycle officer William Dotson of Savannah, Georgia, single-handedly captures four escaped convicts," and emphasized: "Fellow officers mighty proud of Dotson. "The story, reproduced exactly as written, continued:

"Midnight! On the Coastal Highway near Savannah, Motorcycle Officer W. Dotson, acting on a hot tip, crouches over the bars of his trusty Harley-Davidson in the shadows of a wayside filling station. Serious business ahead tonight. Four escaped convicts, heavily armed, are reported heading in Dotson's direction in a high-powered, stolen car. Dotson has not long to wait.

"Far down the road a low hum gradually grows to an angry roar—Dotson tenses himself—that roar means something. No ordinary motorist would take a chance here at that speed. Suddenly the roar dies down, and the driver evidently is about to stop for gasoline. Dotson and the convicts see each other at the same instant. Gears clash as the car, a late model V-8 of popular make, plunges forward into the darkness with Dotson in hot pursuit of the fleeing prisoners.

"Faster and still faster speeds the car, but Dotson, with siren screeching, begins closing in. For five miles the chase continues towards Savannah. The speeding car reaches 76 miles an hour but ficer Dotson, cool and calculating, lets the driver go until the Savannah city limits come into sight. Dotson pulls his service revolver and bangs ay at the rear tire.Then he swings alongside the driver and forces the car over to the curb at gunpoint. He disarms the convicts; two of them d removed their striped shirts to avoid suspicion. He confiscates an axe, a pistol and a double-barreled, hammerless shotgun loaded with ckshot. Two of the convicts are still wearing shackles.

y this time other motorcycle officers arrive. Excited motorists crowd around—at a safe distance. The four prison-breakers are taken to the vannah barracks and held until they can be returned to their Lanier County prison cells.

is not necessary here to point out the details leading to the prison break nor how the car was commandeered by the desperate criminals in ir mad dash to freedom. The fact which stands out in the whole thrilling encounter is Officer Dotson's personal bravery and courage. Under remely disadvantageous circumstances, he chose to perform his duty and to protect the residents of Savannah, knowing as he did that the minals were well armed. To Officer William Dotson, who typifies the spirit of the motorcycle patrol, we take off our hats. He's a man. A real n; we believe no finer tribute can be paid him. But aside from Dotson's fine job, there was another factor—something so important that hout it Dotson could not have made his great capture—we mean his dependable Harley-Davidson, a 1934VLD. In the great test, when Dotson eded perfect, unfailing performance his trusty machine responded. And so, once more we salute Officer Dotson and his motorcycle.

n order to prove the power and performance of the new engine—subsequently dubbed the "Knucklehead" because of the configuration of its rocker boxes, Harley-Davidson headed down to the beaches of Daytona in March of 1937 for an assault on the world one-mile straight-away speed record. Limited to engines of no more than 61 inches, the record of 132 miles per hour had stood since 1926. Factory engineer, Harvey Syvertson, showed up with the curiously streamlined Harley-Davidson machine for which Joe Petrali, not surprisingly, had been selected as rider.

With a disc front wheel, streamlined forks, front cowl and fully enclosed rear body, the "Knucklehead" represented the first use of streamlining in the United States. Equipped with one carburetor for each cylinder, the V-twin was fueled by a mixture of alcohol and benzoyl, producing a whopping 65 horsepower at 5,700 rpm.

After a few days of untimed practice runs, Petrali and the streamliner rolled onto the sand on March 13. It was soon discovered that the rear streamlined tail produced a high-speed wobble, so it was removed for the event. To qualify for a record, two one-way passes were required to neutralize any effects the wind would have on speed. Joe roared down the beach, and on the return run, his speed was sufficient to set a record of 134.83 mph.

Next, he mounted a 45 cubic inch *un*streamlined Harley-Davidson and set a new record of 102.04 mph for that class. Returning to the pits, he said: "I'd like to take another shot with that 61. There's still more in it." And the streamlined motorcycle was rolled out for another two-way run, this time aiming at his own newly established mark. When the sand settled, Joe Petrali had added one more triumph to his long list of accomplishments by establishing a still higher record speed of 136.183 miles per hour.

Mickey Rooney and Judy Garland teamed up for many musicals beginning in the Thirties.

The 1936 61 cubic inch overhead valve engine quickly earned the nickname of "Knucklehead" because of the rounded shapes of the polished rocker boxes atop the heads.

FPG

FPG

Hindenburg disaster, May 6, 1937.

When Douglas "Wrong Way" Corrigan, famed flyer who flew solo from the U. S. to Ireland, visited Milwaukee in 1938, he was escorted by a group of Harley-Davidson police motorcycles and enthusiastically welcomed by thousands. Seeing the 61 inch OHV Harley-Davidsons everywhere he went, former Harley owner Corrigan was prompted to seek a ride on one of the new 1938 models.

Fred Astaire and Ginger Rogers made a perfect dance team in Hollywood musicals.

All-around athlete, Olympic champion and pro golfer, Babe Didrikson Zaharias.

FPG

**J**ust one month later, a cloud was cast over the jubilation at Harley-Davidson when William A. Davidson, vice president and co-founder of the company, passed away on April 21, 1937. Much respected in the industry and well liked by all who knew him, his loss was sorely felt.

Continuing the policy of evolution and refinement, the Harley-Davidson line received updates and improvements late in the decade that enhanced its attractiveness and performance. Rather than making radical changes, the company chose to improve and refine its established products. By 1939, the Harley-Davidson lineup was clearly the most popular in the country. By the end of the Thirties, fully 67 percent of all the motorcycles registered in the U.S. were Harleys.

Like much of the nation, the company had faced the toughest times in its history. And through innovation, sound marketing and solid leadership, Harley-Davidson—while not unscathed— had emerged as the strongest, most popular motorcycle manufacturer in the country.

At a time when the Soviet Union was a large purchaser of Harley-Davidson motorcycles, two young members of the Leningrad Motor Club visited the Milwaukee factory. In the background, left to right: Arthur Davidson, B. H. Bellenson, Walter Davidson and William S. Harley. On December 15, "Gone With the Wind" premiered in Atlanta, Georgia.

## WILLIAM A. DAVIDSON

While William Davidson may have been the last of the four founders of Harley-Davidson to join the initial venture, he brought to the little company a wealth of experience and judgment that went far to assure its future success. As a skilled mechanic, he had been the toolroom foreman at the Milwaukee shops of what later became the Chicago, Milwaukee, St. Paul and Pacific Railroad. He was already a family man, and even the automotive industry provided an uncertain future in those days. But the concept of building a newer form of gasoline propelled transportation intrigued him, and he joined his brothers and William Harley with a dedication for the project, which would become the joy and commitment of his life's work.

As works manager, his desk was always piled high with parts from various stages of the manufacturing process: a semi-finished hub, bearing, shaft or rod. He knew the steel from which it was made, the processes it had undergone and those which were necessary for completion. His was the responsibility of purchasing presses and the other equipment needed to continually improve the manufacturing process, as well as meeting the rapidly growing demand for production of Harley-Davidson motorcycles.

Yet, he was not one to allow his fascination with the technical processes of manufacturing to isolate him from his fellow man. William Davidson was known for his compassion for others, particularly employees who needed advice or a helping hand from time to time. From machinists to dealers, bankers to politicians, he was willing to share his time. And while many people say their door is always open, William A Davidson not only said it but lived by that credo. Well respected throughout the community, he passed away April 21, 1937, at the age of 66.

FPG

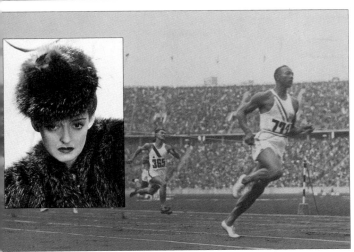

Clockwise from upper left: symbol of the National Recovery Act; the stars of MGM's "Wizard of Oz"; FDR on the cover of *Vanity Fair*; a Harley-Davidson "lucky charm"; Joltin' Joe DiMaggio; the New York World's Fair; Jesse Owens; Bette Davis; signs of hard times; bank robbers Bonnie and Clyde; and a Servi-Car on the job in Hackensack, New Jersey.

This Immense Plant is Devoted Exclusively to the Manufacture of Harley-Davidson Motorcycles

# THE 1940'S

## To War Once More

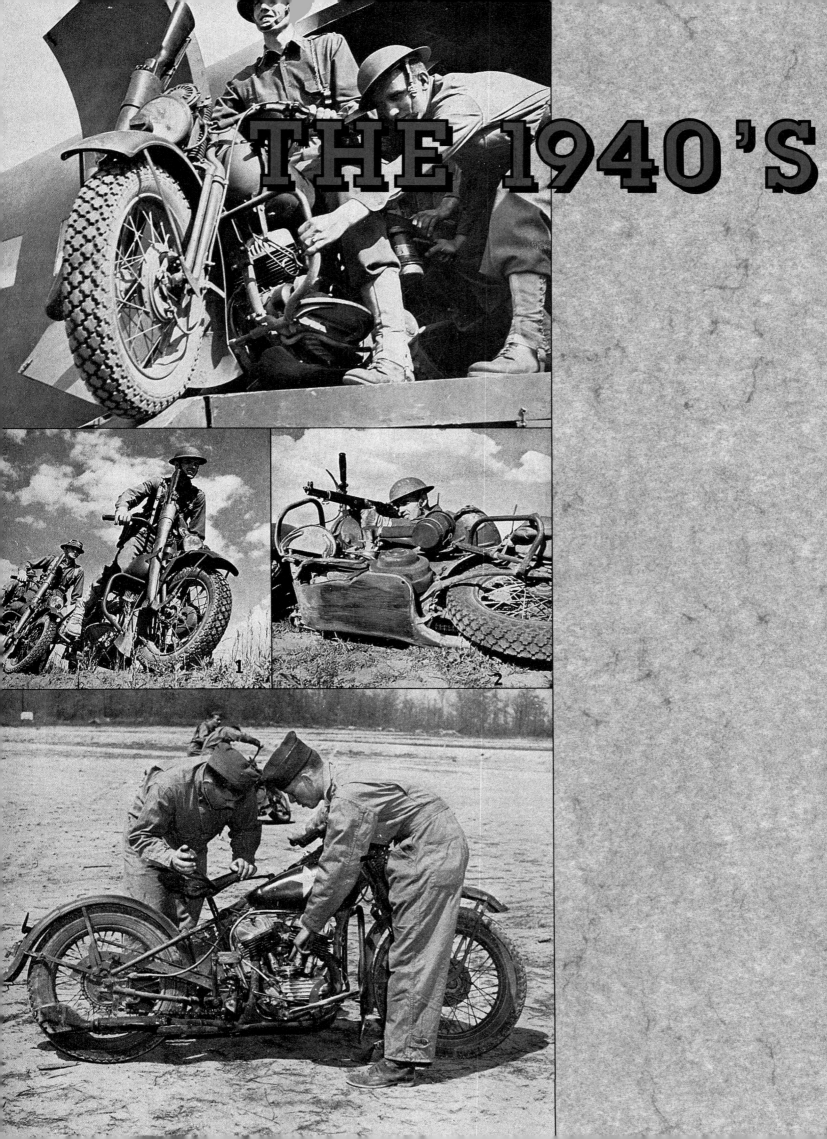

# THE 1940'S

"**A**s 1940 looms ahead and we stand on the threshold of a new season," reads a 1940 Harley-Davidson news bulletin, "it is not amiss to recall that the public does not bestow its favor upon a product by whim or fancy. Only an article of superior value and outstanding merit can hope to win buyer approval year after year. But this favor has imposed an obligation. That which would be passably good is not good enough for the motorcycles bearing our nameplate. It is this challenge that spurs the Harley-Davidson organization to build better and still better.

"Supplied with the latest and best in manufacturing equipment, fortified by ample capital, directed by men of vision and long experience, we can confidently draw back the curtain on Harley-Davidson's offering for 1940.

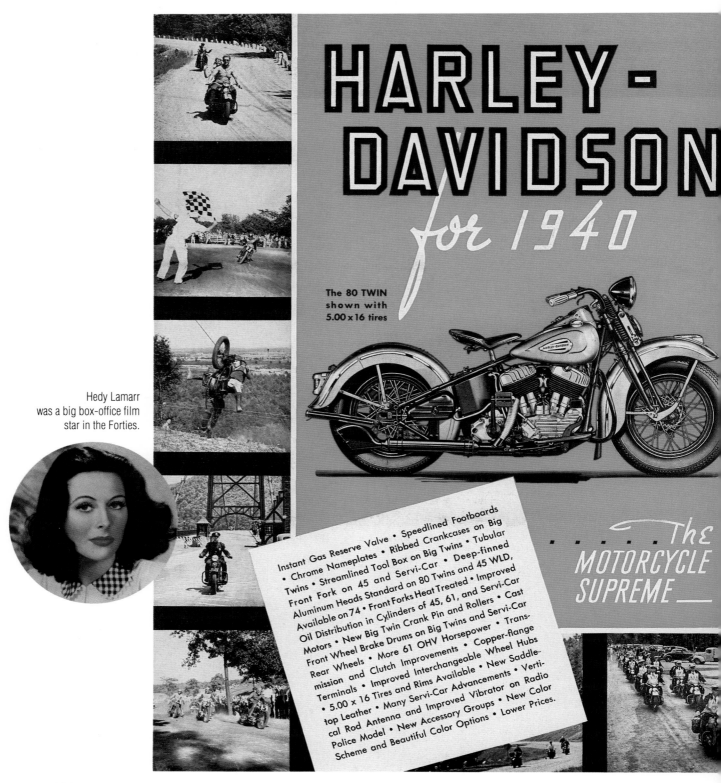

Hedy Lamarr was a big box-office film star in the Forties.

HARLEY-DAVIDSON *for 1940*

The 80 TWIN shown with 5.00 x 16 tires

Instant Gas Reserve Valve • Speedlined Footboards • Chrome Nameplates • Ribbed Crankcases on Big Twins • Streamlined Tool Box on Big Twins • Tubular Front Fork on 45 and Servi-Car • Deep-finned Aluminum Heads Standard on 80 Twins and 45 WLD, Available on 74 • Front Forks Heat Treated • Improved Oil Distribution in Cylinders of 45, 61, and Servi-Car Motors • New Big Twin Crank Pin and Rollers • Cast Front Wheel Brake Drums on Big Twins and Servi-Car Rear Wheels • More 61 OHV Horsepower • Transmission and Clutch Improvements • Copper-flange Terminals • Improved Interchangeable Wheel Hubs • 5.00 x 16 Tires and Rims Available • New Saddletop Leather • Many Servi-Car Advancements • Vertical Rod Antenna and Improved Vibrator on Radio Police Model • New Accessory Groups • New Color Scheme and Beautiful Color Options • Lower Prices.

.......*The* MOTORCYCLE SUPREME

"In a sweep of the eye we can see that these 1940 Harley-Davidsons are NEW! They are distinct, different, streamlined, and breathe the spirit of speed and power."

On this upbeat note, Harley-Davidson launched the decade of the Forties with a renewed sense of optimism. It had survived the previous decade, which had proved so devastating to so many companies, to release the most advanced, powerful and attractive line in its history. In addition to the well-accepted 61 inch OHV, the line now boasted increased power for the 80, 74 and 45 cubic inch models by virtue of deeply-finned aluminum heads that dramatically improved cooling, reduced weight, and provided greater power and performance.

Cosmetically, the new models received semicircular floorboards and a streamlined tool box, both still popular today, plus a stylish metal name-plate and optional 5" x 16" balloon tires and rims. Reflecting the growing militarism of the times, the 1940 models were offered in five colors, with names like Flight Red, Clipper Blue and Squadron Gray.

Police business continued to be a large part of Harley-Davidson's market in 1940, with over 3,500 cities using their products. Motorcycle clubs were also becoming more and more popular, with many members attending large rallies and meets, where they paraded their riding skills and elaborate uniform styles. For many years, Harley-Davidson accepted motorcycle clubs' ideas or sketches and produced custom embroidered emblems to be sewn on uniforms, shirts or jackets.

FPG

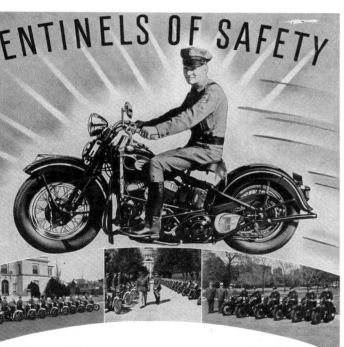

ENTINELS OF SAFETY

Motorcycle mounted officers exemplify the true spirit of public service. They are real guardians of life and property. Motorists and pedestrians alike respect their presence. They prevent accidents and tragedies. They are "Sentinels of Safety" whose alertness and efficiency in solving countless traffic problems build public confidence for police departments. It is significant that an overwhelming majority of the nation's motorcycle officers are mounted on dependable Harley-Davidson Police Motorcycles ... Have your dealer bring over a 1940 model for your inspection.

HARLEY-DAVIDSON MOTOR COMPANY, *Milwaukee, Wisconsin*

ARLEY-DAVIDSON
HE POLICE MOTORCYCLE

**G**radually, events in other parts of the world came to have an impact on Harley-Davidson and, indeed, the nation at large. Japan's aggression in Asia, and especially Hitler's actions in Europe, awakened Americans to the necessity of preparing for eventual war. The German Panzer divisions' startling success in smashing through the French Army in 1940 gave renewed importance to the mechanization of the U. S. Army.

In the newly formed U. S. armored divisions, motorcycle reconnaissance units were created to probe for enemy traps, mines and ambushes; secure

Chrome nameplates of sweeping design were featured in the 1940 Harley-Davidson line, which included (clockwise from upper left): the 61 OHV Twin, 74 Twin, 80 Twin and 45 Twin.

FPG

bridges; and establish forward positions for each division's 400 tanks and 300 scout cars. To meet this need, the Army ordered steadily increasing numbers of 45 WLA Harley-Davidsons, the military version of the 45 WLD model, and other military branches also followed suit.

As England and Russia came under the onslaught of Germany's military might, their motorcycle industries were converted to the production of war-time materials. To round out the military units of our essential Allies and relieve their beleaguered industries, Harley-Davidson motorcycles were shipped to both countries and gratefully accepted.

FPG

FPG

At the end of 1940, with America not yet directly involved in the war, Harley-Davidson announced the new 1941 model line with a 74 cubic inch version of the EL model as flagship. Like other 1941 models, the mighty 74 offered a number of improvements, including a more efficient oil pump, a better clutch, an easier-to-read speedometer and, of course, new color options.

Conditions deteriorated around the globe and friendly countries grew scarce. America offered more support to its Allies and the likelihood of going to war increased. More and more of Harley-Davidson's production was siphoned for military or police use, and raw materials became harder to find. Unable to get enough civilian motorcycles to meet their needs, dealers were urged to sell additional machines to the police, citing the need for increased protection at vital defense industries. Harley-Davidson also continued a high level of advertising to local police forces, both to support national defense and bolster dealers' sales efforts.

The availability of civilian motorcycles decreased and racing activities were curtailed. Club events became more important to the sport. In the *Enthusiast*, the free magazine published by Harley-Davidson, more clubs were featured in an effort to keep motorcycling interest alive. In October 1941, an all-women motorcycle organization, called the Motor Maids, was formed as an auxiliary of the American Motorcyclist Association, acquainting the public with the fact that motorcycles could be handled safely and properly by female riders.

Genuine Harley-Davidson Oil was promoted in this 1940 poster.

Glenn Miller's unique style was making a strong impact on popular music.

## Enjoy Motorcycling More

### With
# HARLEY-DAVIDSON ACCESSORIES

Everything for the Motorcyclist
**APPROVED MOTORCYCLE ACCESSORIES**
for 1940

IF YOUR DEALER CANNOT SUPPLY YOU . . . WRITE DIRECT TO
## HARLEY - DAVIDSON MOTOR CO.
MILWAUKEE, WISCONSIN, U.S.A.
IN U. S. DOLLARS F. O. B. MILWAUKEE, WIS., U. S. A. ALL DUTIES, TAXES, TRANSPORTATION, EXTRA.
QUOTED SUBJECT TO CHANGE WITHOUT NOTICE

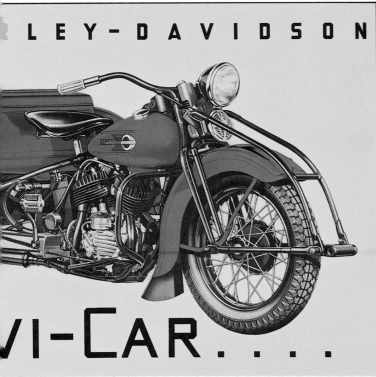

HARLEY - DAVIDSON

VI-CAR . . . .

...vidson Servi-Car with automotive establishments everywhere is based on its ability to de- ...nd produce greater profits. By building greater volume it increases revenue from every ...h shop and service facilities. It saves rent and storage space by solving the pressing prob- ...ave been serviced. Through promotion efforts it will help iron out the slack and rush ...k promote shop efficiency. Out on the streets, it gives you splendid advertising that ...ewspaper or billboard space. Running cost is unbelievably low, only one man is required ...rive a car can handle it. The convenience it affords customers builds good will and in- ...ts use in your business will prove one of the most profitable investments you ever made.

A 32-page catalog offered "everything for the motorcyclist" in Harley-Davidson accessories.

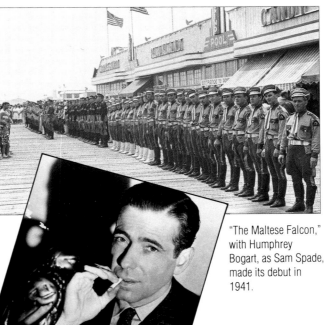

Motorcycle clubs often sported striking uniforms, as evidenced by this gathering in 1941 at Seaside Heights, New Jersey.

"The Maltese Falcon," with Humphrey Bogart, as Sam Spade, made its debut in 1941.

141

# NORTH AFRICAN DESERT PATROL
## By Edward Duncan

A Long Range Desert Group of the Middle East Forces lines up for inspection. The men wear the Arab headdress, a necessary piece of equipment for all who must battle the rigors of the desert. Author Duncan is at the right, nearest the camera.

When I arrived in the Middle East in February of 1940, I little dreamed that I would be assigned to the task of leading patrols and doing dispatch riding for our forces on a Harley-Davidson motorcycle. That same summer, the L.R.D.G. (Long Range Desert Group) was being formed in Cairo. An L.R.D.G. patrol consists of one officer and about fifteen men in five or six motor vehicles. From the beginning, it was clear that navigation on the desert would be a full-time job which the patrol commander could not undertake in addition to his other work, and therefore, it was necessary that each patrol have an official navigator, either an N.C.O. or a Private.

Within the frontiers of Egypt, desert navigation presented no problems, because we were in the possession of fairly good maps. But the maps of the Libyan Desert, beyond the Egyptian border, presented another problem. Naturally, there were no roads but vast stretches of sand for hundreds of miles, from the Egyptian border to the Mediterranean Coast of Libya.

And that is where desert navigation came into the picture. The L.R.D.G. was faced with the task of teaching new navigators, and it took time to train these men. Navigation instruments were hard to obtain as desert navigation is entirely different from sea navigation. The need for navigation, however, as distinct from map reading, came about from the nature of the country.

The interior of Libya in which the L.R.D.G. operated is the most deserty desert in the world—arid and featureless to a degree which the dweller in a northern climate can hardly appreciate. If you were to eliminate rain, you would also remove the natural landmarks by which the inhabitant of Europe or America, with map in hand, could find his way over the country, across streams, lakes, hedges, woods, rivers and valleys. The man-made landmarks—such as roads, villages, towns, railroads and canals—depend directly or indirectly on water for their existence. Thousands of years of heat, cold, wind and blowing sand have formed the desert landscape, smoothing down the features of the past geological eras into vast plains of sand and gravel for hundreds of miles, until it looks like a sea of sand over which movement by patrol trucks in any direction is very restricted. Lack of landmarks compels the deep-sea mariner to rely on sun, stars, compass and log to show him where he is. In the desert, almost equally devoid of recognizable features, the sand sailor must use the same methods. As I have already said, navigation instruments were hard to obtain, so I used to ride on ahead of the patrols for hundreds of miles guided only by a wrist compass which was very much in error. But the speed and distance I could cover on my Harley-Davidson 61 OHV enabled me to make up for such errors, something which a patrol truck could not do. With the kind permission of *Enthusiast* readers, I would like to recall some of my desert experiences with the hope that they may prove interesting.

Among the greatest terrors of the desert are the sandstorms, often called Khamseens, averaging about fifty per month. I always carried at least six pairs of goggles. During a sandstorm, the sand was blown at such an intensity that it penetrated the glasses, rendering them useless. I had a light canvas cover over the engine to keep the sand out of the carburetor, but on top of the fuel tank, it was never unusual to see about two inches of sand. The heat, on an average, was about 142 degrees in the shade. I always left the sand on the fuel tank to prevent the sun from beating down directly on it. I often used to wonder why my spare two gallons of gas which I carried did not catch fire.

One patrol took me into the interior of the Gilf Kebir and into the still little known Eghei Mountains between the Kufra Oases and Tibesti where, as far as I know, not more than a dozen white men have ever been. This region of the desert is still unexplored. I passed through this section at night, and when I laid down to sleep beside my faithful Harley-Davidson, I used to look at my mount and think of what would happen to me if it had broken down, for I was at least four or five hundred miles from civilization. I carried only one water bottle and army rations.

On numerous occasions, I have ridden down sandy slopes for 15 or 20 miles without using any gas whatsoever. As I rode through this blazing inferno, I thought about the people in the United States, for instance, who die from heat waves when the thermometer barely gets over 100 degrees. Here the heat was so intense, I had to wear gloves to prevent my hands from blistering on the handlebars. My shirt had a white coating of salt on it formed by perspiration. You can thus imagine how much I loved my old faithful Harley-Davidson because of the terrific heat and sand it was going through and how it stood up after endless hours of grueling riding. And even though I loved her, I never spared her one bit when it came to the business of pushing on day after day through the scorching sea of sand.

From that hell on earth, I eventually arrived in Alexandria, Egypt, several hundred miles away, and then on to Cairo, another 250 miles. After what I had been through, the temperature was most pleasant and the riding was excellent. Shortly thereafter, I left Cairo for Alexandria again and then I had to journey by water over to Piraeus in Greece when we went to help the Greeks. From Piraeus, I rode through to Mount Olympus in extreme cold and deep snow, and then across the Thessaly Plains to Larissa where General Freyberg, in command of the G.O.C.N.Z. Troops, had his headquarters at that time. From there, I rode through a railroad town called Trikkala, which at that time was occupied by the Germans. I never discovered it until I was half way through. Without warning, the German motorcyclists got after me in a hurry. I made up my mind not to be captured, although my map showed that I would have to ride through a mile-high pass near Metsovo, in and across the Pindus Mountains along a rough Greek road. A blinding snowstorm was raging at the time. How far the Germans followed me, I do not know because I soon lost them. But I am sure they must have sent a radio message to other German motorcyclists near the pass. As I arrived at the pass, I noticed that the road sloped downward in the direction I was going, so I shut off the motor of my Harley-Davidson and was nearly through the pass when the Germans got after me again. By their uniforms, I could see that they belonged to the Adolf Hitler Division of the Elite Guards. They were on motorcycles and immediately it became a battle of motorcycles. A few shots were fired at me but took no effect. And then began a grueling race over a very rough road to Lamia, the gate to the mountain pass of Thermopylae where the Germans hoped to cut me off. But they only wasted their time, for the wonderful power I had under me and the ability of my dependable Harley-Davidson to stand up to the terribly rough roads brought me through safely. Much of the time during that wild chase I was fairly bouncing out of the saddle.

After leaving the pass behind, I followed the road down the mountainside to a shallow river which had about a foot of water in it with the river bed full of gravel. I managed to slip and slide across to the road on the opposite shore which I then followed until I came to the foot of Salamis. From Salamis I got my Harley-Davidson back to Alexandria in Egypt. I went on to Cairo, another 250 miles, and was in time to see Captain James Roosevelt fly his plane over our base camp and Maadi.

Then I went into action with our troops when we entered Fort Capuzzo and then on to the Mediterranean port of Bardia where I was taken prisoner for six weeks by the Italians. They abused my faithful Harley-Davidson something terrible. When I was recaptured again by our own troops, I got my dear old faithful Harley-Davidson back once more. Although she had had a rough spin of it, I had no trouble in getting her going again. From Bardia, I went on, still following the troops to Sidi Azeiz, Sidi Omar and Sidi Rezegh.

This is all barren desert up the coast and hundreds of miles inland all the way to Tripoli and Algiers. After Sidi Rezegh I went on to Gambut, which we captured, then to Bel Hammed, Bir Hachiem, Tobruk, Derna, Sollum and Bengasi, then through the Halfaya Pass, called Hell-fire Pass by our troops because it has a blistering heat of 150 degrees in the shade and is covered with loose gravel and boulders varying in size from 6 inches to 2 feet in diameter. It is several miles in length, and it is painful even to look at. As a matter of fact, it looks well nigh impossible for a man to pass through, let alone a motorcycle. But when I got going on my faithful Harley-Davidson, she took it all right, although she bucked and jumped and turned around to go back to where she had come from.

After going through Halfaya Pass, I went back to the base again for a rest. I also gave my Harley-Davidson an overhaul. Most of the paint had worn off of her and the engine looked as if it was overheated, for it had already done thousands of miles. But when I started it again, I had no trouble. Then when we started our big offensive at El Alamien to drive the enemy out of Africa, I was up there again as usual. She was still going extremely well as I followed the troops' advance right on up to Bengasi. From there I went on to Tripoli and then to Gaves. Several miles farther on, I entered the town of Sfax, and about 30 miles farther, I reached Kairwan, a few miles from Sidi Ahmed Airdrome, then in enemy hands. After we had driven them out of the airdrome, with the help of your P-38s and B-25s, a few miles farther on, I entered Ferryville. Then, after more severe fighting, we entered Tunis and Bizerte where we finally had the Germans run out of Africa. From Bizerte, I went over the road through mountains to Tebourba where I met an American, Colonel Zanuck, who was watching a tank battle taking place between your troops and the Huns. The climb was about 6,000 feet above sea level.

Unlike most military motorcycle riders who rode the side-valve 45WLA Harley-Davidson, Edward Duncan used a 61 OHV Model, like this one, equipped with a sidecar.

From Tebourba, I went on farther to Bone, at which place your troops landed. From Bone I began my return journey. Before I started, I patted the tanks of my faithful Harley-Davidson and said, "Look here, old girl, we have a long way to go—possibly 3,500 miles or more. I am confident you will carry me through to safety." It was a long and tough ride but without driving her, I did it in about 16 days, thanks to the wonderful motor itself and the lighting system, even though the roads were terribly bad. I found the twin headlamps far better than a single one for night riding in a continent like Africa where a man might make a slip and shoot over a precipice.

And that about winds up in a general way my experiences in North Africa on a Harley-Davidson. Some day I hope to come to the United States and see the place where these wonderful machines are made. That 61 OHV Harley-Davidson that I rode surely did its share for our Middle East Forces and aided materially in helping our forces eventually drive the enemy completely out of Africa.

**W**ar now seemed inevitable and production was devoted almost totally to the defense effort. The company discontinued plant tours in November. By December 7, 1941, when the Japanese Imperial Navy launched its sneak attack on Pearl Harbor, Harley-Davidson was building a motorcycle every five minutes. America was completely in the war, and so was Harley-Davidson.

In many ways, Harley-Davidson was fortunate in providing motorcycles for the armed services. By producing motorcycles instead of tanks or machine guns, all the manufacturing processes were kept intact, which ensured more rapid conversion to civilian production at the war's end. It also guaranteed a constant, although limited, supply of spare parts for civilian use. And, the extensive military use of Harley-Davidson motorcycles familiarized tens of thousands of riders with the company's products. In this instance, familiarity bred affection.

During the war, Harley-Davidson produced approximately 90,000 WL military models in various configurations, for use on virtually every front. It was reported in 1945 that the Russian Army utilized 30,000 Harley-Davidson motorcycles in advancing through Eastern Germany toward Berlin. Surprisingly, the Russians chose to copy the German BMW after the war and produced it for decades after.

World War II was also responsible for another unique Harley-Davidson twin. It was called the XA, and displaced 45 cubic inches. What made it unique was the configuration of the twin cylinders: the XA was a horizontally-opposed flat twin and the only shaft-drive Harley-Davidson ever produced. It was designed for use by the Allies in North African desert warfare, since sand had a nasty tendency to devour chains and sprockets. However, only 1,000 were produced before that phase of the war was over. Throughout the war, the Harley-Davidson banner would be carried by the popular, olive-drab 45 WLA models, which consistently proved up to the task.

A horizontally-opposed, shaft-drive Model XA was developed for waging desert warfare.

Greta Garbo retired from the screen after *Two-Face Woman*.

Above, top to bottom: Pearl Harbor attack;
FDR declares war; Army-Navy award
to Harley-Davidson for exceptional
performance in production of war materials;
1941 announcement banner; singer/film star,
Deanna Durbin.

**1940**

President Roosevelt elected
to unprecedented third term.

America prepares for war
with first peacetime draft.

Estonia, Latvia and
Lithuania annexed
by U.S.S.R.

**1941**

Japan attacks Pearl Harbor,
U.S. tools up for war
production.

Ford signs first labor
union contract.

Ted Williams hits .406
season batting average;
Joe DiMaggio hits safely
in 56 consecutive games.

FDR declares
Four Freedoms essential:
freedom of speech and
religion, freedom from
want and fear.

**1942**

First nuclear chain reaction
demonstrated at University
of Chicago.

Battle of Midway is Japan's
first major defeat.

U.S. and British troops
invade North Africa; Marines
land in Guadalcanal.

**1943**

Rationed items include
shoes, canned goods, meat,
cheese, gasoline, sugar,
others.

Mussolini deposed; U. S.
troops invade Italy.

**1944**

Allies launch invasion of
Europe at Normandy on
D-Day, June 6.

President Roosevelt wins
re-election to fourth term.

**A**t home, the nation and Harley-Davidson adjusted to a wartime mode, as concessions were made in everyday life. The service school was transformed into the Quartermaster School for exclusive training of military mechanics. In 1942, the Daytona 200 Mile Race was suspended for the duration of the war. Aluminum for pistons became scarce, and dealers had to turn in old pistons before Harley-Davidson could get their equivalent weight to make new ones. Containers for liquids, like oil, were converted from metal to glass. Shop tools and chains were scarce, and dealers were asked to return empty oil drums to Harley-Davidson so they could be reused. Like the rest of the country, Harley-Davidson learned to cope with shortages.

From top, counterclockwise: The Service School taught military personnel the mechanics of Harley-Davidson motorcycles; Americans being sworn into service; women replacing men in defense plants inspire the song "Rosie the Riveter"; Harley-Davidson in the Army.

FPG

FPG

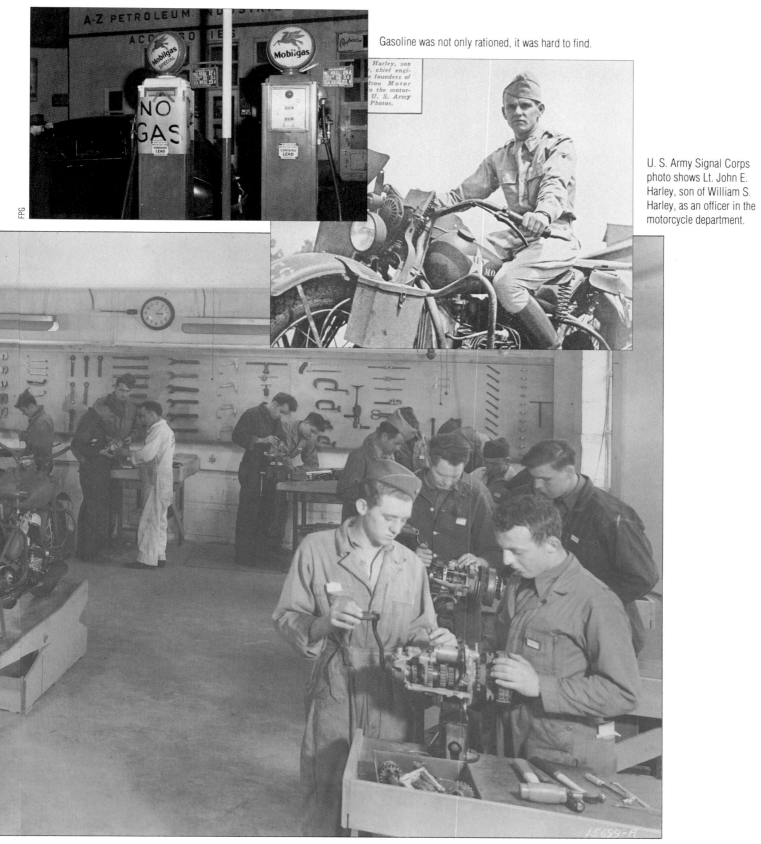

Gasoline was not only rationed, it was hard to find.

U. S. Army Signal Corps photo shows Lt. John E. Harley, son of William S. Harley, as an officer in the motorcycle department.

Far left: WWII cartoon.
Left: All-time classic "Casablanca" with Bergman and Bogart debuted in 1942.

On top of the terrors and hardships of all-out war, personal tragedy struck closer to home in February 1942 with the death of Company President, Walter Davidson. He was succeeded by William H. Davidson, who previously served as a vice president. A year and a half later, William S. Harley also passed away. Of the four founders, only Arthur Davidson remained.

## WALTER DAVIDSON

Early in life, Walter Davidson learned his trade as a machinist, working in railroad shops in Milwaukee and other cities. After lending his talents to help build the first Harley-Davidson back in 1903, it wasn't long before the demand for additional motorcycles convinced him to give up his work with the railroad and devote his full time to the young but growing Harley-Davidson Motor Company.

From building motorcycles to riding them was a short step for Walter Davidson, who soon became one of the most enthusiastic competition riders. In 1908, he was awarded a diamond medal by the Federation of American Motorcyclists for his winning score in the greatest endurance run of that day, made with a single-cylinder Harley-Davidson. The course of the two-day classic started from Catskill, N.Y., went on to Brooklyn, and around Long Island. Shortly thereafter, he established an economy record at Roslyn, Long Island, N.Y., covering fifty miles of hilly road on one quart and one ounce of gasoline. His competition achievements and many victories on hill, road and track did much to bring Harley-Davidson national recognition.

From the twin viewpoints of being a skilled machinist and a competitive rider, Walter Davidson always insisted on the importance of the highest quality standards in Harley-Davidson motorcycles. In later years, he was widely recognized for his expertise in business and, at his death, he was a trustee of the Northwestern Mutual Life Insurance Company, and was a director of the Milwaukee Gas Light Company.

## WILLIAM S. HARLEY

At the age of 15, William Harley started work in a Milwaukee bicycle factory and soon became a draftsman. He and his boyhood friend and neighbor, Arthur Davidson, became dedicated to the development of a motor-driven bicycle for their own use. Combined with the expertise of Arthur's brothers, William and Walter, it became the concept for the first Harley-Davidson motorcycle and the company for which it was named.

After helping develop the first Harley-Davidson motorcycle, William Harley was still fascinated by the more technical aspects of engineering, and enrolled in the School of Engineering at the University of Wisconsin in Madison. He worked his way through school, waiting on tables and doing drafting in a local plant, and after graduation actively rejoined partners Arthur, Walter and William Davidson.

William Harley was also a real motorcyclist who rode some of the first Harley-Davidson motorcycles in many endurance contests, finishing well consistently. Testing out his own designs for years, he understood what the motorcycle public wanted, and his judgement had a profound influence on all motorcycle design.

Always an enthusiast, William Harley could always be counted on to be present at major events of the year, especially the annual races in Daytona Beach, Florida. For twenty-four years, he served on the Competition Committee of the American Motorcyclist Association. An avid outdoorsman and excellent hunter, he also found great fascination in photographing and sketching wildlife. He was active in both the American Motorcyclist Association and the Business Men's Sketch Club of Milwaukee.

# PANAMA PICTORIAL!

Upper left: Deep in the Panamanian jungle a motorcycle instructor, left, and students pose on their Harley-Davidsons in front of a palm-thatched native hut. They are: Pfc. D. Henderson, instructor, and Privates T. Garman, W. Klespies, J. Hendricks and W. Hall. Lower left: Instructor Henderson plunges into a jungle stream. In the rear is Pvt. Garman and farther back is Pvt. Klespies. Upper right: Over rugged jungle trails Pfc. Henderson and the motorcycle students come bouncing along. Lower right: Three members of a Cavalry Reconnaissance unit cross a jungle river on their Harley-Davidsons. They are Sgt. Lester Parker of Hornell, New York, Cpl. John Jacaway, Springfield, Illinois, and S/Sgt. John Randle, Evanston, Illinois.
U. S. Army Signal Corps Photographs.

Bette Davis and Paul Henreid in *Now Voyager*.

# PANAMA PICTORIAL

Left page: In the upper left photo Lieut. R. Reppa writes message to be dispatched by S/Sgt. Randle. At the right two messengers traverse a difficult jungle trail. Below: Three riders line up for a picture in the jungle clearing. They are: S/Sgt. Randle, left, Sgt. Parker and Cpl. Jacaway. Right page: S/Sgt. Randle demonstrates how messengers deliver messages from headquarters on the fly to the leader of an armored vehicle. Below: Cpl. R. Berry of Virden, Ill., skillfully maneuvers his Harley-Davidson through the rocky bed of a jungle stream. On the right Sgt. Parker and Sgt. Randle and their sturdy Harley-Davidsons are shown at the entrance of a dense jungle trail. U. S. Signal Corps Photographs.

Harley-Davidsons continued to be a police favorite in the Forties. This photo from a 1942 *Enthusiast*, captioned "Harley-Davidson in the Lone Star State," shows Texas highway patrolmen on Harley-Davidsons near Houston , examining the credentials of a motorist.

Introducing Officer Bill Curry of the Topeka, Kansas, Police who marks parked cars so fast that even "Believe-It-or-Not" Ripley was amazed.

# MARKED CARS SO FAST RIPLEY DIDN'T BELIEVE IT

Harley-Davidson even rated space in Bob Ripley's "Believe-It-or-Not," according to a May 1942 *Enthusiast* story which read as follows: "You have to do something unusual to rate space in Robert Ripley's famous 'Believe-It-or-Not' Column. And that's just what Officer Bill Curry of the Topeka, Kansas, Police Department has been doing for years. Officer Curry's specialty is marking parked cars and he estimates his yearly total at around five million. He figures he can mark and check 16,000 to 18,000 cars a day.

"So fast and adept is Officer Curry that when a representative of Ripley's 'Believe-It-or-Not' heard about the fantastic number of cars marked, he shook his head. Obligingly the officer asked the representative to get in his car and follow Curry on the Police ServiCar. They moved over to a side street and the officer got busy. He speeded up to 20 miles an hour and stick and chalk flashed in and out beneath the cars. The representative tagged along behind, wide-eyed. He followed the speedy officer for half a day. Then the amazed representative called a halt. He had seen enough. In recognition of the officer's unbelievable speed in marking cars, he was given prominent mention on Ripley's radio program."

Winston Churchill flashes his famous "V-for-victory" sign.

**"HELL ON WHEELS"** division. Tommy guns spitting, they lead tanks into action

# IRON PONIES

### They're the mounts of the 1942 Rough Riders, toughest and fastest of land-army troops

IN THE last war motorcycle troops were "messenger boys."

In this one they are the fastest-moving land branch of the Army.

The medicos' best customers, they suffer more crack-ups in normal work than the tank crews, plane crews and parachutists combined. And although their members are being knocked off regularly, war or no war, they have a peculiar brand of fatalism which impels them to perform even the most routine mission with dash and abandon.

These modern Rough Riders go through a rigorous eight-week course at Fort Knox, Ky. Many of them are famous as dirt track and hill-climbing performers; all have had long experience on cycles. Few soldiers can qualify for the cycles — and not many want to!

The only way to get an appreciative taste of their job would be to ride with one of these wheeled cow-punchers at 40 miles an hour in a total blackout along a rutted country road crowded with fast-moving tanks which take up two-thirds or more of the available space. Your first trip is guaranteed to turn your hair gray!

Roughly — and the word is used advisedly! — they have four missions: scouting and patrolling; traffic control for large troop and supply movements; liaison and courier work; and, finally, as a small harassing force to do the work that horse cavalry used to do.

#### That New Job

IN THIS mechanized era, the second task is vital, but it is the fourth which has made the motorcycle man so different from his 1918 predecessor.

In a tank attack the cycles may either follow right behind the big monsters, tommy guns blazing; or they may precede the tanks if the situation warrants. (Each armored division has about 200 cycles.) On scouting work they must be keyed for surprise attack and quick action, since theirs is usually the first contact with the enemy. In such a situation it is breath-taking to see a swiftly moving squad of cyclists plunge headlong off the road like a band of Hollywood stunt men, spilling their wheels in the grass or brush while they unlimber their sub-machine guns and cover the enemy until the tanks lumber up.

Strangely enough, one of the outstanding developments in this wild-and-woolly branch of the service is a new type of motorcycle infinitely quieter than the standard commercial cycle.

So the enemy will soon find hell descending on him without so much as a "put-put" of warning.

— PAUL W. KEARNEY

**TOUGH.** He takes hardest knocks in the Army

**QUICK.** Enemy sighted, split-second dismount

**NON-STOP.** Even rivers can't slow him down

Teddy Roosevelt could probably not have pictured the "Rough Rider" described in a 1942 issue of *This Week* magazine.

Films co-starring Spencer Tracy and Kathryn Hepburn were big box-office hits, even back in the Forties.

Man the GUNS Join the NAVY

151

**I**n April 1943, Harley-Davidson was presented with the prestigious Army-Navy "E" Award by Under Secretary of War, Robert P. Patterson, for exceptional performance beyond the normal execution of duty in the production of war materials. With the award, Company President William H. Davidson received a large banner for Harley-Davidson to fly along with the American flag.

On behalf of Local No. 209, Union President, Leonard Hackert, said: "The employees of Harley-Davidson are working long, hard hours. We're buying war bonds and accepting shortages. Most of us are staying on the job, day in and day out, often working on days when we aren't well—days we would lay off in peace time. That's the way we are dealing blows to our enemies. By winning this grand award, the boys in our Armed Forces and our Allies are saying, 'Thank you for your production.' And they may rest assured that we, the employees of Harley-Davidson, will never let them down."

## SAN DIEGO MOTORCYCLE OFFICER GETS HIS MAN

The following article from a mid-Forties issue of the *Enthusiast* illustrates Harley-Davidson's longtime promotion and recognition of Harley-Davidsons as effective law enforcement tools.

"Seldom are the thrilling captures made by the Nation's motorcycle officers, in line of duty, given the publicity they deserve. This is regrettable because their effective law enforcement work is not always fully appreciated by the public. Therefore, it is with satisfaction that the recent experience of Officer Vic R. English, San Diego, California, is briefly recounted here.

"As Officer English was leaving the police station on his Harley-Davidson 74 OHV one day recently, he was informed by Lt. F. E. Wolfe that a car, stolen in Van Nuys, was reported heading south toward San Diego. Officer English proceeded to Gillette Street and waited. Soon the car was spotted and the chase was on! Faster and faster roared the desperate driver, aware now that he was being followed. Officer English, crouched low over the tanks, siren screaming, and red pursuit light flashing, began to close in on the car. The needle of the

Officer Vic English is shown on the 74 OHV Harley-Davidson, which he piloted through the streets of San Diego in the successful pursuit of a fleeing law breaker.

speedometer raced across the dial to 50—60—70—80—90 miles an hour and still it moved! As the frantic driver approached Juniper Street, a girl stepped down off the curb. The car driver applied his brakes, swerved to miss the pedestrian, went into a skid and slid broadside into a signal standard. Officer English quickly came to a stop, took the uninjured driver into custody, and another traffic menace was soon deposited in a safe place. The officer's prompt, courageous action undoubtedly prevented a more serious and perhaps even a fatal accident. A salute to Officer Vic English and to the other motorcycle officers who, like him, are determined to make our streets and highways safe."

Right: Roddy McDowall starred in the original "Lassie Come Home" in 1943.

Far right: Bob Hope, Dorothy Lamour and Bing Crosby helped lift the spirits of the nation with their series of "Road" movies in the Forties.

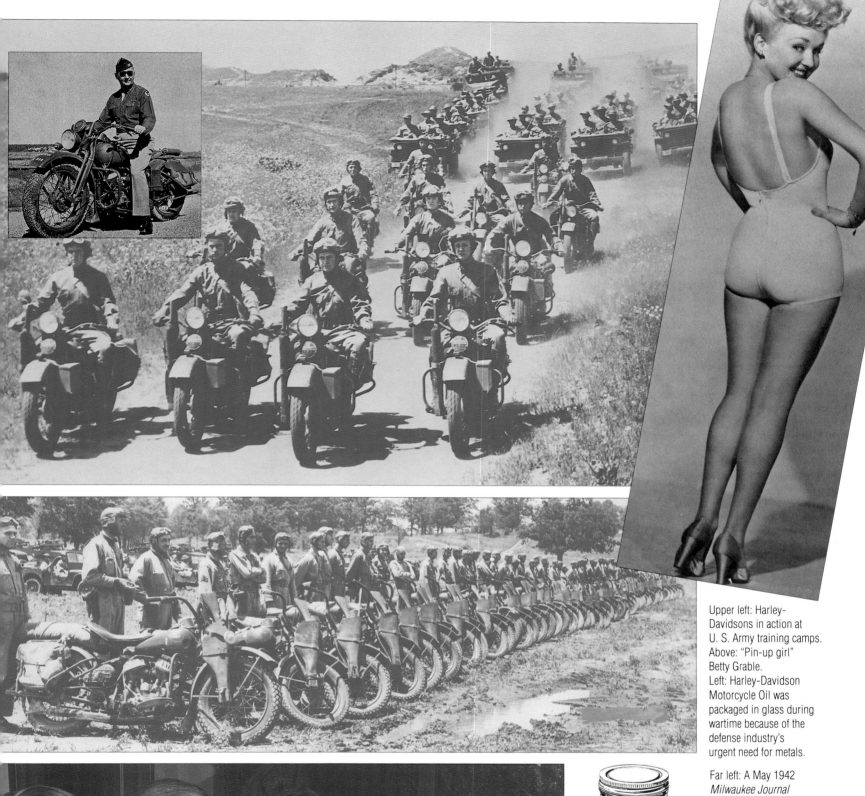

Upper left: Harley-Davidsons in action at U. S. Army training camps.
Above: "Pin-up girl" Betty Grable.
Left: Harley-Davidson Motorcycle Oil was packaged in glass during wartime because of the defense industry's urgent need for metals.

Far left: A May 1942 *Milwaukee Journal* photo of (left to right): Gordon Davidson, William H. Davidson, Arthur Davidson, William S. Harley.

At right: The Model XS was a version of the XA with a sidecar. The wheel of the sidecar was powered by a driveshaft running off the rear hub of the motorcycle. Very few XS models were actually built.

Bottom right: An American Army motorcyclist in England uses his Harley-Davidson as a shield while firing during maneuvers. Bottom left: "Marcus Welby" star, Robert Young, was a Harley-Davidson enthusiast back in the Forties.

Upper left: The 1949 model sported innovations like the Hydra-Glide front fork and the full-skirted fenders.

Above: Before Evel Knievel's time, this daredevil attempted a "12-man jump."

# The 1950's

Celebrating Our
Golden Anniversary

The 1950's

*T*he Fabulous Fifties debuted on a note of optimism in the country as the aftereffects of World War II were relegated to history. At long last, scarcities of raw materials were no longer an issue and a booming economy cranked out consumer goods at a record pace, all of which competed with the motorcycle dealer for the customer's dollar. The Fifties became a market for eager consumers and with so many products available to enhance the average American's everyday life, it became more difficult to attract new buyers to the motorcycle marketplace.

Recognizing the need for a more aggressive marketing stance, Harley-Davidson dealers were encouraged to get out from behind the counter and work more closely with their potential customers. They were urged to advertise and promote not only their products, but the sport of motorcycling in general. For the first time ever, each dealer was supplied with a demonstrator motorcycle, and advised of the importance of giving demo rides to prove the comfort, power and performance of the new Harley-Davidson motorcycles. Also, by the 1950s Harley-Davidson was continually expanding its already considerable line of accessories and clothing in order to maintain the interest of enthusiasts already involved in the sport.

To help combat some negative images generated by certain motorcyclists, the 1950 models sported new mufflers that produced a deeper, mellower tone compared to the harsh, staccato sounds of earlier years. This quieter, more pleasing exhaust note was created despite a ten percent increase in power developed through redesigned and enlarged cylinder inlet ports on the 61 and 74 OHV engines.

1950 74 OHV FL Model.

Ava Gardner starred in many films in the Fifties.

In the postwar motorcycling world, racing continued to play an ever-increasing role as Harley-Davidson riders scored victory after victory in all types of two-wheeled competition. Gerald McGovern won the 1950 Jack Pine Endurance Run, marking the twenty-first win for Harley-Davidson in the twenty-four times the event had been held. Bill Huber won Langhorne, Roger Soderstrom took the checkers at Peoria, and Larry Headrick scored double wins at Springfield and Milwaukee, just to name a few. In all, Harley-Davidson riders took 18 of 24 National Championships in 1950, establishing six new racing records in the process.

Clubs, too, enjoyed increasing popularity as organized motorcycling attracted more and more riders. Many of the clubs worked diligently at improving the motorcyclists' image through civic activities such as organizing fund raisers, providing escort services, arranging muffler inspections, helping the needy and working for civil defense.

Some of the women riders of the Augusta, Georgia Motorcycle Club who took part in the Augusta Crusade for Cancer drive.

**B**ecause of international tensions heightened by the 1950 Communist invasion of South Korea, America was gripped by the fear of nuclear war. Several cities staged mock civil defense exercises in which motorcycle club members played key roles in keeping the lines of communication open after a simulated nuclear attack. When all other forms of communication failed, motorcycle dispatch riders kept information flowing. In every instance, the motorcyclists were praised for their dedication and performance.

A sad note was rung in the final days of 1950 when Arthur Davidson, secretary and general sales manager and the sole surviving founder of Harley-Davidson, was killed along with his wife in a tragic automobile accident. The task of running the company had now been fully passed to the second generation of Harleys and Davidsons.

Opposite page, top center; An arresting picture! In the Fifties, it was a pleasure to get "curbed" in Sullivan County, N.Y. Instead of issuing tickets, a special corps of Courtesy Copettes on motorcycles presents a list of cardinal safety rules of Sullivan County and explained how safety pays. The method was said to be successful *and* popular.

## ARTHUR DAVIDSON

Teaming up with boyhood friend William S. Harley, Arthur was the first of the Davidson brothers to join in the production of the original Harley-Davidson motorcycle. And as the new Harley-Davidsons gained in popularity and production increased, it was Arthur who took charge of sales, covering the country from coast to coast and establishing a sound network of dealers. Arthur also appreciated the importance of competent mechanics to serve Harley-Davidson owners, and the Harley-Davidson Service School is a tribute to his foresight.

In the early days of advertising, Arthur was quick to recognize it as a new force in selling and always insisted that the merits of Harley-Davidson products be promoted constantly before the public. When the trend toward installment buying was recognized, the Kilbourn Finance Corporation was organized in 1923, and he served as its president for many years. He also served the last six years of his life as president of the American Motorcyclist Association and helped develop many of the policies and programs instituted to enlarge its scope and influence. During those same years, he was also president of the Motorcycle and Allied Trades Association, an organization of members of the motorcycle industry.

Always interested in youth activities, he served in many capacities with the Boy Scouts of America and received scouting's highest award for distinguished service. He was also a board member of the Milwaukee Boys' Club and active in the Y.M.C.A. A great lover of the outdoors, he was a lifetime member of the Izaak Walton League. Because of his keen business and financial insight, Arthur Davidson served as a director for several firms, such as the Koehring Company, the Kellogg Seed Company and Wisconsin Pharmacal Company.

While many young Americans celebrated the spring of 1950 with formal dances, others entered South Korea to help fight the North Korean Communist invaders.

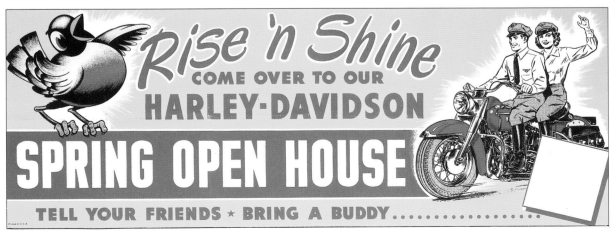

In the early Fifties, a number of newspapers around the county employed young riders on Model 125's to deliver their papers, like this group of boys from the Denison Herald in Texas.

171

*A*s good as the new Harley-Davidsons had become, 1951 saw even more innovations, with chrome-plated piston rings on the OHV motors and—an industry first—hydraulic rear brakes on the Servi-Car, which was still an important boon to police and business concerns. The Model 125, the junior Harley-Davidson, also received an update with a telescoping Tele-Glide front fork patterned after that of its bigger brothers.

Perhaps the biggest news in 1951 was the founding of the Harley-Davidson Mileage Club. Based on mileage accumulated since January 1, 1951, Harley-Davidson owners could earn recognition for their riding achievements by receiving a handsome pin and membership card in three classifications: 25,000 miles, 50,000 miles and 100,000 miles. Remarkably, by the end of the Club's fourth year, 73 members had already topped the 100,000 mile mark.

"The Honeymooners" was a TV favorite.

The Fifties
were *Howdy
Doody Time.*

Long before
the TV series,
Harley-
Davidson
promoted
"Happy Days."

## THROUGH NORWAY ON A HARLEY-DAVIDSON

Steve and Karen Slaby of Detroit toured Norway in
1952 on a Harley-Davidson 125. Fully loaded with
gear and two passengers, the spunky little 125 had
a gross weight of 570 pounds, yet was able to
handle the mountainous terrain and gravel roads
with little difficulty. In one instance, the pair was
forced to navigate an almost continuous grade for
50 miles, riding in first or second gear, resulting
in the engine getting so hot it even ran with the
ignition turned off. Nonetheless,
the motorcycle never failed them
and they were able to enjoy the
remarkable scenery of that
beautiful northern country.

General Douglas MacArthur returned to
his boyhood home of Milwaukee.

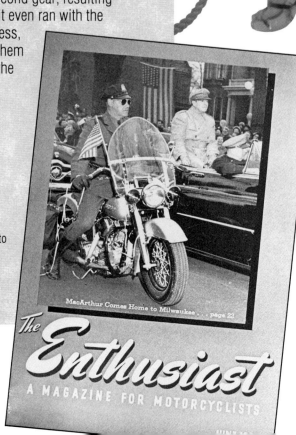

MacArthur Comes Home to Milwaukee... page 22

*The*
*Enthusiast*
A MAGAZINE FOR MOTORCYCLISTS

*I*n 1952 the venerable 45 WL, which had been in the line since the Thirties, was dropped in favor of an excitingly different motorcycle called the Model K. Powered by an all-new 45 cubic inch side-valve motor, the Model K represented the most modern and technologically advanced Harley-Davidson ever produced. Features included an integrated four-speed foot-shift transmission, hand-operated clutch, hydraulic-suspension front and rear, and sleek, sporty looks. The K was an instant success on the streets, and its sporty racing brothers, the KR and KRTT, were equally successful on the nation's race tracks. At the 200-mile 1953 National Championship race on the sands of Daytona Beach, it was Paul Goldsmith on a pepper red KR who took the lead just before the halfway point and held it all the way to the checkered flag, winning by a margin of over two miles and setting a new course record.

The next year saw two models disappear from the model line. Succumbing to increasing demands for the more powerful 74 OHV, the 61 OHV was dropped. To appeal to riders seeking a lightweight motorcycle with a little more power, the Model 125 was replaced by a 165cc model. It still averaged an impressive 80 miles per gallon and yet, could travel up to 60 miles per hour, a necessity for the increasingly faster traffic of the times.

More significant was the fact that 1953 marked the fiftieth year of business for Harley-Davidson. To commemorate the event, a handsome logo was designed, depicting a "V" symbolic of the engine configuration, crossed by the company name and accompanied by the legend: "50 years—American made." This logo, in the form of a brass medallion, would grace the front fenders of all 1954 models.

The 45 cubic inch Model WR dominated dirt tracks until it was replaced by the more advanced KR in 1952.

Honoring Harley-Davidson's Golden Anniversary
September 3, 1953 were (left to right): John
Harley, product engineer; Walter C. Davidson,
secretary; William H. Davidson, president;
Gordon Davidson, vice president; William J.
Harley, treasurer and chief engineer.

At a dinner honoring the anniversary, Company President William H. Davidson remarked, "Harley-Davidson looks back on its past with humble pride. Harley-Davidson looks to the future in eager anticipation of meeting tomorrow's challenge. Our assets are many as we start our second half century. Never have we had a finer array of models than our new Golden Anniversary line. No motorcycle manufacturer, anywhere in the world, has a range as complete as Harley-Davidson.

"The present Harley-Davidson organization owes much to the sterling example and sound pattern which the founders—the three senior Davidsons, William, Walter and Arthur, and William Harley, Sr.—so firmly established. Never has a finer business heritage been handed down from one generation to the next. Let me assure you that my generation holds this heritage in highest esteem and that we have the same unwavering faith in America's future as did our fathers before us.

"Harley-Davidson's achievements over the years, including the announcement of our splendid Golden Anniversary models, now in full production, are adequate evidence that we are firmly committed to an aggressive program of steadily moving forward. Harley-Davidson is sharply conscious of our ever-shifting economy, and the need for intelligent and constant change."

The reason for the company's need to remain vigilant was an influx into the United States of a number of foreign-made brands of motorcycles which, because of the lower labor rates in their home countries, made them cheaper than comparable Harley-Davidson models. Because of constant product line improvements, innovations and quality, plus rider loyalty and an outstanding racing record, Harley-Davidson was more than able to hold its own against the competition and remained the dominant force on the American motorcycle scene. This was also a time that its oldest and best known competitor, Indian, ceased production, leaving Harley-Davidson as the only American manufacturer in an industry that once saw several hundred brands competing in the U. S. market.

1954, © Walt Disney Productions

Fess Parker's portrayal of Davy Crockett created a national frenzy for coonskin caps.

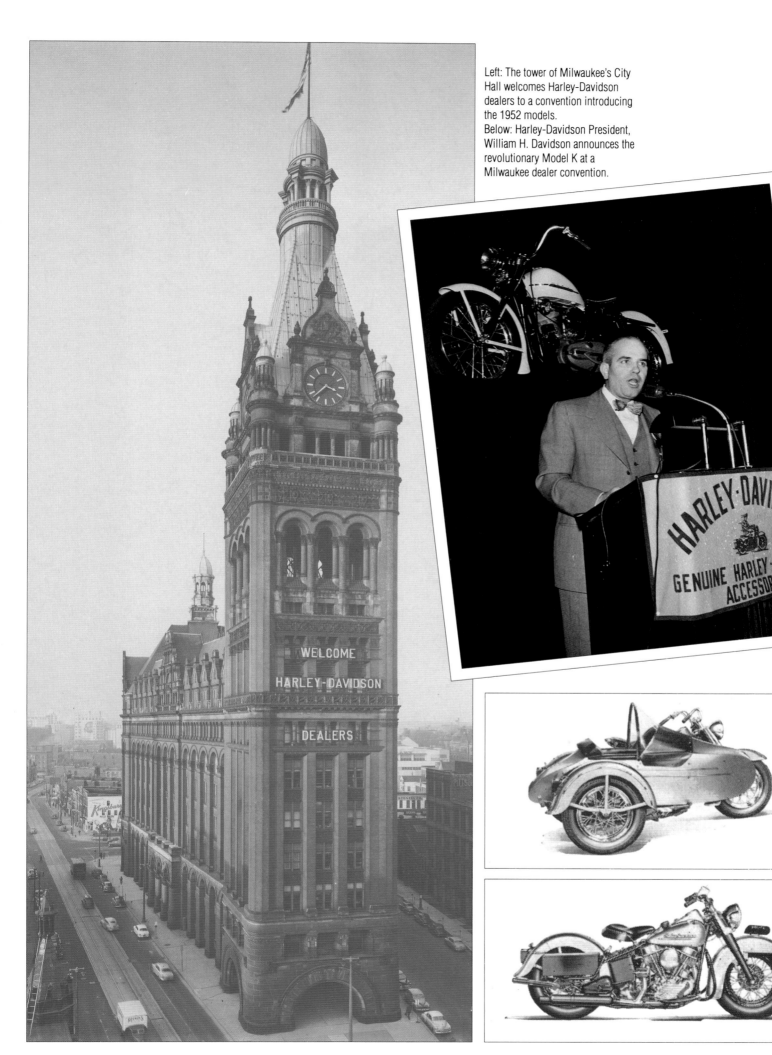

Left: The tower of Milwaukee's City Hall welcomes Harley-Davidson dealers to a convention introducing the 1952 models.
Below: Harley-Davidson President, William H. Davidson announces the revolutionary Model K at a Milwaukee dealer convention.

*I*n 1954, the American Motorcyclist Association changed its method for naming the Grand National Champion, awarding it to the racer who accumulated the most points at a select group of dirt track, road racing and speedway Nationals held throughout the season. When the dust settled that year, it was Joe Leonard racing on the invincible Harley-Davidson KR model who earned the coveted Champion's number plate with its bold Number One. Trailing Leonard were fellow KR riders, Paul Goldsmith and Charlie West.

To satisfy the demands of the American riding public for more horsepower, the K evolved into the KH in 1954, growing to 55 cubic inches. In September of 1953, Don Pink won the twenty-seventh running of the Jack Pine on one of the new KHs and Bert Cummings won Class A Heavyweight top honors, also on a KH, proving the power of this new motor.

Since the early days of motorcycling, Daytona has always been the scene of hot racing action. 1955 was no exception as 19-year-old Brad Andres led a 1-2-3 Harley-Davidson sweep of the 200-mile road race, beating the old record set in 1953 by K-mounted Paul Goldsmith. In 1956, John Gibson also won on a KR, and Joe Leonard scored back-to-back, record-breaking victories in 1957 and 1958. Brad Andres brought his KR home to the checkered flag once again in 1959, rounding out a decade of Harley-Davidson dominance at this historic and prestigious event.

But it wasn't only the V-twins that could win for Harley-Davidson. On Labor Day weekend in 1956, a young rider named Leroy Winters from Ft. Smith, Arkansas, won the Jack Pine aboard a single-cylinder Model 165, defeating 526 other competitors in the process. This marked the first time a lightweight motorcycle ever won overall honors at the event, which was traditionally dominated by the bigger, more powerful twins.

A beautifully restored 1954 Model KH.

Kim Novak starred in the 1955 film production of "Picnic."

When a championship winner like Joe Leonard uses nothing but Genuine Harley-Davidson Oil in race after race, you know it must be mighty good oil. The oil that helps Joe win will also win you dependable service under the most grueling conditions on or off track or highway. It's the championship oil that is good to your motor regardless of the rugged demands you may make upon it.

You are always ahead and you can't lose when you insist on the Genuine Harley-Davidson Oil made expressly for high-speed, air-cooled engines. Make your motor happy by always using it. This championship oil is now available at all Harley-Davidson dealers.

**HARLEY-DAVIDSON MOTOR CO.**

MILWAUKEE 1, WISCONSIN, U.S.A.

Leroy Winters made Jack Pine history in 1956 by winning the grueling 500-mile off-road event on a Harley-Davidson 165.

The powerful KR racing model was unmatched on America's dirt tracks in the Fifties.

**1955**

U.S. agrees to help train South Vietnamese army.

Supreme Court orders "all deliberate speed" in integrating public schools.

**1956**

First transatlantic telephone cable begins operation.

First aerial H-bomb tested over Bikini Atoll.

**1957**

President Eisenhower sends federal troops to Little Rock, Arkansas to enforce court-ordered school integration.

The Space Age begins as Russians launch Sputnik I into orbit around earth.

**1958**

First U.S. satellite, Explorer I, launched at Cape Canaveral.

**1959**

Cuban President Batista resigns and flees; Castro takes over.

Alaska and Hawaii admitted as 49th and 50th states.

Soviet Premier Krushchev makes unprecedented tour of U.S.

Organized club activities remained very popular throughout the Fifties.

"Rebel Without a Cause" featured James Dean, while Marlon Brando starred in "The Wild One."

The old Jack Pine winner, Oscar Lenz, presents cowbell and trophy to Gerald McGovern.

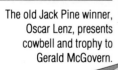

HARLEY-DAVIDSON
SPORTSTER
Takes
JACK PINE
LANSING, MICHIGAN
SEPT. 2, 1957

GERALD McGOVERN on HARLEY-DAVIDSON SPORTSTER
Wins Grand Championship of 500-Mile Jack Pine Endurance Run-959 points
Wins Heavyweight Championship-948.37 points
CECIL LANE riding HARLEY-DAVIDSON Wins Sidecar Championship-937 points
ERNEST KIMBALL
ROBERT KIRCHER  on HARLEY-DAVIDSON

During the 1959 season, the Milwaukee Braves used a specially-equipped Topper with a sidecar to ferry pitchers from the bullpen to the pitcher's mound at County Stadium.

The first motorcycle hobby kit ever produced was the 1958 Harley-Davidson Duo-Glide.

Competing against 101 expert racers in the Daytona 200-mile road race, it was Harley-Davidson's Brad Andres, Number 4, who finished first. Congratulating him and third place finisher, Tony Murquia, are William H. Davidson, right, and Walter Davidson, center.

DAYTONA MOTORCYCLE CLASSICS 1959

The north turn of the first lap of the 1959 200-miler on the beach at Daytona. A parade of six Harley-Davidsons, headed by Bart Markel, leads the pack.

**H**arley-Davidson closed the decade on a note of revolution rather than evolution as it introduced the Topper motor scooter. Advertised as "tops in beauty and tops in performance," the Topper was a handsome machine with its fiberglass body and two-tone paint. Powered by a 10 cubic inch two-stroke engine, the scooter boasted such features as automatic transmission, leading-link front suspension, rubber-mounted engine and two-wheeled brakes.

Innovative, maneuverable and fun to ride, the Topper nonetheless arrived on the scene a little too late in a declining scooter market. It faded from the product line after only a few years.

The Fifties were Fabulous, not only for the country but for Harley-Davidson as well. The company not only enjoyed a landmark celebration with its Golden Anniversary, but also launched a number of new and highly significant models and product improvements that would form the basic product line for years to come.

Doris Day in "Pillow Talk," the number one hit of 1959.

## MAN ABOUT THE WORLD scoots about on nimble Topper...

Harley-Davidson Topper Model A and AU starting at $430 f.o.b. Milwaukee    Denim Terry Topper. $5.95    Seersucker Quilted Terry Shawl Topper. $15.00    Sparkle Plaid Surfer Jac. $10.00    Meteo
Ticking Surfer. $5.00    Seersucker Quilted Terry Surfer. $10.95    Sparkle Plaid Surfer. $7.95    Coords

Topper is thrifty, easy to handle and parks anywhere. *Scootaway* automatic transmission is smooth and effortless — places Topper above all other scooters. Economy? The greatest — up to 100 miles per gallon. Perfect balance, hefty brakes and large wheels produce comfortable, safe ride. Fashioned in fiber- glass, stainless steel and aluminum — for the modern man in motion.

**TOPPER BY HARLEY-DAVIDSON**

Harley-Davidson Motor Co., Milwaukee 1, Wisconsin

**wears new, sl**

New Surfers with a salty l by the sea. Easy-care cott back into action. McGregd a sun-basker, surf-rider, baker type — add lively your life. See them at you

New! A Scooter by

# HARLEY-DAVIDSON

Tops them all in beauty and performance
...it's the *Topper*

Fun-loving Jacks (and Jills, too) are jumping at the chance to meet the new Harley-Davidson Topper. And why not? There's not another motor scooter like it — combining clean, smart beauty with the newest mechanical secrets of success. *Scootaway* automatic transmission makes riding a snap . . . lowest center of gravity makes handling a dream. See the new Topper at your Harley-Davidson dealer. Or write for free, colorful folder.

**HARLEY-DAVIDSON MOTOR CO.,** Milwaukee 1, Wisconsin, Dept. SC
*World's leading manufacturer of lightweight motor vehicles*

This advertisement will be seen by over 15,000,000 readers in the following magazines: SPORT, August: MOTOR LIFE, August: HOT ROD MAG, August: MOTOR TREND August: NATIONAL FUTURE FARMER, August-September: SCOOTER MAGAZINE, July: BOY'S LIFE, August: POPULAR MECHANICS, August: POPULAR SCIENCE, August, 1959.

*Derby Helanca Shawl Topper, $10.95*
*Derby Helanca 21'er Surfer, $6.95*
*Punjab ADM Boat Knit Topper, $5.00*
*Punjab Surfer, $8.95*

*...fers* and **Toppers** by **McGregor**

...s porpoise—colorful as a seascape—they're designed for fun
...nd cool as ocean-spray — washes in a jiffy — bounces right
...fers in mad colors to mate with carefree Toppers. If you're
...r, or clam-
...Surfers to

# McGREGOR.

Also Boy-Sized, Boy-Priced. Made in Canada, too. McGregor-Doniger Inc., N.Y. 19, N.Y.

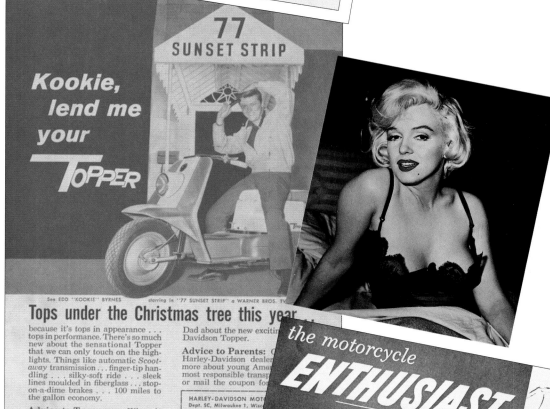

## 77 SUNSET STRIP

*Kookie,
lend me
your*

# Topper

See ED "KOOKIE" BYRNES starring in "77 SUNSET STRIP" a WARNER BROS. TV

## Tops under the Christmas tree this year . . .

because it's tops in appearance . . . tops in performance. There's so much new about the sensational Topper that we can only touch on the highlights. Things like automatic *Scootaway* transmission . . . finger-tip handling . . . silky-soft ride . . . sleek lines moulded in fiberglass . . . stop-on-a-dime brakes . . . 100 miles to the gallon economy.

**Advice to Teenagers:** When it comes to combs and scooters, never a borrower or a lender be. Instead, start dropping hints to Mom and

Dad about the new exciti... Davidson Topper.

**Advice to Parents:** ... Harley-Davidson dealer... more about young Ame... most responsible transp... or mail the coupon for...

HARLEY-DAVIDSON MOTO...
Dept. SC, Milwaukee 1, Wisc...

Send me more inform...
Harley-Davidson...

Name...

Address...

*Harley-Davidson*
MOTOR CO.
MILWAUKEE 1, WISCONSIN

Even Ed "Kookie" Byrnes of TV's "77 Sunset Strip" became part of Harley-Davidson's promotional efforts for the Topper motor scooter.

*the motorcycle*

# ENTHUSIAST

*in action*

THE MAGAZINE FOR MORE MOTORCYCLING PLEASURE

DECEMBER 19...

ENTRANCE Dino's Lodge PARKING

TOPPER SHARES SPOTLIGHT WITH "KOOKIE" ON TV
(See Story Page 2)

A fleet of radio-equipped 1958 Duo-Glides ready to be shipped to the California Highway Patrol.

This all-chrome Duo-Glide was ordered by a man in Venezuela from Arthur "Bub" Tramontin, Harley-Davidson dealer in Clifton, New Jersey, and was completely chrome from the nuts and bolts right up to the motor. The saddlebags and seat were hand-tooled. It took Tramontin approximately five months to complete it, and cost $3,500.

# THE 1960'S

A Decade of Diversification and Change.

**A**s the decade began, America was filled with a renewed feeling of optimism. Entering the White House with his attractive family was the nation's youngest President, John F. Kennedy. He was handsome, enthusiastic and full of vigor, and a new feeling of awareness was dawning in America.

Early in 1960, Harley-Davidson President, William H. Davidson, announced a program of overseas expansion to better serve the European market and substantially improve the company's position in the United States, particularly in the growing lightweight motorcycle market.

Harley-Davidson International, a wholly-owned Swiss-based subsidiary, was established to provide central control, administrative and technical assistance in the overseas marketing of motorcycles, parts and accessories, and scooters, particularly in Europe where the Common Market had recently been created.

Following a two-year study of motorcycle and scooter manufacturers in various foreign countries, Harley-Davidson purchased a half interest in an Italian firm, Aeronautica Macchi, and Aermacchi Harley-Davidson was formed. Already marketing its own line of touring and sport motorcycles for European enthusiasts, Aermacchi Harley-Davidson was to produce a line of lightweight Harley-Davidson motorcycles for the American market. The first of the Italian lightweights to be offered with a Harley-Davidson nameplate was the 1961 250cc Sprint.

Powered by a horizontal four-stroke, single-cylinder engine, the Sprint was a needed addition to round out the bottom end of the product line. Reliable and dependable, the Sprint's torque and power helped it slip comfortably into the product line, and it soon grew in popularity. At the same time, Harley-Davidson was also offering the domestically produced Topper motor scooter and the new 165cc Super-10—"keen wheeling for teen wheeling," according to the sales brochure.

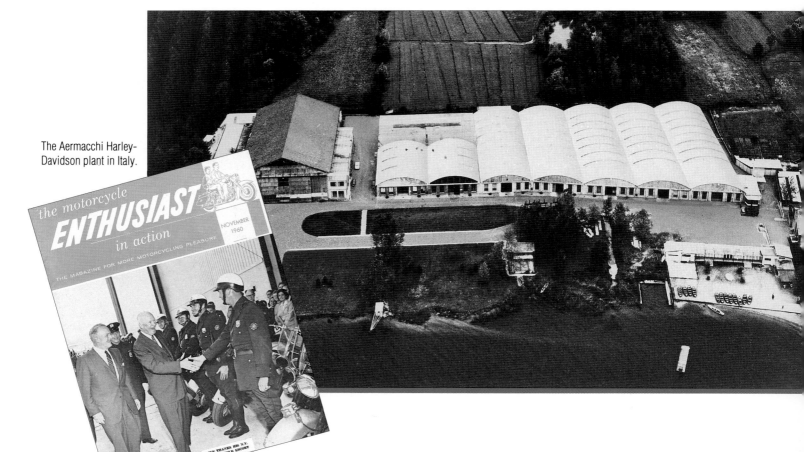

The Aermacchi Harley-Davidson plant in Italy.

DUO-GLIDE FLH

DUO-GLIDE FL

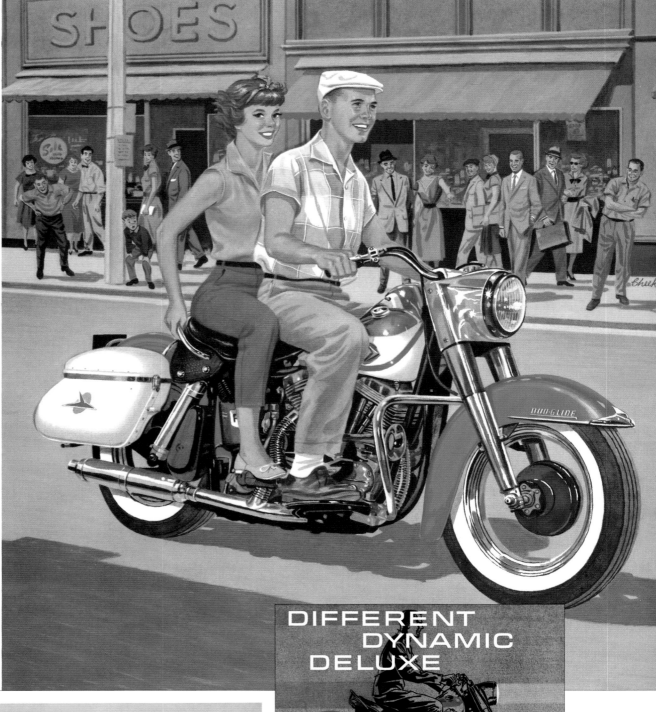

DIFFERENT
DYNAMIC
DELUXE

'60 HARLEY-DAVIDSON
DUO-GLIDES

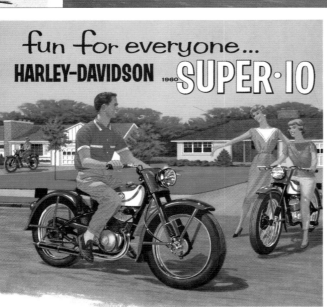
Robert Stack in
TV's "The Untouchables."

y 1960, there were more motorcycles registered in the United States than ever before, totalling well over a half million. Interest in the sport was on the upswing, and Harley-Davidson enjoyed a sixteen percent increase in business that year. William H. Davidson expected sales to continue growing, largely because the company was now able to offer motorcyclists a complete range of price and performance choices. Rounding out the top of the line were the stylish Duo-Glide and powerful Sportster models.

Harley-Davidson continued its racing successes into the Sixties, most notably with a resounding sweep of the 1960 Daytona road races. In the 200-mile National, it was veteran racer, Brad Andres, who scored his third Daytona victory while leading thirteen other Harley-Davidson racers to the top fourteen places. Tommy Seagraves led a top seven Harley-Davidson record-setting sweep in the 100-mile Amateur race, marking the third consecutive win in the event for Harley-Davidson.

The next year, the famed race was moved from the hard-packed beach to the newly opened Daytona International Speedway, where the 200-mile event consisted of 100 laps over a twisting infield course and spectacular high-banked turns. Leading all but the very first lap, Roger Reiman piloted his Harley-Davidson KR racer to a win in that inaugural race. At the same time, five Harley-Davidson 165s swept the Lightweight Road Race, and Bob Hamilton proved the mettle of the new Sprint by scoring a win in the Class 5 Road Race.

In 1961, William J. Harley was named chairman of Aermacchi Harley-Davidson, and William H. Davidson's son, John, joined the company in the dealer relations department. Carroll Resweber, the transplanted Texan living in Cedarburg, Wisconsin, captured an unprecedented fourth consecutive title of Grand National Champion in motorcycle racing, a feat that has never been equaled.

John A. Davidson

The product line remained relatively unchanged for 1961; however, the next year saw several significant additions and changes. The 165 was enlarged to 175cc and offered in three versions, tailored to distinctly different riding tastes. The Pacer was a conventional street motorcycle; the Scat served a dual purpose as an on-road/off-road lightweight; and the Ranger was pure off-road, stripped of lighting and sporting aggressive tires.

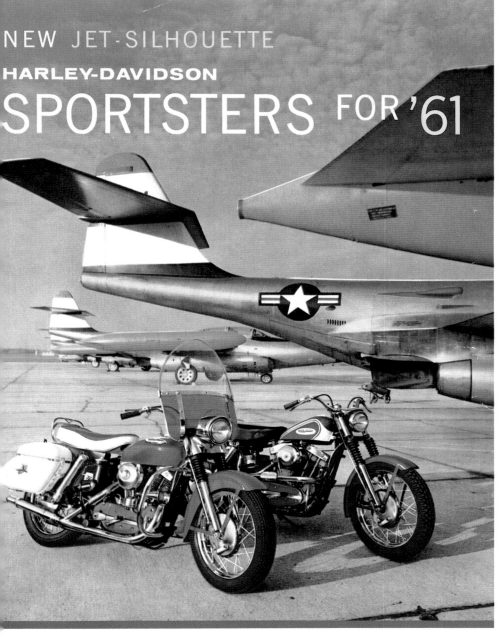

NEW JET-SILHOUETTE
HARLEY-DAVIDSON
SPORTSTERS FOR '61

"Gunsmoke" was a top-rated television series.

At the 1960 International Sports and Vacation Show in the Los Angeles Coliseum, one of the top attractions was a demonstration of the Harley-Davidson XLCH Sportster's awesome power and climbing ability. Mounting a wooden ramp erected over the Coliseum seats, the Sportsters rode the 400 feet from the arena floor to the uppermost rim at grades of 45° to 55°.

The stunt had five riders performing three or four times a day for ten days, and was sponsored by the Rich Budelier Company, the L.A. Harley-Davidson dealer, to dramatize how safe a motorcycle can be when ridden properly by an experienced rider.

Right: An artist's sketch of the manmade hillclimb from the floor to the rim of the Los Angeles Coliseum. Below right: Metal trusses supported the wooden track above the seats.

# ROGER REIMAN WINS 1961 DAYTONA 200

Roger Reiman of Kewanee, IL, led every lap but the first on his Harley-Davidson to win the 200-Mile National Championship on the Daytona International Speedway AMA road course. Reiman averaged 69.25 mph in the twisting, tortuous 100-lap road race. His winning time was 2 hours, 53 minutes, 17.51 seconds.

Harley-Davidson riders took three of the first six places. George Roeder was third and Bart Markel took fifth. In the time trials, Reiman was the top qualifier with a speed of 72.310. Carroll Resweber had the second fastest time—71.856. Larry Williamson, a Harley-Davidson rider from Peoria, Ill., took the first place spot at the start of the race, only to lose it to Reiman who kept the lead for the distance. Chief challenger up to the midway mark was Resweber on a Harley-Davidson. He held the number two position only 13 seconds behind Reiman for 50 laps! However, Resweber was forced out in the 51st lap. Lone former Daytona 200 winner in the field, Dick Klamfoth, had clutch trouble and only completed 28 laps. The number of riders in the front was whittled down rapidly. Larry Palmgren had the number three spot up to the 73rd lap when he went out. Garnet Koehler, a Canadian rider, was among the front five. Engine trouble sent him to the pits for two extra stops in the 86th and 89th laps. He finished eighth. As the race wore on, the fans realized that nothing could stop Reiman. He kept pouring it on, though, and ran the last 100 miles even faster than the first 100!

A crowd in excess of 7,500 attended the race, held for the first time on the Speedway's two-mile AMA road race course. It had six sharp turns which necessitated 3,000 gear shifts and at least 600 brake applications during the 100-lap event. There were 54 machines in the starting lineup. Only 27 survivors were still running when Reiman took the checkered flag. Of these, 15 were Harley-Davidsons! Once more, the superior power, performance and durability of the Milwaukee Brand had been proven in this gruelling test of man and machine!

# THE REMARKABLE CARROLL RESWEBER

On August 20, 1961, factory racer Carroll Resweber accomplished what no man before him had ever equaled. On that date, Resweber won the 50-mile national race at Springfield, Illinois to earn his

fourth title as Grand National Champion. The fact that he won his four titles in consecutive years make his feat even more remarkable.

Like fellow Harley-Davidson rider Joe Petrali in the Thirties, Resweber was almost unbeatable in the late Fifties and early Sixties. In 1961, for example, he won ninety-five percent of all the races he started.

Small of stature, the wiry Resweber was a transplanted Texan who moved to the small town of Cedarburg, Wisconsin, just north of Milwaukee. At a testimonial dinner in his honor after clinching his third title, over 300 residents of Cedarburg gathered to pay tribute to the champion and his accomplishments.

As a token of their esteem, the well-wishers presented Resweber with the keys to a fire-engine red 1961 Chevrolet. The car was purchased from a fund which received contributions fromCedarburg residents and industry, motorcycle dealers and racing friends from all over the United States and Canada.

After recovering his composure, the grateful Resweber told the crowd: "This is the greatest thing that has ever happened to me. All I can do in return is to say thank you! If I seem to be getting the best part of the deal, I hope you will all understand."

But he did give them more than a simple "thank you." The next year he gave his fans the best year of his career, as he raced to his fourth and still unequalled national title.

Below, with his trophies providing the background, Carroll Resweber, second from right, is congratulated by Tom Vasey of the Cedarburg Chamber of Commerce. Looking on were Mayor Merlin G. Rostad (left) and Lin Kuchler, executive secretary of the AMA. Below right, Carroll Resweber--where he could usually be found in a race--out in front.

## 1960

America launches 17 space satellites and probes, including first weather satellite.

Francis Gary Powers shot down in U-2 spy plane over Russia.

## 1961

U.S. breaks diplomatic relations with Cuba.

Cuban "Bay of Pigs" invasion attempt to overthrow Castro is repulsed.

## 1962

John H. Glenn Jr. becomes first American to orbit the earth.

Cuban missile crisis: Kennedy blockades Cuba until Soviets agree to dismantle missile bases.

## 1963

President Kennedy is assassinated in Dallas; Lyndon B. Johnson becomes president.

Lee Harvey Oswald, Kennedy's accused assassin, shot by Jack Ruby.

U.S. troops in Vietnam total over 15,000 by end of year.

## 1964

Seven men convicted of conspiracy in Mississippi killing of three civil rights workers.

Seeking to expand its business interests even further, Harley-Davidson purchased a company in Tomahawk, Wisconsin, which had previously been devoted to the production of fiberglass boats. Because of the growing versatility of fiberglass in the motorcycle industry, it quickly became apparent that the company needed its own source to manufacture a growing number of components. In 1962, the Tomahawk Division was established.

It was also a time when Harley-Davidson decided to branch out into a totally unrelated field of leisure products and began production of three-wheeled golf cars. With their all-fiberglass bodies, they also became an end user for the Tomahawk plant, and the golf car bodies became one of the primary products manufactured there for nearly two decades. Harley-Davidson also produced a commercial version of the golf car called the Utilicar, which was ideal for use as a light-duty truck or personnel carrier. By the end of the decade, Harley-Davidson's fine gasoline and electric-powered golf cars had secured approximately one third of the U. S. market, and were used overseas as far away as Japan.

Other than the addition of an off-road version of the Sprint, 1963 saw no major changes in Harley-Davidson models, but subtle refinements were made in existing features to enhance riders' comfort and enjoyment. For example, the Duo-Glide—flagship of the line—received a fishtail muffler, brilliant Hi-Fi colors, huskier brakes and new backswept optional fiberglass saddlebags.

To help riders get the most out of the sport, Harley-Davidson marketed an extensive line of motorcycle accessories as well as motorcycle clothing and novelties. Using nothing but genuine Harley-Davidson accessories, a Harley-Davidson motorcycle owner could customize his mount to suit his own personal taste and riding style by installing his choice of a number of chrome racks, bars, lights, horns, windshields, or dozens and dozens of other items.

the motorcycle
ENTHUSIAST
in action
AUGUST 1962
THE MAGAZINE FOR MORE MOTORCYCLING PLEASURE

In the early Sixties, Harley-Davidson entered the golf car business with a reliable, well-built three-wheeled car that came to be a dominant force in the market by the end of the decade.

# and now... another new Sprint by Harley-Davidson

a new 250 cc champion

the *Sprint*

Doris Day, the number one box office star, for five years straight.

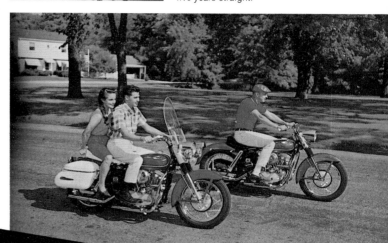

## a new Sprint model with real way ahead stay ahead power the HARLEY-DAVIDSON *Sprint*

The New 250 cc Sprint H combines the lean, lithe lines of a thoroughbred with winning performance proven by the 1-2-3 finish in the AMA National Short-Track Championship at Santa Fe!

On road, track or trail the Sprint H packs the performance features to put you way ahead ... and keep you there!

With a compression ratio of 9.2 to 1, oversize intake valve and port, the Sprint H has added zip. Its streamlined gas tank, bobbed fenders and hi-flo exhaust give it a distinctive custom look. Larger wheels for higher clearance get you through the rough stuff with ease!

Ride a Sprint H and FEEL the way ahead-stay ahead power. Try it today!!!

**features**

**engine ...** With a compression ratio of 9.2 to 1, oversize intake valve and port, the Sprint H overhead valve 250 cc engine delivers 21 solid, reliable horsepower.

**tank ...** A stream-lined 2.6 gallon gas tank with bold red and white color styling make the SPRINT H a standout in appearance as well as in performance!

**exhaust ...** Bobbed fenders for a distinctive custom look in a real road, track and trail machine. Thrill to the dynamic, virile note of its Hi-Flo tuned exhaust!

**brakes ...** Brake back plates specially designed to keep out dirt and water. Large, safe 7" brakes are fast stoppers, every time!

**wheels ...** Large 18" wheels mean greater ground clearance for scrambles, track or grassy trails to take you through the rough stuff with ease.

**frame ...** A sturdy, large diameter, reinforced, single-strut frame designed to take it no matter how rough the going! Engineered for maximum strength.

SPRINT H EXTRAS • Specialized Crankcase Breather • Shrouded Air Cleaner • Tuned Exhaust System • Rubber-mounted Handlebars • Big ⅜ inch Control Cables • 60 Watt Output Generator • New Improved Battery • Ball-end Control Levers

## and... for road or show it's the *Sprint* with the custom look!

Commands attention wherever it goes! Distinctively different and smartly styled to take you out of the ordinary in motorcycling pleasure. The Sprint is completely engineered for full riding performance. Hydraulically damped front and rear suspension shares the load to give you a real joy ride. For you or two ... costs less to buy ... costs less to run with 70 miles per gallon economy. For style, spirit and really enjoyable motorcycling it's the Sprint by Harley-Davidson!

**and** for the track ask your Harley-Davidson dealer about the *Sprint*

commercial version of the golf car was offered number of configurations, shown here as ght-duty carrier.

1961 Sprint, the first motorcycle resulting n Harley-Davidson's Italian merger, ured a horizontal single-cylinder, cc four-stroke engine.

HARLEY-DAVIDSON MOTOR

**A**new employee started that year, one who would have a deep, far reaching and lasting effect not only on Harley-Davidson but ultimately, the whole sport in America in future years. Fresh from a series of outside positions involving product design and styling, William G. Davidson joined the company as director of styling. The oldest son of William H. Davidson, he assumed responsibility for designing all subsequent Harley-Davidson models and many of their accessories. Riders nationwide would come to know him as Willie G.

With the company's diversification into the golf car business, Harley-Davidson felt a change in the company logo was warranted in 1964, to better reflect the broader scope of its leisure vehicle business. The familiar bar and shield trademark, which dated back to the first decade of the century, was dropped as the corporate logo. In its place, to identify the leisure vehicle business, was a stylized logo with the words "Harley-Davidson" flanked by two elongated triangles. Gone were the words "Motor Cycles." However, the old trademark continued to be used in various forms on motorcycles, parts and a wide range of consumer products for some time and was resurrected for corporate use much later.

JFK's tragic death stunned the nation and the world.

FPG

The third-generation William Davidson, William G. Davidson, joined the company as director of styling in 1963.

"Cleopatra," starring Elizabeth Taylor, cost and lost more than any film ever had before.

Sean Connery's series of James Bond films were big hits in the Sixties.

Late in 1963, the American Motorcycle Association sanctioned the use of fairings for streamlining motorcycles on road race courses, and the 1964 Daytona event marked their first use in a competitive event. Repeating his 1961 victory, Roger Reiman streaked to a thrilling win over an elongated 3.81-mile course in a record speed of nearly 95 miles per hour. The following year, Reiman was to repeat his win once again.

Capitalizing on Reiman's skill at controlling a motorcycle at high speeds, the company selected him to pilot its Sprint-powered streamliner in a 250cc class speed record attempt on the Bonneville salt flats of Utah in September. The old mark of 150 mph had stood unbroken since 1956. Despite a projected top speed of nearly 200 miles per hour, the streamliner's performance was hampered by poor surface conditions resulting from freakish summer storms. Nonetheless, Reiman managed to set new records for both the mile and the kilometer of over 156 miles per hour.

Under better racing conditions thirteen months later and powered by the new Sprint CR racing engine, George Roeder propelled the streamliner to an even higher mark of 177 miles per hour, the fastest speed any 250cc engine using gas or fuel had ever attained.

The engine used in Roeder's record attempt debuted in a 1965 model called the Sprint Scrambler. A competitive winner on the European racing circuit, it was added to Harley-Davidson's model line to fill a need for a competition —or pure off-road—high-performance 250. Also from the Aermacchi operation came a nifty little model called the M-50. A 50cc two-stroke in a step-through frame, it claimed an amazing 180 miles of breezy enjoyment per gallon.

Mickey Mantle and the Yankees dominated the American League in the early Sixties.

Teammates Roger Reiman (#1) and Mert Lawwill (#18) finished one-two in the 1965 Daytona 200 miler. Lawwill earned his own Number One plate for the 1969 season.

# WORLD SPEED RECORD SET BY HARLEY-DAVIDSON SPRINT

One year and a month after Harley-Davidson set the 250cc world speed record at Bonneville, the Sprint streamliner returned to the salt and blasted the record up to an incredible 176.817 mph for the mile and 177.225 mph for the kilometer.

On October 21, 1965, under the guidance of top-notch racer George Roeder, the 250cc Harley-Davidson Sprint smashed all records in class A or class C runs with its two-way 177 mph average. The streamliner was powered by the new 1966 Sprint CR racing engine and burned standard pump gasoline. No 250cc bike had ever gone faster using gas or fuel. The historic speed runs were timed by the United States Auto Club (USAC) and sanctioned by the American Motorcyclist Association (AMA).

Clear, bright skies dried the flats for two weeks before the Harley Davidson Sprint was set to run. Under the direction of Stormy Mangham, airline pilot and record setter, the Sprint shell was brought up from Texas where it had spent the last year being refurbished and the updated Sprint engine was installed. Mangham was in charge of the 1964 Sprint record runs at Bonneville when Roger Reiman piloted the 15 cubic inch machine to 156.24 mph for the world's record.

At that time, the salt was mushy at all hours of the day, and the high-revving 250 could not get adequate traction to really let out. This time the salt was far from perfect, but it was considerably better than the previous year. By late morning, the old problem of water seeping onto the flats made good traction impossible, so most runs had to be made in the first few hours after sunrise.

On Tuesday morning, October 20, Roeder pushed the Sprint to a 170 mph two-way average to shatter Harley-Davidson's previous record. But it wasn't good enough for the crew on the salt. On the next day, the 14-foot Sprint streamliner was positioned 4-1/2 miles down the run from the timing traps and Roeder squeezed into the tight cockpit. Strapped down with only inches to turn his head, Roeder revved up the newly designed engine and was push-started down the course. The Sprint's five-speed transmission drove the bullet-nosed streamliner through the traps twice for the 177 mph mark average, and retained the Harley-Davidson 250's title as the fastest 250cc motorcycle in the world.

Below:
Nikita Khrushchev
and Fidel Castro.

**F**or the first time, a Harley-Davidson leisure motorcycle received an electric starter to crank its two massive pistons. Gone was the Duo-Glide; in its place was the Electra Glide. Riders never had it so good—not until 1966, at least.

That was the year Harley-Davidson doled out liberal doses of extra horse power. The Electra Glide received an updated engine with redesigned "power pac" aluminum heads, which put out ten percent more horsepower. Because of the shape of their combustion chambers, these new heads earned the engine the nickname of "shovelhead."

Not to be outdone by its bigger brother, the Sportster also got a fifteen percent boost in power by virtue of a new carburetor and cams.

Added to the bottom end of the line was a sport model of the M-50, as well as a new 175cc model. Called the Bobcat, this newest lightweight sported a

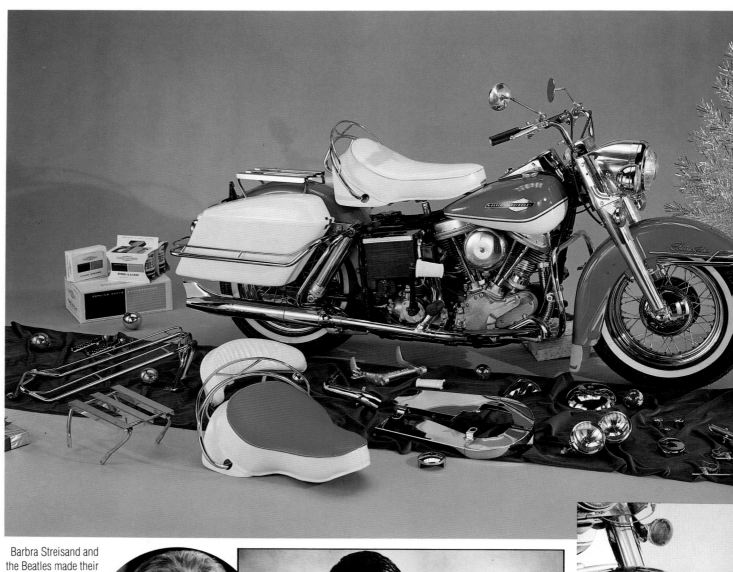

With Harley-Davidson accessories, a rider could tailor his Electra Glide to suit his own personal tastes.

Barbra Streisand and the Beatles made their impact on American Music.

unique one-piece molded ABS resin body, which covered both the gas tank and the rear wheel. The Bobcat was the last of the domestically produced lightweights and, despite its modern looks, was gone from the line a year later. From then on, all the Harley-Davidson lightweight models were produced in the Italian plant.

More changes to the line for 1967 saw the XLH Sportster receiving an electric starter, while the M-50s got a boost in displacement to 65cc. The Sprint underwent styling changes to both the engine and its sheet metal, especially the H model which received a five gallon, road-race style gas tank. Companion to the Electra Glide was a smoothly-styled, more contemporary fiberglass sidecar. Except for the introduction of the 125cc Rapido, the model line changed little for 1968.

Above: A promotional piece for the 1966 Bobcat; a cutaway view of the 1966 Big Twin engine; Julie Andrews in "The Sound of Music." Left: The 1965 Sportsters.

205

Far right:
Raquel Welch.

Hottest
Thing
Going
On
two
Wheels

SPORTSTER

H

electrifying!

PUSH BUTTON STARTING

positive, heavy-duty **electra glide type** with new 4-pole starter motor

Push the button . . . ZAP . . . and away you go. It's electrifying . . . it's unbelievable . . . it's new SPORTSTER H instant starting. Powerful 12 volt system, using a 32 ampere hour battery, leaps to your command to pulse SPORTSTER H's charging horses into action. Battery-oil tank combo is rubber mounted to isolate all vibration. Heavy duty system allows more power, too, for your favorite accessories. Make your fun more electrifying this year on a new SPORTSTER H.

*NEW SPORTSTER H ELECTRIFYING STYLING* — Stand back . . . take a look! Catch the sparkle of the new **twin tach-speedo** instrumentation. It's right up front where you can see it . . . but not the hidden drive cables. **New Headlight Nacelle** is really a beauty. An **Indicator Lamp Panel** is built right into the nacelle with aircraft design. New **Neat-Pleat All-Model Buddy Seat** has California styling that says "class" from the word go!

206

Above: "Spy" stories remained popular, as in TV's "The Man from U.N.C.L.E." Left: The 1967 Harley-Davidson model line.

NEW HOT AND SWINGING... '67 HARLEY-DAVIDSON M-65's with 62% more horsepower

Above: "Bonnie and Clyde" shot 'em up on film, while Rowan and Martin broke 'em up on TV.

'67 electrifying HARLEY-DAVIDSON SPORTSTERS H&CH

fun for YOUNG AMERICA at any age

Never before has a lightweight sportcycle won so many hearts as the Harley-Davidson. Now, add the punch of more power and you've got a two-wheeled wildcat loaded with get-up-and-go! Safe power, too! Perfect for keeping up with traffic . . . ideal for long ride leisure. Yes, no matter what your riding pleasure, you'll love these neat and nimble lightweights . . . they're a barrel of fun for everyone.

HARLEY-DAVIDSON MODEL M-65 and M-65 SPORT
Sleek for Sightseeing ■ Shopping ■ School ■ Work or Play

**D RIDING LEATHERS**
Lightweight, competition-styled garments of
select black leather. Nylon lined, form-fitting
for comfort and safety.
98140-60V Leather Shirt,
   Sizes 34-48 . . . . . . . . . . . . . . . $37.30
98145-60V Leather Pants,
   Sizes 28-42 . . . . . . . . . . . . . . . $39.50

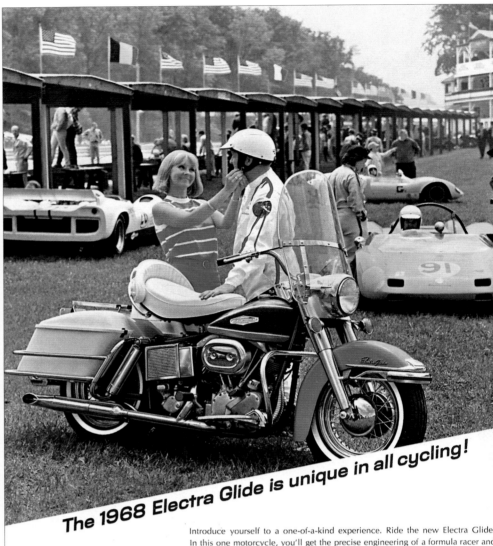

## The 1968 Electra Glide is unique in all cycling!

Introduce yourself to a one-of-a-kind experience. Ride the new Electra Glide.
In this one motorcycle, you'll get the precise engineering of a formula racer and
the handcrafted luxury of a custom roadster. Here too, are the stamina, balance
and ride that have made the 1200 cc Electra Glide the world's foremost cycle.
Now add electric starting, new instrumentation and futuristic styling. This is
Electra Glide for 1968. On display right now at the Harley-Davidson dealer
nearest you. A limited edition of unlimited excellence. Stop in for a test ride soon.

## HARLEY-DAVIDSON

The Harley-
Davidson
accessories line
continued to grow
in the Sixties.

## I CYCLE CHAMP AND CYCLE QUEEN JACKETS

Form-fitting, fashioned from choice black leather, both have quilted nylon lining, zipper closing, snap-down lapels, wind-tight sleeves, plenty of pockets.

| | |
|---|---|
| 98100-58V Champ, Sizes 34-48 (with belt) | $47.50 |
| 98105-46V Queen, Sizes 32-42 (with belt) | $43.75 |
| 98130-58VA Belt, Sizes 32-48 | $ 2.75 |

Townsman Coat (not shown) — Black leather, hip length, belted coat, sizes 34-48.   98101-53V   $49.75

The Beach Boys,
Sandra Dee and Troy Donahue in "A Summer Place."

209

**R**acing action continued hot and heavy with Harley-Davidson excelling in virtually every area of two-wheeled competition. From drag racing to hillclimbing to Bonneville record runs, it was the Sprints, Sportsters and KR racers from Milwaukee that set the pace and broke records on strips and courses all over the country.

Perhaps the greatest accolade to symbolize Harley-Davidson's dominance of motorcycle competition in the late Sixties was the nickname bestowed on its team of Class C dirt trackers and road racers. "The Wrecking Crew" was so powerful in 1968 that it won 18 of the 23 National Championship races held that year, wrecking everyone else's hopes of having a winning season.

The most stunning ride of the year was turned in by team road racing ace Cal Rayborn, as he rode his streamlined KR to victory at the Daytona 200 miler a full four miles ahead of the second place man. Rayborn's win was

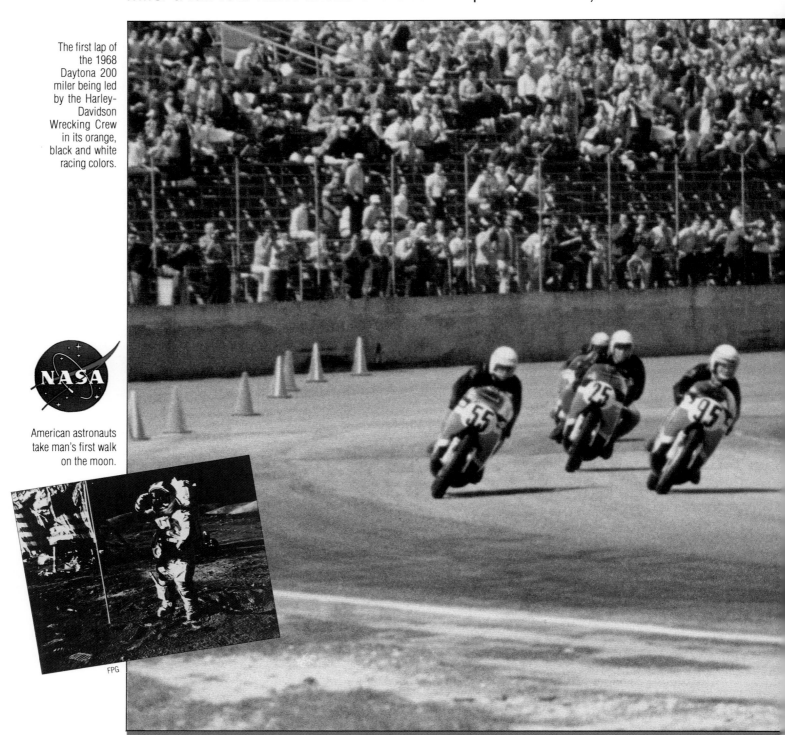

The first lap of the 1968 Daytona 200 miler being led by the Harley-Davidson Wrecking Crew in its orange, black and white racing colors.

American astronauts take man's first walk on the moon.

FPG

one for the record books as he ran the race at an average speed of 101.290 miles per hour, the first motorcycle racer to crack the 100 mph barrier on the famed course. He also became the first racer to do it a second time when he won again in 1969, once more at an average speed over 100 miles per hour after having lapped the entire field.

The final year of the decade saw the Sprint engine receive an increase in size to 350cc along with its racing counterpart, the ERS, which took a first overall in the Greenhorn 500-mile National Championship Enduro in California.

Cosmetically, the dependable little Rapido received an update which gave it a cleaner, more modern look. Demonstrating the reliability and performance of the spunky little two-stroke, three adventurous motorcyclers made a trek of nearly 2,000 miles across the treacherous wasteland of the Sahara Desert on a trio of fully-loaded Rapidos in the early months of the year.

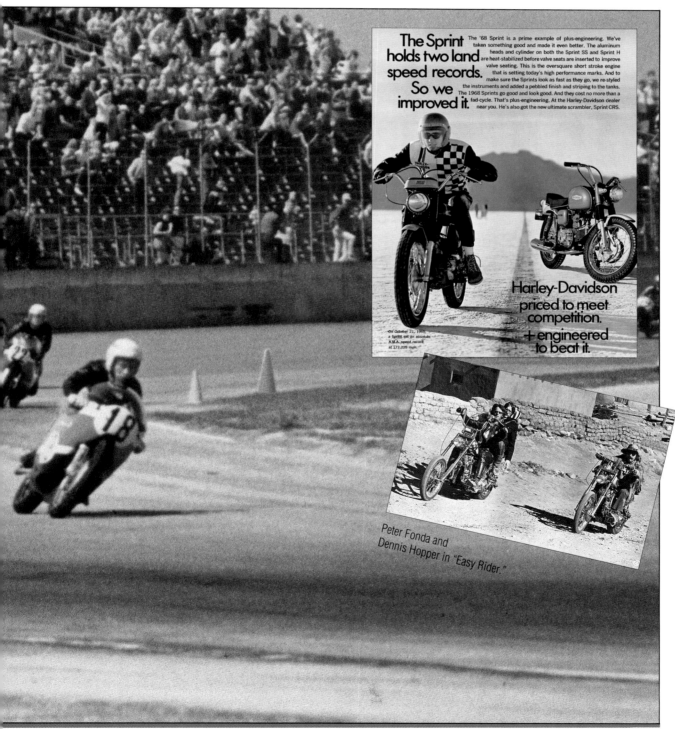

Peter Fonda and Dennis Hopper in "Easy Rider."

# CROSSING THE SAHARA DESERT ON RAPIDOS.

Early in 1969, five American adverturers set out on the motorcycle journey of a lifetime, across the barren landscape of North Africa's fabled Sahara Desert. Their purpose was to make a photographic and cinemagraphic record of what was to become a long and arduous trek. Their motorcycles of choice were not thumping 250cc trail bikes, but rather the nimble 125cc Harley-Davidson Rapidos.

While all five men arrived in Casablanca in mid-January to start the journey, two of them would drop out and go home before the trip was even half over. The remaining three were Russel Rehm, Dick Ewing and Frank Fanger.

The plan was to set up their motorcycles and leave from Casablanca as soon as possible, in order to get across the desert before the March sandstorms began. As so often happens, the best laid plans don't always work the way they should, and the group faced two weeks of delays as they grappled with paperwork, indifferent officials and missing motorcycles. Four of the five Rapidos were being shipped directly from Aermacchi Harley-Davidson via the Italian port of Genoa and had not arrived on time.

With the bikes arriving from the docks by horsecart, the crew was finally able to begin assembly. In addition to normal setup, each bike was fitted with a high exhaust pipe so it could better negotiate the obstacles posed by desert travel.

Finally, the big day arrived on January 31. Up at 5:30 a.m., the men loaded—then unloaded and reloaded—the Rapidos, rearranging and discarding equipment in their attempts to balance the loads. Despite their best efforts, the bikes handled poorly that first day, causing several spills as they picked their way cautiously over the rugged roads. Fortunately, no one was seriously injured, and after that their skills at packing the little 125s got progressively better.

Heading northeast and then east through Rabat, Fex and Oujda, the travelers were treated to a variety of impressions as they witnessed everyday life in North Africa. Scenes such as town markets, vineyards, groves of fig and date trees, and Roman ruins all conjured up biblical images as they slowly motored eastward.

Pushing for Oujda, they encountered a cold front with 40° temperatures and driving rain. After 150 miles over miserable roads, the group opted for hot food, warm beds and clean sheets in the town's best hotel, rather than spending a night camping in the chilly weather.

Entering Algeria, they turned their motorcycles south and headed into the true desert. Crossing a plateau 3,500 feet high, they encountered an old, abandoned and shot-out fort where they spent the night under the stars. Their room for the night had apparently been used by wandering shepherds to pen their sheep, and smelled accordingly. But animal scents were the least of their worries. As they traveled, they continuously worried about the availability of gasoline and were plagued by the indifference of Algerian police and minor officials, who seemed more intent on making their lives difficult than speeding them on their way. They were constantly warned against taking pictures, and often were threatened with having their equipment and film confiscated.

As they rode southward, stopping periodically for gas, they were continually followed by the local police, and occasionally stopped for questioning. In a fit of frustration, they sent a telegram to the president of Algeria but, of course, received no reply.

"Broadway Joe" Namath led the New York Jets.

FPG

# THE 1970'S
## Under the AMF Banner

# THE 1970'S

Entering the Seventies, Harley-Davidson motorcycles and golf cars continued to be in great demand despite the growing number of foreign-made competitive products flooding the marketplace. While it was no longer the fastest motorcycle on two wheels, the Sportster still retained its image as the ultimate macho machine and was highly sought after by enthusiasts. Because the demand so greatly exceeded the supply, it was not uncommon for a rider to wait months for delivery of a new Sportster, or fly a thousand miles to purchase one available on the showroom floor of a remote Harley-Davidson dealership.

The 1970 Sportster featured an updated, more modern look which included a boat-tail fiberglass seat/fender combination which jutted out the back like a torpedo, totally covering a cutoff rear fender. To Sportster purists, it was too radical a departure from the motorcycle's classic look, and the Sportster seat aftermarket flourished among riders anxious to change them.

New for that year were two hot competition machines. The Baja was introduced as a 100cc high performance, off-road model. With its aggressive tires and long-legged stance, it proved ideal for moto-cross, enduros and desert racing and quickly ran up a string of victories in Southern California's District 37 desert racing.

The other hot performer was a full-blown racer, designed to compete on the Class C professional racing circuit. Powered by a destroked Sportster engine, the XR 750 debuted on America's racetracks as a powerful successor to the time-honored KR. Because its powerplant was essentially a street engine with cast-iron cylinders and certain performance modifications, the XR was really a stopgap race bike, designed to be campaigned while development proceeded on a more advanced version. Despite the engine's many inherent limitations, it still proved itself a worthy competitor. In its most impressive win of what proved to be a short career for the "iron XR," the machine was campaigned by the late, great Harley-Davidson team racer, Cal Rayborn, at a series of six 1970 Anglo-American match races in England. In a performance that stunned the European road racers and spoke more of the rider than the motorcycle, Rayborn rode the XR to three firsts and three seconds in the six races.

The 1970 XR-750.

The U.S. invasion of Cambodia caused widespread antiwar demonstrations.

Racing Director Dick O'Brien, left, and Jules Horky of the AMA inspect a massed array of XRs prior to the start of the 1970 racing season.

221

In October of 1970, the Sportster was a headliner once more in motorcycle publications, as Harley-Davidson journeyed to the Bonneville salt flats for an assault on the motorcycle land speed record. As in past record-setting attempts, the company again called on its premier racer to pilot its Harley-Davidson down the course. This time, it was Cal Rayborn. Laying almost flat on his back with a souped-up Sportster engine right behind his head, Rayborn steered an orange, cigar-shaped streamliner resembling a jet fighter's wing tank down the course, setting a two-way record of 265.492 miles per hour. It was the fastest speed any motorcycle-powered vehicle had ever attained.

The year closed with even more news as Harley-Davidson entered a totally different arena of leisure vehicles. After years of testing and evaluating other machines on the market, in late 1970 the company unveiled its brand new snowmobile, a 398cc beauty made available that season on a limited basis. Harley-Davidson felt that many snowmobile manufacturers would soon fall by the wayside and customers would want a product backed by a solid, established dealer network. Snowmobiles went into full production the next year and were highly praised for their quality, comfort and reliability, if not for their sizzling performance.

In October of 1970, Harley-Davidson went to the salt flats of Bonneville near Wendover, Utah, to prove that a single Harley-Davidson engine could break an absolute motorcycle land speed record held previously by twin-engine machines.

The vehicle they chose to make the record run was a computer-designed monocoque streamliner which measured nineteen feet long and a scant 25 inches high. The streamliner was so low that its driver, veteran road racer Cal Rayborn, had to lay almost flat on his back and look out either of two side windows to steer the machine down the course.

With 1930s Harley-Davidson racing great Joe Petrali present as the official United States Auto Club timer, Rayborn blasted down the ten-mile course to clock a speed of 266.785 miles per hour for the measured mile. His return run of 264.200 was good enough for an average of 265.492 and another page in the record books for Harley-Davidson.

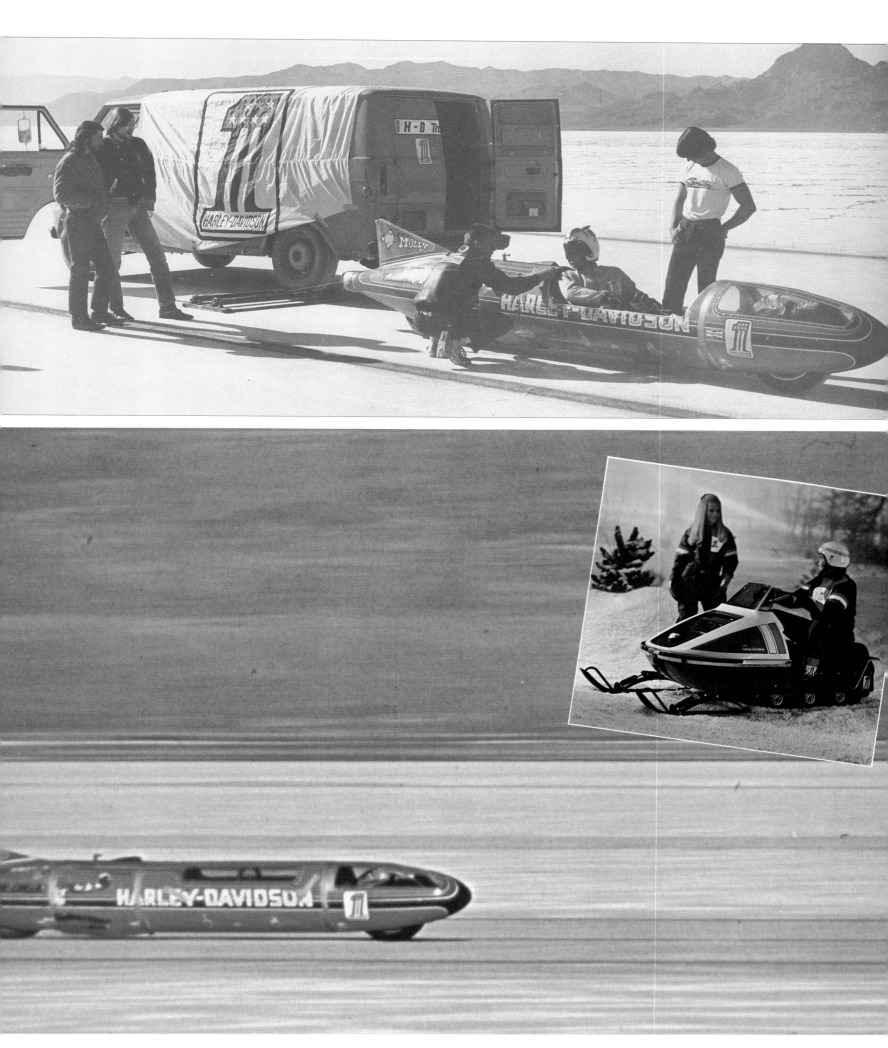

S ince the merger between Harley-Davidson and AMF, the influence of the corporate parent received little notice by riders and dealers as the company proceeded more or less with business as usual. The fact that Harley-Davidson was no longer master of its own destiny became evident soon after the addition of the AMF corporate logo to all 1971 motorcycle gas tanks. From that time on, the company was to be known as AMF Harley-Davidson, a decree that rankled enthusiasts everywhere.

That summer, AMF flexed its corporate muscles even more by naming a new president and elevating William H. Davidson to chairman. For the first time in sixty-eight years, someone other than a Davidson sat in the president's chair. At the same time, John Davidson was promoted from vice president of sales to executive vice president. Earlier that year, William J. Harley, engineering vice president, passed away. His brother, John, remained as the last Harley to hold a position of responsibility in Harley-Davidson Motor Company until his death five years later.

There was a bright spot in 1971—or perhaps a solar flare-up would be more appropriate—as Harley-Davidson unveiled a new heavyweight motorcycle destined to change the face of American motorcycling forever. Customizing and personalizing Harley-Davidsons had long been a right and privilege of owners, who tailored their motorcycles to their own tastes. This growing trend reached its zenith by the Seventies, and Harley-Davidson felt it was time to take an active part.

Clint Eastwood's movie role as Harry Callahan began with "Dirty Harry."

The 1971 Harley-Davidson Outperformers.

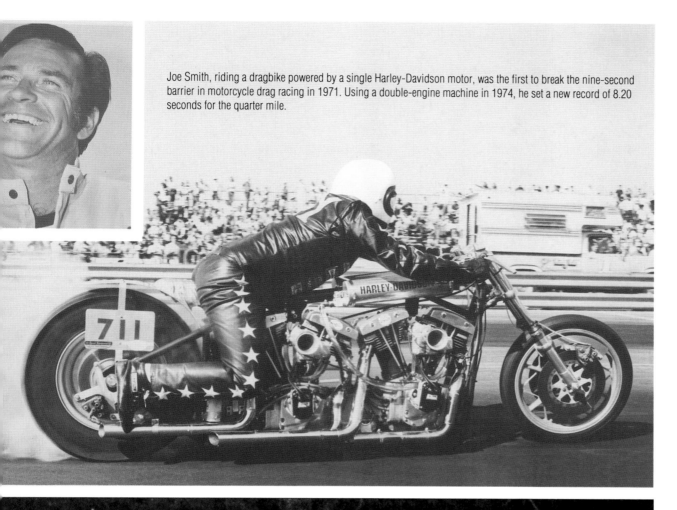

Joe Smith, riding a dragbike powered by a single Harley-Davidson motor, was the first to break the nine-second barrier in motorcycle drag racing in 1971. Using a double-engine machine in 1974, he set a new record of 8.20 seconds for the quarter mile.

al Rayborn leads Briton Ray Pickrell through a curve at
allory Park in England during the 1971 Anglo-American
atch races.

225

**1970**

News of U.S. invasion of Cambodia results in campus violence and demonstrations.

George C. Scott wins Oscar for role as Patton, but refuses it.

**1971**

The 26th Amendment to the Constitution, lowering voting age to 18, is approved.

Charles Manson found guilty of 1969 slaying of Sharon Tate and six others.

U.S. and South Vietnamese military enter Laos.

**1972**

Alabama Gov. George Wallace shot and seriously wounded by Arthur H. Bremer.

Five men arrested for break-in at Democratic headquarters in Watergate office complex.

**1973**

OPEC oil embargo causes long lines at gas stations and shuts down factories.

Charged with tax evasion, Vice President Agnew resigns; succeeded by Gerald Ford.

Last U.S. troops leave Vietnam March 29.

**1974**

President Nixon resigns under threat of impeachment; Gerald Ford becomes president.

Fresh from the design studio of Willie G. Davidson came the boldly massive FX 1200 Super Glide. The FX got its name and custom looks by mating the frame and running gear of the FL series to the lighter, sportier front end of the XL series. The FX was derived by using the first letter of FL and first letter of XL. Like the earlier Sportster, the Super Glide also sported a fiberglass seat/fender, although in a more detailed form. Rounding out the custom look was a red, white and blue color scheme the factory called "Sparkling America." While the fiberglass seat/fender never gained widespread popularity, the "Sparkling America" versions became instant collectors' items.

In the middle of the product line, a new on-road/off-road version of the 350cc Sprint made its appearance in the rugged SX 350. The street version with its low exhaust disappeared, at least for 1971, but was to reappear in mid-1972.

In addition to its new models and racing successes, Harley-Davidson was also gaining publicity from unusual quarters. Early in the decade, the company began working with a super showman whose career was just beginning to rise. In what proved to be an interesting and rewarding relationship, Harley-Davidson began supplying motorcycles and support to a charismatic daredevil by the name of Evel Knievel.

While jumping over long lines of cars parked side by side was his main stock in trade, Knievel attracted considerable attention to himself and Harley-Davidson through his flamboyant lifestyle and by his abortive attempt to pilot a rocket-powered "skycycle" over the Snake River Canyon. While many serious motorcyclists scoffed at Evel Knievel's antics, he gained a great deal of favorable publicity for Harley-Davidson through personal appearances and two feature-length films dramatizing his adventures.

Donald
Sutherland
and Jane
Fonda in
"Klute."

The Sprint
SX 350.

Clockwise,
from upper left:
the 1971 Super Glide
in "Sparkling America"
red, white and blue;
Robert Blake in
"Electra Glide in Blue";
Olympic star Mark
Spitz; a composite
photograph illustrating
Evel Knievel's
technique as he
hurtles his XR 750
over nine trucks.

In 1972, the Sportster was the hot news again as it grew in size to 1000cc or 61 cubic inches. The Sportster also received a baby brother called the Shortster in the form of a sturdy little 65cc minibike. Also, the Sportster-based XR 750 was replaced by a more advanced, more powerful version with a new aluminum alloy engine. So strong was the new XR that it propelled team racer Mark Brelsford into the title of Grand National Champion for 1972, Harley-Davidson's first Number One plate since Mert Lawwill's achievement in 1969 on the KR.

Celebrating the fiftieth anniversary of Harley-Davidson's 74 cubic inch engine, the majestic FLH Electra Glide was fitted with a mighty 10 inch front disc brake, making it the first production motorcycle to have hydraulic front and rear brakes. Little wonder it was often referred to as "King of the Highway."

Liza Minneli in "Caberet."

The 1972 Shortster.

The Electra Glide,
in blue and white.

The Beatles changed
the face of popular
music.

A blueprint drawing of the
1972 alloy engine XR 750
road racer.

Harley-Davidson has had a
long history of speed records
at the Bonneville salt flats. In
1972, Warner Riley set a new
two-way speed record of
206.544 miles per hour on a
nitro-fueled Sportster.

"The Godfather" starred
Marlon Brando.

229

Big changes were brewing in the world of Harley-Davidson in 1973. Actual assembly of motorcycles and golf cars was moved from Milwaukee to a modern 400,000-square-foot, single-story AMF plant in York, Pennsylvania. Harley-Davidson's headquarters, racing division, and parts and accessories operation remained at Milwaukee's Juneau Avenue plant, while its Capitol Drive plant was used chiefly to produce engines, transmissions and component parts to support the York assembly line.

William H. Davidson, who had served as chairman for two years after twenty-nine years as company president, retired in 1973. Later that year his son, John, was promoted to the position of president.

Almost the entire line underwent changes for 1973, the most extensive improvements being in the line of Italian lightweights. All the model names were dropped in favor of letter and number designations, which was more in line with the rest of the industry. In addition, numerous features like oil injection were incorporated in an effort to put the motorcycles more on a par with others in their class. New tanks, frames, fenders and graphics were all part of this upgrading process.

The minibike got a bigger, better engine and transmission and was reborn as the X-90. Replacing the Rapido was the TX-125, and a smaller version of it became the Z-90. The Sprints received electric starters in addition to their many other improvements and became known simply as the SX-350 and the SS-350.

The old Sprint gas tank, a streamlined teardrop, was added to the Super Glide for a longer, leaner look and more of a custom appearance. The fiberglass seat was history. By 1973, all of the heavyweights had received a front disc brake.

Harley-Davidson continued to expand its line of riding apparel.

The addition of the York plant gave Harley-Davidson sorely needed room for expanded production.

230

# Discover the shortest distance between two points.

The new Harley-Davidson TX-125.

An on-road, off-road, 5-speed, oil injected goodtime machine.

With a look that moves people to envy and delight.

A double downtube frame makes the riding so sweet, that before you know it, you're where you want to be.

Sun-drenched, tingly and feeling like new money.

The Harley-Davidson TX-125.

Restyled. Eager.

The nicest way you'll ever go from one place to another.

AMF Harley-Davidson,
Milwaukee, Wisconsin 53201
Member Motorcycle Industry Council

**AMF**
**Harley-Davidson**

## Harley-Davidson TX-125.
## The Great American Freedom Machine.

Below: Robert Redford starred with Paul Newman in "The Sting" and with Barbra Streisand in "The Way We Were."
Bottom: Harley-Davidson snowmobiles and golf cars continued to be in demand.

In Europe, the Ameracchi Harley-Davidson plant began to campaign an awesome 250cc, twin-cylinder road racer in Europe called the RR-250. In the hands of a skilled road racer like Italy's Renzo Pasolini, it quickly became a force to contend with. Later, Walter Villa rode the RR-250 to three consecutive World 250 championship titles in 1974-76, a feat never previously accomplished. The RR-250 debuted in the U.S. in 1974 when team racer Gary Scott won the 250cc road race at Loudon, New Hampshire, marking the first time Harley-Davidson had won an American 250cc road race in four years.

After the extensive improvements to the product line in 1973, few changes occurred the following year. The most significant event was the addition of an electric starter model to the Super Glide line, the FXE. Now riders who favored the laid-back, low-down look of the Super Glide were able to choose between a button starter or kick starter. Also, a brand new 2-stroke 175 was unveiled, which was head and shoulders above the other Harley-Davidson lightweights for style and performance.

A year later, Harley-Davidson introduced a larger version of the 175 in the form of a 250, both of which received the SX designation for their on-road/off-road abilities. The Sprint, long past its prime in the motorcycle world, was dropped from the line. By 1975, after three relatively snowless winters, Harley's snowmobile also faded quietly from the scene.

Richard Nixon met his Watergate in 1973.

AMF
Harley-Davidson
SX-175

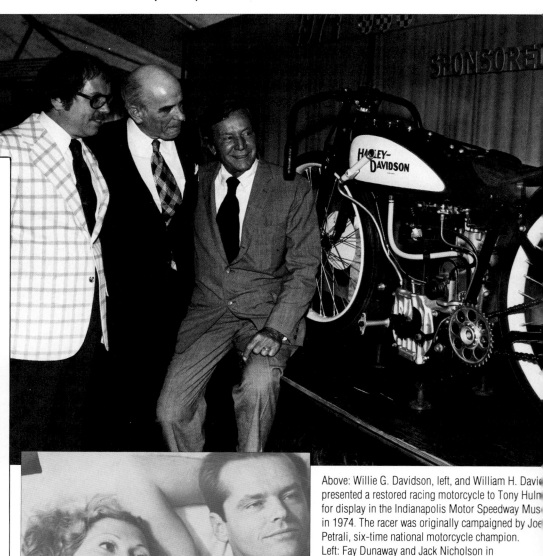

Above: Willie G. Davidson, left, and William H. Davi[d]son presented a restored racing motorcycle to Tony Hulm[an] for display in the Indianapolis Motor Speedway Mus[eum] in 1974. The racer was originally campaigned by Joe[ ]Petrali, six-time national motorcycle champion.
Left: Fay Dunaway and Jack Nicholson in "Chinatown."

Actor Sam Elliott playing the title role in the TV movie "Evel Knievel."

In 1975, Harley-Davidson advertising materials promoted The Great American Freedom Machines and rider's accessories.

America's bicentennial year, 1976, was a cause of great celebration throughout the country. Everyone was swept up in the fervor of a two-hundredth birthday party, and Harley-Davidson was no exception. As America's sole remaining motorcycle manufacturer, it was logical and fitting that the company do something special to commemorate the event.

For years, Harley-Davidson had been making the circuit of consumer motorcycle shows, displaying its products to an enthusiastic public. The biggest show, which traditionally kicked off the start of the motorcycle season, was held annually at Daytona Beach in conjunction with the week of races in March. Hordes of riders flocked south for sun, fun and racing. All major motorcycle manufacturers and many from the aftermarket regularly showed their products at a large show in a hotel on the beach.

To celebrate its American heritage, Harley-Davidson pulled its booth out of the regular motorcycle show and put together its own exhibit several miles down the beach, in the ballroom of a luxury hotel. With motorcycles from its extensive collection of antiques plus existing new products, Harley-Davidson created a stunning display entitled "A Salute to American Motorcycling." Thousands of motorcyclists and enthusiasts endured long lines to view Harley-Davidson's show, the likes of which Daytona Beach had never seen.

Originally intended to be a bicentennial event only, Harley-Davidson's extravaganza proved so successful that the decision was made to hold it every year and to make it bigger and better. The events surrounding the show gradually multiplied, as Harley-Davidson worked to get more riders involved in the sport by making more activities available to them in Daytona. As activities increased in the following years, there were poker runs, field meets, ride-in shows, a special section for Harley-Davidson riders at the speedway and much more.

Above, the 1976 Liberty Edition Superglide and, at right, the Liberty Edition FLH.

The hit of the 1977 show was a beautifully-detailed Willie G. Davidson creation called the FXS Low Rider. Featuring mag wheels, lettered tires, drag style handlebars, plus special paint and engine treatments, it epitomized everyman's ideal of what a custom motorcycle should be. The Low Rider was an instantaneous success and launched a whole new generation of motorcycles, the factory customs.

Later that year, a second Willie G. factory custom, the XLCR Cafe Racer, made its appearance. Based on a Sportster engine, the XLCR was a black-on-black beauty that capitalized on the prevailing cafe racer popularity in vogue at the time. Unlike the Low Rider, which went on to unprecedented popularity, the XLCR proved to be too much of a departure from traditional Harley-Davidson styling to ever gain widespread acceptance and was only produced through the 1978 model year. However, a lasting legacy of the Cafe Racer was the extensive auditing and road testing to ensure a top quality product, which eventually filtered into the other motorcycles coming out of the York operation.

With a history as long and varied as Harley-Davidson's, the company felt it should be shared with its many devotees, and opened a museum at the York plant in Pennsylvania. After viewing a selection of landmark motorcycles from the company's past, viewers would be free to tour the production facilities. With different vintage Harley-Davidson models rotated on a regular basis, the museum hosted tens of thousands of visitors annually until it was closed in late 2000 in anticipation of a new, much larger museum in Milwaukee.

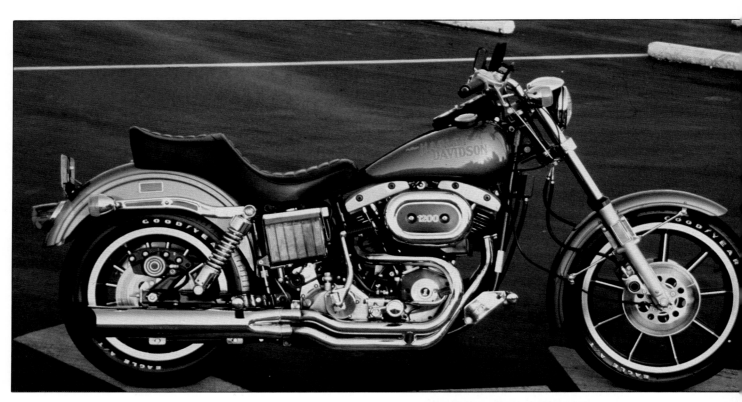

"Laverne and Shirley" was a successful spinoff from TV's "Happy Days."

## or the man who wears he Harley-Davidson Brand

There's a kind of man who wears the Harley-Davidson brand. It burns deeper every time he swings into the saddle and lights the fire. And it smokes when the unbroken asphalt ribbon unwinds.

That's the kind of man who'll get off on our new leathers.

Exciting styling. Comfortable and color co-ordinated to match the distinctive silver-gray paint on the lowdown Low Rider . . . Harley-Davidson's mean new machine.

Pants are bib-overall styled, with wide-buckle shoulder straps. And big, massive zippers where you need 'em . . . full-length front and at the ankles.

The jacket has double-snap collar and waist tabs, with padded reinforcements at shoulder caps and elbows. A full-length zipper up front and at the wrists. Pockets, too . . . with zippers, likewise.

Jacket and pants both are tailored with a deep-pleated action back for free and easy movement in the saddle . . . and for added warmth over the kidneys.

Your partner does a dual number with her own jacket in similar style. Lookin' a little like a lady. And you both can choose from a line of color-coordinated helmets. Full-face X-100 or Compact Combination styles.

If you're a man who wears the brand, see your Harley-Davidson dealer. Then light the fire and let the road unwind.

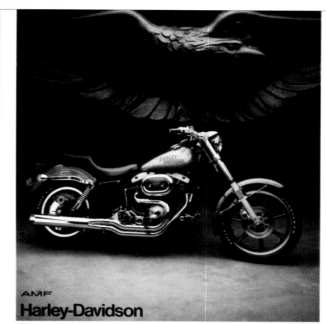

Left: A 1977 ad for Harley-Davidson leathers. Below: A promotional brochure touted the Low Rider as "one mean machine."

AMF
**Harley-Davidson Low Rider**

Above: Sylvester Stallone's star rose in "Rocky," while "Happy Days" used Milwaukee as a sitcom setting. Left: The Harley-Davidson Cafe Racer.

237

As happens nearly every decade, a star rose from the galaxy of motorcycle racers to shine as the outstanding performer in motorcycle competition during the second half of the Seventies. A youngster from Michigan first burst on the scene as a privateer in 1975, campaigning a Harley-Davidson XR-750 on the nation's dirt tracks. Because of his successes, he quickly caught the eye of Harley-Davidson's longtime Director of Racing, Dick O'Brien, and Jay Springsteen was signed for the 1976 factory team.

Riding in a spectacular style that pleased crowds and subdued competitors, Springsteen—or Springer, as his fans called him—fulfilled O'Brien's confidence in him by winning the title of Grand National Champion his first year on the team. At 19, Springsteen became the youngest man ever to wear the Number One plate. He repeated as Champion in 1977, and again in 1978.

Below: Michael Jackson originally caught the public's fancy as a member of The Jackson Five.

Right: The 1977 Daytona show featured a salute to Harley-Davidson racing. Bottom left: Walter Villa rode the potent RR-250 to three successive World 250 titles.

238

Top left: John Davidson cuts the ribbon, opening Harley-Davidson's 1977 Daytona Show. On his right is World 250 Champion Walter Villa and on his left is AMA Grand National Champion Jay Springsteen. Left center: Springsteen in action. Right center: John Travolta in "Saturday Night Fever."

Late in 1977, the company began making plans for the kind of event that only Harley-Davidson can pull off successfully. The next year was to be Harley-Davidson's seventy-fifth anniversary and John Davidson, who was chairman, and Vaughn Beals, who had just become president, agreed that a massive ride of Harley-Davidson executives would be just the thing to draw attention to this very special occasion.

Sixteen executives, ranging from managers to the chairman, departed from points on the perimeter of the United States and followed seven different routes across the nation, with a final rendezvous at the Louisville motorcycle races in early June. Riding in teams of two or three riders, the men collectively traveled over 37,000 miles, visiting over 160 Harley-Davidson dealers along the way. At almost every stop, the riders were greeted by throngs of well-wishers, and were often interviewed by local media. The fact that the people who ran the company were all riders—and that they would take two weeks out of their busy schedules to get out on the road and meet their customers—impressed everyone who came into contact with them.

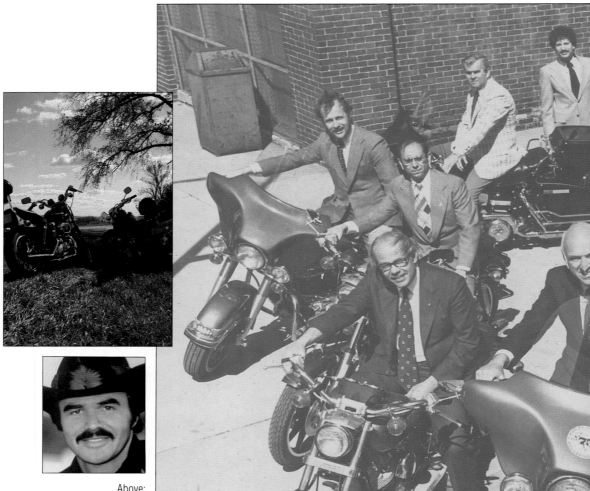

Above: Burt Reynolds was a big box office star in the mid-seventies. Right: Led by (front row from left) John Davidson, Vaughn Beals and Willie G. Davidson, sixteen Harley-Davidson executives toured the country in celebration of the company's seventy-fifth anniversary.

**Harley-Davidson**
**V-Twin Motorcycles**
AMF

## WE DON'T WANT OTHER PEOPLE'S PARTS IN OUR MOTORCYCLES.
### (A Less Than Tolerant Viewpoint From Harley-Davidson.)

This should be a polite message that attempts to persuade you to use only genuine Harley-Davidson parts.

We don't feel all that polite about the subject, however.

Our engineers and designers, quite frankly, lack tolerance. They seem to take great joy in constantly reminding us that Harley-Davidson motorcycles are expected to be classics.

Naturally, with that kind of pressure from within, we've become somewhat exacting and inflexible.

For example, the piston to cylinder wall fit on a Harley-Davidson FX-1200 motorcycle is between .001 and .002 of an inch. That's 1/3 the thickness of a human hair!

So you can see why we come unglued when instead of seeing your authorized Harley-Davidson dealer and using only genuine Harley-Davidson replacement parts, you put in somebody else's heads, valves, pistons, cables, and even oil and oil filters.

Worse yet, when you don't use our parts, you don't use the one guy out there who we trust to be just as tenacious as we are—your Harley-Davidson dealer.

To you it's no big deal. To our guys, you're violating a basic law of physics.

**The Whole Equals the Sum of its Parts.**

## A CHOICE BETWEEN COMFORT OR STYLE IS NO CHOICE AT ALL.
### [A Less Than Tolerant Viewpoint from Harley-Davidson]

You see it all the time. Some poor joker takes one look at some fancy leathers modeled by a California actor leaning on a rented motorcycle and before you know it, he's out on the highway in them. Touring Milwaukee in late October, freezing his ——— off.

Or he turns practical. And winds up in an outfit that looks like something from a late night, Science Fiction, TV show.

**Nobody wins.**

Naturally, we feel a great deal of sympathy when this happens. For us, The Human Icicle and Space Oddity don't exactly make great ads for motorcycling. So, in the interest of your image, and ours, we cordially suggest a way you can avoid all that.

**A clothing store for motorcyclists.**

Simply visit an expert with such a wide variety of styles he could stock a clothing store—your Harley-Davidson dealer.

The first thing he'll tell you is that no style looks good on a shivering rider. Then he'll show you some features to look for.

Like the specially sewn-in wind flap that's on our Pioneer leathers and Cycle Champ jackets. A wind flap that's not just covering the front of the zipper, but rather, is on the inside, behind the zipper where the wind can't get at it.

He'll show you the special sleeve closures on many of our jackets, to keep the wind from whistling up your arms. And specially-designed, pleated "action backs" to give you freedom of movement when you bend forward on the cycle.

**Common sense.**

He'll show you the common sense thinking behind our snap-down collars. And demonstrate how they're designed to keep you from being flapped to death at 40 MPH.

And he'll show you how to determine the proper length riding jacket so that it's long enough to protect you from wind whistling up under it, yet short enough not to bunch up beneath you.

You'll be able to choose intelligently from more jackets, vests, boots, gloves and riding apparel than you'll see from any other motorcycle manufacturer.

And you'll hit the highway confident that Harley-Davidson would never leave you out in the cold.

**It takes a warm body to tame cold steel.**

## ANYBODY CAN DRESS UP A HARLEY-DAVIDSON. NOT EVERYBODY CAN DO IT RIGHT.
### [A Less Than Tolerant Viewpoint.]

Too many riders treat the purchase of a set of pipes or a sissy bar as though they were buying a star for the top of their Christmas tree. So long as it stays on, everything's fine.

Well, everything isn't so fine.

To most of you this won't be news, but you don't hang pipes on a Harley-Davidson motorcycle. You fit them. Perfectly. So they become part of the machine.

The Sportster shown here illustrates our point. It's dressed with a chrome-finished sissy bar, padded backrest, flat black cast wheels, independent staggered dual exhaust pipes, chrome oil cooler and chrome point cover. And it's 100 per cent Harley-Davidson. Because every part on it is a perfectly tooled-to-fit genuine Harley-Davidson accessory.

What's more, every Harley-Davidson accessory—from coolers to highway pegs to touring seats—is available at any Harley-Davidson dealer. So when you dress your Harley-Davidson motorcycle, you can dress it right.

Look at it this way. You've already committed yourself to riding one of the finest motorcycles the world has ever known. A cycle built to such exact tolerances that the piston to cylinder wall fit on an FX 1200, for example, is between .001 and .002 of an inch—1/3 the thickness of a human hair!

That's what you paid for. That's what you got. This is no time to start making compromises.

**Part of a motorcycle. Not parts on a motorcycle.**

For a free accessories catalogue see your Harley-Davidson dealer or write Harley-Davidson direct at 3700 W. Juneau, Milwaukee, Wisc. 53201, desk J-1.

---

**1975**

Last U.S. citizens are airlifted out of Saigon as South Vietnam falls.

President Ford escapes two assassination attempts.

Mitchell, Haldeman, Ehrlichman and Mardian found guilty of Watergate cover-up.

**1976**

Jimmy Carter elected President.

The Viking II sets down on Mars.

**1977**

President Carter signs treaties transferring control of Panama Canal to Panama by 2000.

President Carter pardons most Vietnam War draft evaders.

Scientists identify bacterium as cause of mysterious "Legionnaire's Disease."

**1978**

Airline Deregulation Act passed by Congress, signed by President Carter.

**1979**

Shah of Iran overthrown by Ayatollah Khomeini; 90 hostages taken by militants.

Radioactive gases escape in accident at Three Mile Island, Pennsylvania, nuclear power plant.

Federal government announces $1.5 billion loan-guarantee to aid Chrysler Corporation.

This long-established practice of mingling with the people who use the product has since grown to become one of Harley-Davidson's most important and consistent policies. Following the Seventy-Fifth Anniversary ride, Harley-Davidson executives and employees have participated in several similar marathon rides, plus hundreds of local, regional, national and international motorcycling events.

Further commemorating its three quarters of a century mark, Harley-Davidson produced special anniversary XL and FL models in black with striking gold trim. In addition, the Electra Glide had its engine increased in size to eighty cubic inches, or 1340cc.

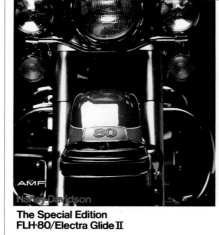

**The Special Edition FLH-80/Electra Glide II**

Top: The 75th Anniversary Sportster.
Right: The Special Edition
Electra Glide II.

With the exception of the Sportster, the products changed little in 1979. The XL received an updated, state of the art frame and a two-into-one exhaust. Also, because the Low Rider proved so successful, a similar Sportster-based version called the XLS Roadster was produced. The most notable change throughout the product line was the addition of large "ham can" air cleaners, which were needed to meet federally mandated noise limits. Federal regulations regarding noise and emissions were to play an increasingly prominent role in Harley-Davidson's product development in the coming years.

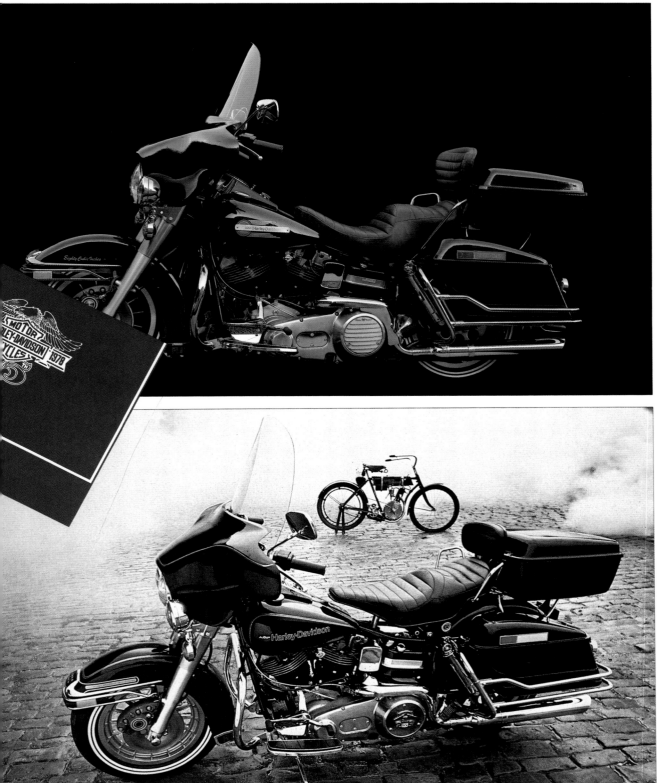

Left: The 1978 Electra Glide. Below: TV hits ranged from Donnie and Marie to "Charlie's Angels." Bottom left: The 75th Anniversary Electra Glide.

**B**y 1979, after thirty years of making lightweights, Harley-Davidson had stopped producing the smaller machines, choosing instead to concentrate all its efforts on the V-twin heavyweight models. As the decade rolled to a close, Harley-Davidson experienced its most successful sales year ever. Thanks to a large influx of capital from AMF for needed machinery and the addition of the York assembly plant, Harley-Davidson was able to produce a record number of motorcycles in 1979. Despite all of AMF's efforts at making the company a more powerful and effective manufacturing force, many riders and enthusiasts came to blame the parent company for a number of Harley-Davidson's shortcomings, real or imagined. The truth of the matter is that AMF provided Harley-Davidson with the necessary funds to modernize and a facility to increase production, at a time when both the market and the competition were growing.

As the company prepared to enter the Eighties, customer dissatisfaction with AMF continued to fester. It was their fascination with the product, combined with mammoth public relations efforts of people like Vaughn Beals and Willie G., that sustained customer loyalty and kept them interested in Harley-Davidson.

# The 1979 Electra Glide "Classic" with Sidecar

The unequalled prestige of riding a 1979 Electra Glide "Classic" can only be enhanced by showing off the enviable utmost in touring fun: The 1979 Electra Glide "Classic" with Sidecar.

Designed by Willie G. Davidson for availability as a complete vehicle unit, the 1979 limited edition Electra Glide "Classic" with Sidecar is Willie G.'s "piece de resistance" — for the die-hard tourist who *thought* he had everything. The two-tone tan and creme color scheme and hand-applied brown pinstriping which perfectly match the "Classic" are just the beginning. Willie G.'s eye for making the unusual dramatic insisted upon equipping the Sidecar with the same black cast mag wheel that you see on the "Classic".

You'll find other little details similarly rewarding, like the Sidecar drum brake, matching brown vinyl Sidecar bench seat and color coordinated snap-on tonneau cover.

Did Willie G. do it up right? We think it's a knock-out!

**Harley-Davidson**

*Until you've been on a Harley-Davidson, you haven't been on a motorcycle.*

Subject to E.P.A. approval available 3-15-79.

FPG

President Jimmy Carter was completing a turbulent term.

Bo Derek was a perfect '10."

245

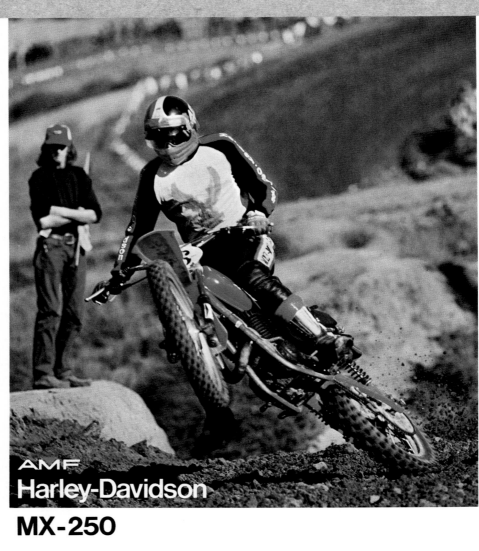

AMF
**Harley-Davidson**

**MX-250**

# THE 1980'S

## The Eagle Soars Alone

THE 1980'S

The Eighties burst upon the scene in a flurry of excitement for Harley-Davidson that was to continue through the entire decade. More events of major significance occurred at Harley-Davidson during those years than in any previous decade, as the company produced an array of the most exciting, trend-setting motorcycles the sport has ever seen, and they engaged in a variety of events that set the industry and the nation buzzing.

The 1980 model year brought several exciting introductions. The 80 cubic inch FLT Tour Glide was born, with five-speed transmission, oil-bath-enclosed rear chain and a vibration-isolated engine. Together with a totally redesigned frame and steering geometry for "sport bike handling," the FLT was destined to become the inheritor of the FLH's "King of the Highway" crown. Also introduced was the 80-inch Wide Glide factory custom and the Sturgis.  What made the latter so unique was that the 80-inch engine transmitted its power to the road through a twin belt drive. Thus the belts, which are lighter and simpler than a shaft, smoother than a chain and required no lubrication, made a comeback after a several-decade absence—with the latest in modern technology applied, of course.

The company also held an increasing number of consumer promotions, like the annual motorcycle show at Daytona during Bike Week and sponsorship of the "Bikers' Fight Against Muscular Dystrophy."

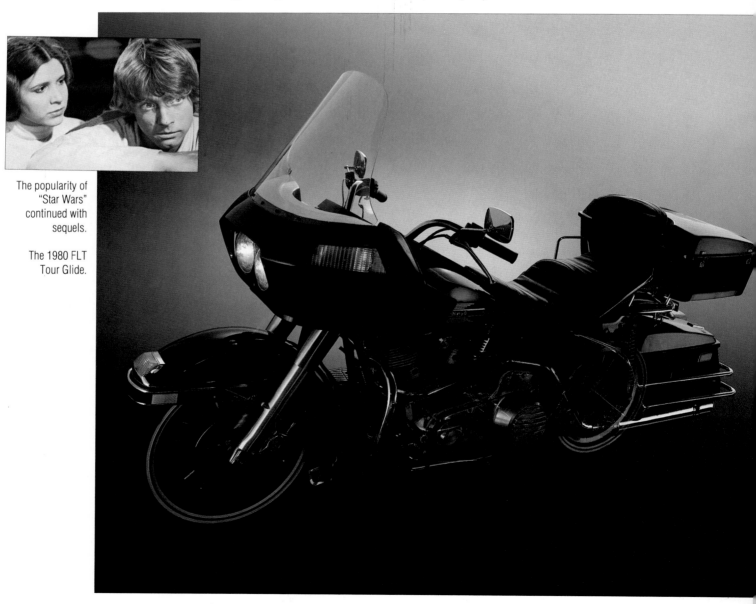

The popularity of "Star Wars" continued with sequels.

The 1980 FLT Tour Glide.

Top: The 1980 Sturgis marked the return of the drive belt, but with the technology of the Eighties. Left: The flamed Wide Glide personified the factory custom motorcycle.

At the 1981 Daytona activities, the air was full of big news concerning the company's future. It had begun on February 26, 1981, when a group of senior Harley-Davidson executives signed a letter of intent with AMF to purchase Harley-Davidson Motor Company from AMF. The purchasing group was headed up by Vaughn Beals, an AMF executive in charge of Harley-Davidson operations, and included Charles Thompson, company president; William G. Davidson; and others in the company.

During a press conference at Daytona Beach on March 3, 1981, Beals talked about the positive aspects of the AMF and Harley-Davidson association, "From 1969 through 1980, AMF's substantial capital investment in the motorcycle and golf car businesses permitted Harley-Davidson revenues to grow from $49 million to approximately $300 million . . . "

Beals went on to say, "AMF helped the Motor Company through a critical stage of growth . . . the most tangible evidence of their success is the company's ability to now stand on its own once again and to look to the future with pride and expectation."

The return to private ownership was completed June 16, 1981 as the shareholder group of the new Harley-Davidson company celebrated the event with a York-to-Milwaukee ride, proclaiming "The Eagle Soars Alone."

Signing documents to mark the return of Harley-Davidson to stand-alone status in June 1981, were (from left): Ralph Swenson, Charles K. Thompson, and (seated) AMF President Ray Tritten and Vaughn Beals.

REAGAN

The first non-AMF motorcycle to roll off the York assembly line receives a gold dipstick from Vaughn Beals as company officers look on. From left: Ralph Swenson, Charles Thompson and Willie G. Davidson.

Christopher Reeves as "Superman."

# RUN TO THE SUN.

*The 1981 Harley-Davidson Wide Glide, Low Rider, Roadster and Sportster. Valdosta, Georgia to Daytona Beach, Florida.*

It happens every year. The classic union of Harley-Davidson® motorcycles and the men who ride them down to Bike Week in Daytona Beach. But the run means more. Because you're on more than a machine. You have the unique sound and feel of our legendary 1000 cc and 1340 cc V-Twin engines, the heartbeat of every Harley-Davidson. No other motorcycle built can match it.

You have our tradition of custom styling. The look that *means* American. You see it in all our gas tanks, from the original teardrop Peanut to Fat Bob. You feel it with our pullback buckhorn handlebars, low stepped seats with sissy bars and the unique Harley riding position. And chrome is where it belongs: on the hardware and the staggered shorty duals.

We do more with custom paint, too. There's matching painted tanks and fenders. Hand-applied pinstriping. Unique tank graphics and dramatic engine finishes. Yet every 1981 Harley-Davidson has a

distinctive character completely its own.

The Wide Glide.™ From extended front forks and custom bobbed rear fender to the flamed bob-and-a-half tank, it's the first factory built custom.

The Low Rider.® It's where custom styling begins. Extended front forks, 9-spoke cast wheels and a riding position just 27" from the ground.

The Roadster.™ With flashing new 2-tone silver metallic paint with black pinstriping and a lot of Low Rider style.

Then, to this custom trio add our stylish '81

Sportster.® Latest edition of the classic American street machine. The one so many riders choose to join the Harley-Davidson tradition.

Your own Run to the Sun starts the moment you get on a Harley. Now you're part of a 78 year tradition that announces your commitment to motorcycling. That's a Harley-Davidson. It's more than a machine.

We support the Motorcycle Safety Foundation and the A.M.A. and recommend you ride with lights and helmet. Specifications subject to change without notice.

**Harley-Davidson** Support the Bikers Fight Against Muscular Dystrophy.

Above:
Painted illustrations supplemented photography to promote Harley-Davidsons in the early Eighties.
Left: Pop idols Tom Selleck as "Magnum" and super model Christie Brinkley.

253

The buy-back was accompanied by an even firmer resolve to build motorcycles in the best American tradition of quality and durability. An internal program called "I Make The Eagle Fly" was instituted in all areas of the company and in dealerships, with a commitment to build, sell and service the products with a new level of quality. Two models introduced for 1982—the FXR Super Glide II with its rubber-isolated, five-speed power train, and a new welded and stamped-frame Sportster—quickly became prime examples of the company's commitment to a future of exciting products.

After nearly 80 years as the leader of America's motorcycles, Harley-Davidson was embarking on a course that was very much a reflection of the company's pioneering spirit and founding standards of excellence.

Top: Bruce Springsteen. Bottom: Tony Dorsett, Dallas Cowboys vs. Minnesota Vikings, ran the longest run from scrimmage, 99 yards.

This pioneering spirit would be essential to the survival of the new privately-held Harley-Davidson. In 1982, the demand for motorcycles in the 651+cc market (Harley-Davidson's niche in the motorcycle industry) dropped by

Below right: The introduction of the 1982 FXR heralded the beginning of a new era of performance and handling for Harley-Davidson motorcycles.

Soar with

Motorcycle Week
Mar 4-8, Daytona Hilton

over 33,000 units compared to 1981 figures. Harley-Davidson laid off employees to bring production and inventories in line with demand, while Japan continued to export in record numbers.

In September of 1982, Harley-Davidson petitioned the International Trade Commission (ITC) for tariff relief from Japanese manufacturers who were building up inventories of unsold motorcycles. On April 1, 1983, upon ITC recommendation, President Reagan imposed additional tariffs on all imported Japanese motorcycles 700cc or larger. The additional tariff was to be effective for a five-year period ending in April 1988, at annually declining rates of 45, 35, 20, 15 and 10 percent.

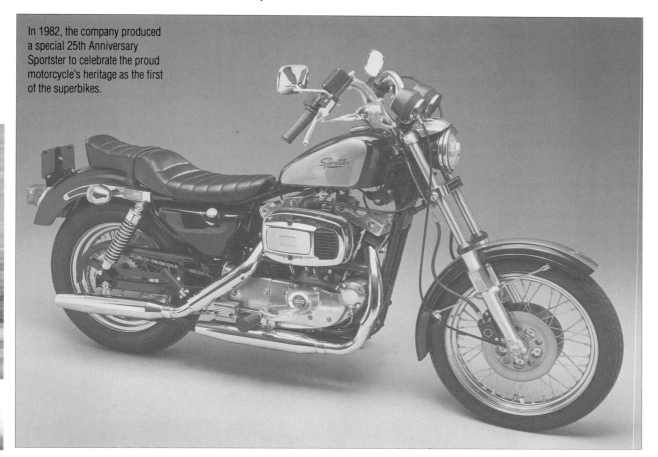

In 1982, the company produced a special 25th Anniversary Sportster to celebrate the proud motorcycle's heritage as the first of the superbikes.

he Eagles.

Harley-Davidson had made it clear from the beginning that special tariffs were not aimed at preventing free market competition. According to Vaughn L. Beals, Jr., Harley-Davidson chairman and chief executive officer, "We simply wanted the U.S. government to restore order to a motorcycle market under siege by Japanese manufacturers who increased production in the face of sharp market decline."

One of the major factors in the ITC's decision to recommend tariffs was the fact that Harley-Davidson had started a major revitalization campaign in the late 1970s. The campaign was aimed at improving efficiency and product quality through programs like Just-In-Time manufacturing, Employee Involvement and Statistical Process Control.

A different campaign was aimed at getting Harley-Davidson owners more involved in the sport of motorcycling. The Harley Owners Group (H.O.G.), the only factory-sponsored motorcycle club in the world, was formed in 1983. H.O.G. played a significant role in the company's revitalization as it refocused attention to customer satisfaction after the sale. H.O.G.'s special benefits and motorcycle rallies helped boost membership to over 90,000 in six years.

The company also took steps to resolve another problem. For years, some people from time to time had been using the Harley-Davidson name and logos on various products without company permission. In some instances, the name was used on items of questionable taste or in conjunction with profanity or vulgarity. To remove these products from the marketplace, Harley-Davidson mounted a vigorous trademark-enforcement campaign, prosecuting trademark infringers. Soon after, it embarked on a broad program of licensing its name and trademarks. An array of items ranging from neckties to jewelry to wall hangings soon began appearing, not only in motorcycle shops but also in department and specialy stores. These broad merchandising efforts, combined with the company's enforcement efforts, gradually cleaned up the bootleg product market and served to boost the company's image in the eyes of the general public.

Sylvester Stallone as *Rambo*, and Arnold Schwarzenegger as *Conan*.

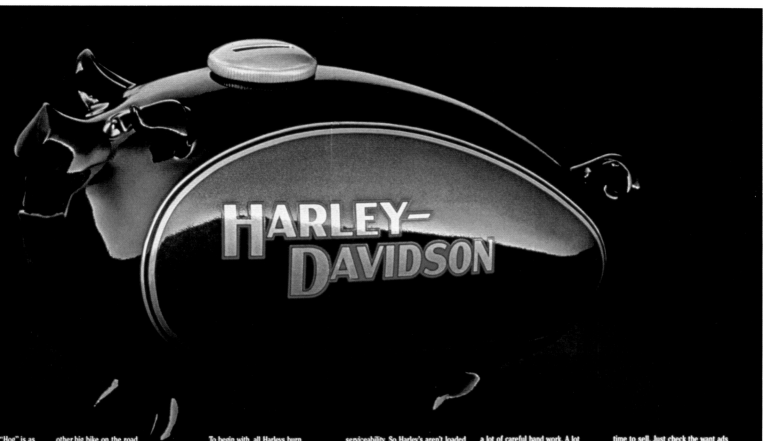

## HOG?

To some, the term "Hog" is as [...] as mud. But to the thousands of [Har]ley-Davidson owners who affec-[tion]ately refer to their motorcycles [as H]ogs, there is no confusion.

A Harley-Davidson is not fat. [It do]esn't eat you out of house and [hom]e. And it's definitely not a gas [hog]. With its incredible resale value, [it's l]ike money in the bank.

Let's take it point by point. First, [Har]ley-Davidson is not fat. Throw [a] leg over one and see. Harley's [l]onger, lower and leaner than any other big bike on the road.

A Harley-Davidson is not overweight either. Don't compare a Harley with some little lightweight bike; there is a world of difference and we'd like to keep it that way. The key is balance. A Harley has the power to match the weight. When you're off the scales and on the highway, that weight translates into stability. And that's exactly what you need in this age of 18 wheelers and gusty Interstate highways.

A Harley-Davidson is not a gas hog.

To begin with, all Harleys burn less expensive regular gas. And they burn less of it than you'd imagine. On average, our motorcycles get between 47 and 54 MPG on the highway*. Compared with engines of similar displacement, our 1000cc and 1340cc V-Twins, by design, are a couple of the most efficient internal combustion engines made.

A Harley-Davidson won't eat you out of house and home after you buy it. Simplicity of design is the best way to insure durability, dependability and serviceability. So Harley's aren't loaded down with high-tech complexity. For instance, we use only one carburetor. You don't pay for four and the hassles later. In fact, many of the routine maintenance tasks can be performed by the rider.

Harley-Davidson is the best grade of motorcycle you can buy. Actually as the quality of many products is going down, the quality of Harley-Davidson motorcycles is going up. Because we don't turn out motorcycles like popcorn. There's a lot of careful hand work. A lot of meticulous assembly and constant quality control. The result. This year, our motorcycles are the best handling, the best all around performance motorcycles we've ever built.

Harley-Davidson motorcycles are not cheap. We don't build them that way, so it stands to reason we can't sell them that way. We put more into a Harley. So you get more out of your Harley. You get more every time you ride down the street. And you get more down the road, when it comes time to sell. Just check the want ads in your paper. You'll see. A Harley may be called a Hog. But don't be confused. There's no better place to put your money.

**MOTORCYCLES. BY THE PEOPLE. FOR THE PEOPLE.**

Harley-Davidson Motor Co., Inc. P.O. Box 653, Milwaukee, WI 53201

*[...] on our own test results. Your mileage may vary depending on your personal driving habits, weather conditions and trip length.

The FXRT
Sport Glide.

During this time period, Harley-Davidson was also working on further improvements to the product. In 1983, Harley-Davidson introduced a critically acclaimed "anti-dive" air-assisted suspension system on a sport-touring model called the FXRT, as well as the first computer-controlled ignition. Although the new designs did a lot to improve the motorcycles, the big V-Twin shovelhead engine didn't live up to the current levels of consumer expectations for function and durability.

In 1984, Harley-Davidson introduced the 1340cc $V^2$ Evolution engine on five models. The product of seven years of development, the Evolution engine produced more power at every engine speed and was also lighter, cooler and cleaner running, and extremely oil-tight. It was designed for high reliability and durability with a minimum of scheduled maintenance.

Revolutionary new motorcycles like the FXST Softail, an industry trendsetter in styling, and the XR1000, with an engine based on the XR 750 racing power plant, were also introduced in 1984 and did a great deal to help increase sales.

For the first time in years, Harley-Davidson motorcycles were given good grades in motorcycle magazine reviews. Belt-drive, five-speed transmissions, and rubber-isolated engines improved the product line. To get the word out to the public, the company created an industry "first" when it started a "Super Ride" demo program at dealerships nationwide. A fleet of demo bikes was also put into service at all major motorcycle rallies, to let riders everywhere experience the new Harley-Davidson quality.

Harley-Davidson also won the California Highway Patrol contract in 1984. This was the first time in ten years that a Harley-Davidson motorcycle was able to meet the rigid standards of the CHP—a tribute to Harley-Davidson's improved quality and performance. The contract awards were repeated in 1985, 1987,1988 and 1989 increasing the number of Harley-Davidsons in the CHP fleet.

The sight of a highway patrol officer mounted on a Harley-Davidson is becoming more common in California.

Top left, actor Sam Elliott riding a Harley in a scene from the movie *Mask*. Top Right Cher and Sam Elliott in *Mask*.

Left: The 80 cubic inch Evolution motor and unparalleled styling helped make the 1984 FXST Softail one of the most popular motorcycles.

Harley-Davidson beer, produced in limited quantities, quickly became a collectible.

A view of the powerful 1340cc Evolution V-twin engine.

With an engine based on the potent XR-750 power plant, the XR-1000 was the most powerful street machine Harley-Davidson ever produced.

arley-Davidson's 1985 motorcycles received a special AIW/IAM union label. The label was a tribute to the two international unions that represent the Harley-Davidson work force: the Allied Industrial Workers of America and the International Association of Machinists and Aerospace Workers. AIW Local 209 President Jerry Knackert said, "The union label is a reassurance to consumers that the people responsible for the product have confidence enough to put their seal of approval on it."

Harley-Davidson also created three special "Liberty Edition" models in 1985, with a total of 1,750 Liberty Edition motorcycles in all. In a salute to the Statue of Liberty and the loyal riders of American-made Harley-Davidsons, the company donated $100, for each Liberty Edition purchased, to the Statue of Liberty/Ellis Island Foundation, Inc., for restoration of the statue. Harley-Davidson also organized a cross-country "Ride for Liberty."

Vaughn Beals traveled on a northern route from the west coast to the east and Willie G. Davidson took a southern route. They rendezvoused in Washington, D.C., and led thousands of riders to Liberty State Park, New Jersey. At the concluding ceremony there, Vaughn Beals presented a check for $250,000 to the Statue of Liberty/Ellis Island Foundation.

The big product news for 1985 was the introduction of Harley-Davidson's 1986 $V^2$ Evolution Sportster 883. The 883cc aluminum V-Twin engine gave Harley-Davidson its first entry in a decade in the smaller-than-1000cc market and carried a suggested retail price of $3,995—eight hundred dollars less than the 1985 XLH 1000. The Evolution XLH 883 Sportster gave Harley-Davidson a full line of Evolution-engined motorcycles.

Below: Bill Cosby and Eddie Murphy.

Yet, with all the hoopla over the new Sportster and Liberty Editions, Harley-Davidson didn't forget about its own heritage. A new addition to the FL family emerged in the Heritage Softail, a motorcycle with the timeless look of the 1950s backed by the technology of the 1980s. The Heritage front end sported a wide front fender and a front suspension that looked like the first telescopic fork on the 1949 Hydra-Glide. The rear end of the Heritage Softail had the no-suspension, hard-tail look of the 1950s and a contemporary soft ride, due to the concealed gas-charged, horizontally-mounted rear shocks.

UNION MADE

Marking the end of an era, the last Shovelhead Sportster engine rolls off the assembly line followed by the first Evolution Sportster engine. Opposite page: A column of riders heads for the capitol of the U.S. on the final leg of the Liberty Ride.

Word of Harley-Davidson's improved quality had spread far beyond the motorcycle industry. In April of 1986, Harley-Davidson Chairman and Chief Executive Officer Vaughn L. Beals, Jr. accepted the prestigious Corporate Quality Award from the three Colorado sections of the American Society of Quality Controls (ASQC). The ASQC is a nationwide organization of more than 50,000 professional members dedicated to the improvement of quality and productivity in American industry.

Also in 1985, the buy-back team learned that the leading member of the four financing banks wanted to back out of the deal. The company needed to round up cash in a hurry. To the rescue was Harley-Davidson Chief Financial Officer Rich Teerlink. Teerlink successfully negotiated a loan-refinancing package with a new lead lender in late December. By placing the company on a firmer financial footing, Teerlink was then able to guide the company to public ownership, in June 1986, by offering two million shares of common stock and a concurrent offering of $70 million principal amounts of subordinated notes due 1996.

This public offering helped reduce outstanding debt and also enabled Harley-Davidson to acquire Holiday Rambler Corporation, the world's largest privately-held producer of recreational vehicles and a major supplier of specialized commercial vehicles. Headquartered in Wakarusa, Indiana, Holiday Rambler Corporation was a perfect complement to Harley-Davidson. Teerlink said, "We found Holiday Rambler to be a natural fit because it is in a closely-related industry and because of the many similarities it has to Harley-Davidson. Like Harley-Davidson, Holiday Rambler is a manufacturing-intensive, leading producer of premium quality recreational vehicles."

From its inception in 1953, Holiday Rambler Corporation developed a strong brand name recognition, a reputation for high-quality products, and a broad base of loyal dealers and customers. The acquisition helped Harley-Davidson to broaden its earnings base.

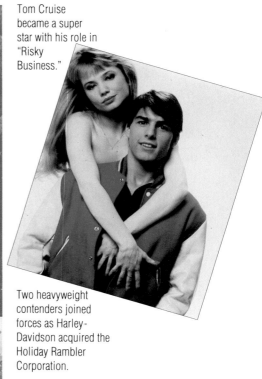

Tom Cruise became a super star with his role in "Risky Business."

Two heavyweight contenders joined forces as Harley-Davidson acquired the Holiday Rambler Corporation.

"Dynasty" became a top-rated nighttime TV soap opera.

"Miami Vice" becomes a TV hit, as Robert Redford hits a homer in "The Natural."

**HRC**
HOLIDAY RAMBLER CORPORATION ®

n 1987, Harley-Davidson initiated a bold, new marketing strategy that guaranteed a resale value of $3,995 on the Evolution Sportster XLH-883 motorcycle. Riders who traded in their 883 within two years for an FL or FX model Harley-Davidson would be allowed $3,995 for the trade-in, a program that was unprecedented in any industry.

Four new motorcycles were introduced in the 1987 model line. The FLHS Electra Glide Sport, FLSTC Heritage Softail Classic, the FXLR Low Rider Custom and the 30th Anniversary 1100cc Sportster. The 30th Anniversary Evolution Sportster marked the first time the XL engine received the chrome and black engine treatment found on many of its FL and FX relatives. Available in limited quantities, the 30th anniversary Sportster featured a special orange and black paint scheme with 30th anniversary graphics on the gas tank and front fender.

The FLST Classic featured a black and chrome power train and custom two-tone paint, similar to the colors that were original specification on Harleys during the 1950s. The Special also featured some touring amenities: windshield and passing lamps, leather saddlebags, and a two-piece seat and backrest, all complete with studs and conchos. Wire wheels and floorboards were also standard equipment.

The FLHS Electra Glide Sport, a sportier version of Harley's premium touring machine, featured lighter, more nimble handling in the style of traditional American touring bikes of the '50s. And the FXLR celebrated the 10th anniversary of the Low Rider. It featured a unique handlebar and gas tank complete with a 10th anniversary leather center strap.

The XLH Sportster 883.

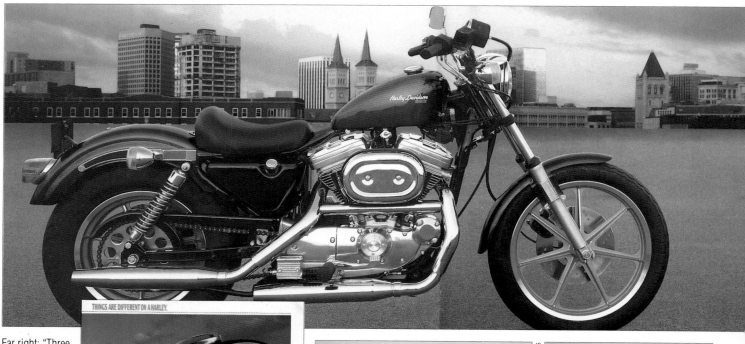

Far right: "Three Men and A Baby" and "Good Morning Vietnam."

But the new bikes were not the biggest news for Harley-Davidson in 1987. On March 17, 1987, Harley-Davidson petitioned the International Trade Commission for early termination of the five-year tariffs on heavyweight motorcycles. The move was unprecedented! No other American company had asked for removal of import protection, and it was hailed by the press as one of the best public relations moves in history.

"We have informed the ITC that we no longer need tariff relief to compete with the Japanese," said Vaughn L. Beals, Jr. "We're taking this action now because we believe we're sending a strong message out to the international industrial community: U.S. workers, given a respite from predatory import practices, can become competitive in world markets."

To celebrate Harley-Davidson's successful turnaround, Mr. Beals invited President Ronald Reagan to visit Harley-Davidson's final assembly plant in York, Pennsylvania. On May 6, 1987, a presidential helicopter landed at the test track behind the York plant. Accompanied by presidential aides and security people, representatives from Harley-Davidson led President Reagan on a tour of the final assembly facility. After touring the assembly line, President Reagan started the engine of a newly built 30th Anniversary Sportster. He then met with a group of employees in a round-table forum, prior to delivering a speech hailing the company's comeback.

"We looked at you carefully," said Reagan. "We asked, 'Is Harley-Davidson really serious about getting into shape?' And the answer came back, a resounding 'Yes.' Harley was hard at work with new products and finding better ways to make better bikes. And Harley's shape-up was not relying just on the top management. Everyone from the board room to the factory was involved. No matter how we looked at it, we could see that everyone at Harley-Davidson was serious about getting into fighting shape," said Reagan.

"Who Framed Roger Rabbit?"

1988. ® Walt Disney Productions

Dolly Parton.

FXLR Low Rider Custom and FXST Softail.

As Chairman Vaughn Beals looks on, Ronald Reagan addresses a group of Harley-Davidson employees at the York plant during his 1987 visit.

A pparently the people at the New York Stock Exchange (NYSE) felt the same way about Harley-Davidson's accomplishments. On July 1, 1987, Harley-Davidson, Inc. was approved for listing on the NYSE. Harley-Davidson, Inc. had been listed on the American Stock Exchange since its initial public offering in July 1986.

According to Vaughn Beals, the move "provided Harley-Davidson with improved market liquidity and visibility and will bolster our stature as a broadly-diversified, international company."

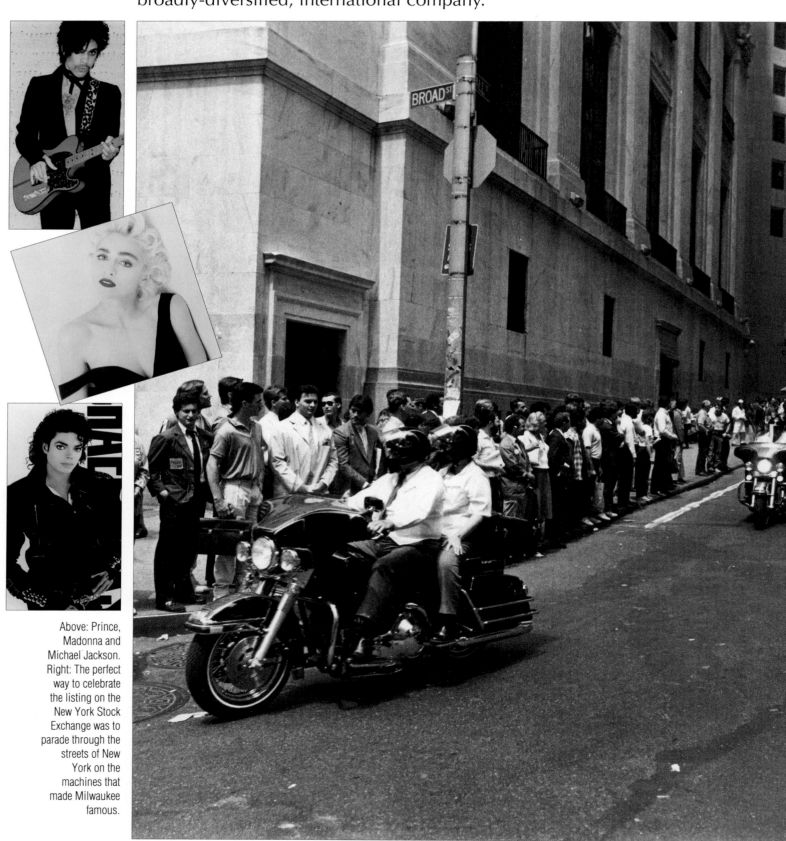

Above: Prince, Madonna and Michael Jackson. Right: The perfect way to celebrate the listing on the New York Stock Exchange was to parade through the streets of New York on the machines that made Milwaukee famous.

On October 10, 1987, acquired the design and worldwide manufacturing rights for its model MT500 military motorcycle from Armstrong Equipment of North Humberside, England. "This purchase is part of Harley-Davidson's plan to continue looking at new opportunities to expand its earnings base," said Richard F. Teerlink, president and chief operating officer of the Motorcycle Division of Harley-Davidson. The MT500 is a single-cylinder, 500cc four-stroke, off-road motorcycle.

Chairman Vaughn Beals and President Rich Teerlink monitor the ticker on the day Harley-Davidson was listed on the American Stock Exchange.

Armstrong's general purpose military motorcycle is designed to be strong, for use in off-road conditions. A range of engines can be fitted into the welded steel, box-section frame. It features heavy-duty suspension, sealed-wheel bearings, and dust- and water-resistant brakes.

The 1988 product line featured the biggest Sportster ever. The Sportster 1200, with its 74 cubic inch engine and 40mm constant-velocity carburetor, put out 12 percent more horsepower and 10 percent more torque than the 1987 1100cc Sportster. The 1200 Sportster also featured a 39mm front fork and revised rear suspension.

The FXRS Low Rider was also revamped for 1988. Its twin-cap Fat Bob gas tank sported a built-in fuel gauge and brought back fond memories of the 1977 Low Rider. The new 39mm fork replaced the former 35mm unit on all FXR and XL models.

Also new for 1988 were the special 85th Anniversary motorcycles. Four models sported special 85th Anniversary graphics in celebration of the company's 85th birthday. One bike created especially for the 85th Anniversary was the FXSTS Springer Softail. The "Springer" front end was the subject of more computer-aided design and finite elements computer analysis than any other component in Harley-Davidson's history.

Harley-Davidson also organized a special 85th Anniversary celebration and tied-in a cross-country ride—all to benefit the Muscular Dystrophy Association. Riders departed from ten points around the United States and headed for festivities in the motorcycling mecca of Milwaukee.

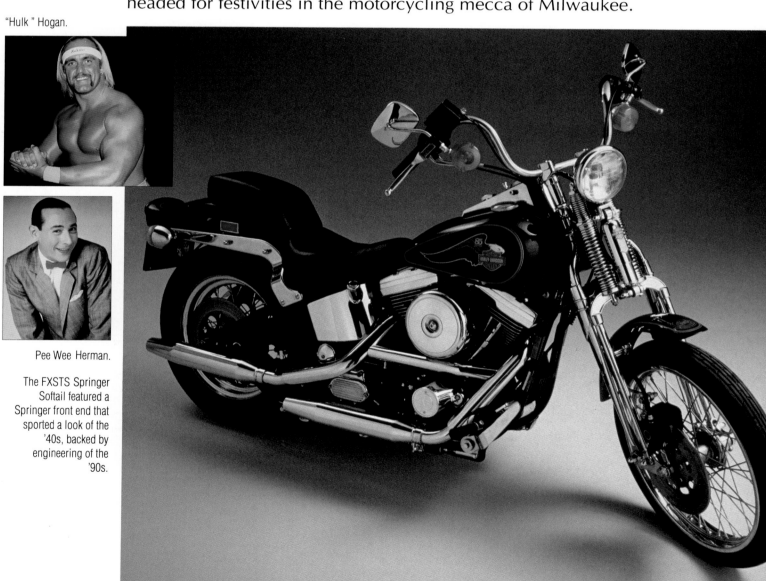

"Hulk" Hogan.

Pee Wee Herman.

The FXSTS Springer Softail featured a Springer front end that sported a look of the '40s, backed by engineering of the '90s.

The event was attended by over 35,000 motorcycle enthusiasts and helped raise nearly $600,000 for Muscular Dystrophy. It typified Harley-Davidson's close-to-the-customer philosophy and changed some people's image of what a Harley-Davidson rider is really like. The Milwaukee Ride for MDA was one of the biggest motorcycling events of the century and did a great deal to fuel the fight against muscular dystrophy.

Over 35,000 motorcyclists flocked to Harley-Davidson's celebration on the shores of Lake Michigan following the 85th Anniversary Milwaukee Ride.

The 1988 version of the FXRS Low Rider.

Above: Tom Cruise in "Top Gun"; Tom Selleck as "Lassiter"; William Hurt in "Body Heat"; Mel Gibson is "Mad Max"; Harrison Ford as "Indiana Jones."

In 1988, Harley-Davidson took its heritage on the road in the form of a traveling museum, housed in a huge semitrailer truck painted with the company's award-winning graphics. The photos above and on the opposite page offer a brief "tour" inside.

Major accident at Soviet nuclear power plant in Chernobyl.

1987

TV evangelists Jim Bakker and wife Tammy Faye resign.

Worst stock-market crash in history drops Dow Jones Industrial Average 508 points.

Senate and House hold public hearings investigating Iran-contra affair.

1988

U.S.S.R. agrees to end its military intervention in Afghanistan after 8-1/2 years.

President Reagan holds summit conference with Soviet leader Gorbachev in Moscow.

1989

George Bush becomes the 41st president of the United States.

Death of Ayatollah Khomeini leaves Iran in political uncertainty.

Over 2,000 peaceful pro-democracy demonstrators killed by government troops in China.

As the events of summer in 1988 began cooling down, the race for the presidency of the United States started heating up. Vice President George Bush, the Republican candidate, and Democratic candidate Michael Dukakis both mentioned Harley-Davidson as success stories in their campaign speeches.

In a different kind of election in August of 1988, the board of directors of Harley-Davidson, Inc., elected Richard F. Teerlink to the new post of president and chief operating officer of Harley-Davidson, Inc., and James H. Paterson to the position of president and chief operating officer of the Motorcycle Division.

Meanwhile, Harley-Davidson was aiming for a successful 1989 model line with the introduction of some new motorcycles. A line of touring machines called Ultra Classics with luxurious standard equipment was introduced. The Tour Glide and Electra Glide Ultra Classics featured cruise control, fairing lowers with a built-in glove compartment, an 80-watt four-speaker stereo system with volume and tuning control for the passenger, built-in CB, and special silver and black paint.

The special 85th Anniversary Springer Softail was carried over for 1989 and offered in a variety of colors. The FL touring models received a newly designed gas tank, 32 amp alternator and also featured self-cancelling turn signals controlled by a microprocessor.

As Harley-Davidson headed for the 1990s, the emphasis on technological improvements was balanced by the emphasis on the rich heritage of the past. America's only surviving motorcycle manufacturer hasn't lost sight of what it has taken to get this far and plans to keep improving into the 21st century.

Right: Few heads of large corporations would spend as much time on the road on company products as Vaughn Beals and his wife, Eleanore.

The Eighties was the decade of Harley-Davidson as the company prospered and grew, and ultimately became not only an American success story but the very image of success itself. By keeping in close touch with its devoted and dedicated customers—and never wandering far from its heritage of building basic and stylish motorcycles—Harley-Davidson prepared to enter the Nineties as the most successful manufacturer of motorcycles marketed in the United States and perhaps the world.

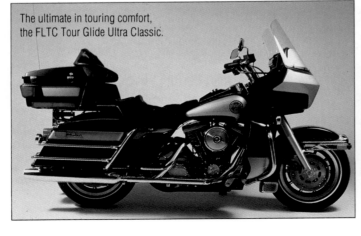

The ultimate in touring comfort, the FLTC Tour Glide Ultra Classic.

The selection of fashions & collectibles created exclusively for Harley-Davidson continues to expand.

FPG

FPG

Presidential candidates Republican George Bush and Democrat Michael Dukakis.

Harley-Davidson's traveling ambassadors of goodwill and probably the most recognized couple in the sport, Nancy and Willie G. Davidson.

The FLSTC Heritage Softail Classic is one of the most visually striking motorcycles in the Harley-Davidson lineup.

273

# THE 1990'S

## A Decade Of Record Growth

# THE 1990'S

# "Hey, Fat Boy."

O n this humorous note, Harley-Davidson ushered in its 1990 model year with what many perceived to be Willie G. Davidson's most customized factory creation to date, the FLSTF Fat Boy. Based on the popular Heritage Softail model, the Fat Boy featured shotgun exhausts, gently flared fenders and disc wheels front and rear. Finished in fine metallic silver, including the frame, and accented with subtle yellow engine highlights and a genuine pigskin seat with hand-laced leather details, the Fat Boy projected an image unlike any previous Harley-Davidson motorcycle. The Fat Boy went on to become one of the Motor Company's most sought after models through the decade.

Early in the year, it became evident to company management that a growing demand for Harley-Davidson products necessitated a more concentrated effort on the part of the Motor Company to meet the growing demands of a world market. Realizing it was only scratching the surface in terms of global potential, Harley-Davidson shifted its international offices from Connecticut to its headquarters in Milwaukee. This move allowed the utilization of corporate resources and the capacity to triple the staff. It also opened a European parts and accessories warehouse near Frankfurt, Germany stocked with many of the fastest-moving products.

Below, sultry Michelle Pfeiffer in "The Fabulous Baker Boys."

The 1990 Fat Boy, distinctive silver on silver with subtle yellow accents.

Actor Mickey Roucke rode a Harley on and off the set.

Farom sixteen percent of production in 1987, exports of Harley-Davidson motorcycles grew steadily to over thirty percent by 1991, even as total production continued to rise significantly. Top export markets included Canada, West Germany, Japan and Australia with channels of distribution in virtually every other industrialized nation in the world. Because of the Company's success in the overseas market, Wisconsin Governor Tommy Thompson remarked, "Harley-Davidson is a great example of a respected American manufacturer bouncing back from adversity. It's great to see another fine Wisconsin product take the offensive in our global economy."

So successful had Harley-Davidson become by that time that its Board of Directors approved a two-for-one stock split. In exactly four years, Harley-Davidson stock had soared from an original issue price of eleven dollars a share to around fifty-six dollars. The split, the first of many in the next years to come, served to bring the cost of individual shares down to a more generally affordable level and allowed more investors to join the Harley-Davidson family.

The 1991 model year saw two very important product developments. The first was the addition of belt drive and a five-speed transmission to all Sportster models. These were improvements riders had been asking for since they appeared on the Big Twin models earlier and served to make the entire Sportster line more attractive to a host of enthusiasts.

Left,
the ledgendary actress Greta Garbo
and the 50's love godess Ava Gardner
made their exits.

The second, and more significant, announcement was the introduction of an updated version of an old favorite, the Sturgis model. Similar in appearance to its 1980 predecessor, the 1991 Sturgis was built a on new platform called the Dyna Glide chassis. The first Harley-Davidson model devised from the ground up using computer-aided design technology, the FXDB Sturgis featured a totally new frame, a two-point rubber isolation system for the drivetrain, an oil tank located under the transmission, a more accessible rear drive belt and redesigned locks using high-security round keys. The new black-on-black Sturgis combined the look of the ever-popular rigid-mount FX models of the Seventies and Eighties with the tight handling and smooth ride enthusiasts expected in a Nineties motorcycle. The Sturgis was just the first of what was to be a full line of Dyna models.

Wisconsin's Governor Tommy Thompson

Sequels made box office bonanzas for Bruce Willis in "Die Hard 2" and Mel Gibson in Lethal Weapon 2." While Arnold Schwarzenegger rode his FLSTF Fat Boy to another multi-million dollar success in "Terminator 2"

The Sturgis resurrected images of its 1980 predecessor in a Nineties chassis.

The summer of 1991 saw the world plunged into turmoil as the massive military forces of Iraq poured across the border to invade neighboring Kuwait. As the nation and the world condemned the aggression of Saddam Hussein, the U.S. and its allies mounted a coalition of forces to assemble in nearby Saudi Arabia not only to free tiny Kuwait, but to secure the region from further encroachments by Iraq. Through the balance of the year, Iraqi forces held their positions as the Coalition gradually built its forces.

This holding action, dubbed Desert Shield, ignited the fervor of the U.S. citizenry in an outpouring of support for military action unheard of in decades. As American reservists were called to active duty, Harley-Davidson stepped forth in its traditional support of military personnel and announced one of the most generous military leave policies in the country for employees who were called up. Early in 1992, the U.S. and its allies unleashed a high-tech military operation on the forces of Iraq that brought the invaders to their knees in a matter of weeks.

Above, General "Stormin' Norman" Schwarzkopf led allied forces to quick and decisive victory in Operation Desert Storm.

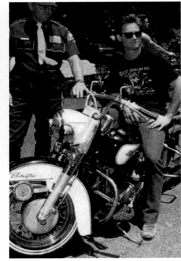

Right, "Backdraft" star, Kurt Russell astride his Harley, and above, actor James Marshall played a Harley enthusiast in the TV series "Twin Peaks."

The 1992 Dyna-Daytona featured Harley-Davidson's first true pearl production paint.

By 1992, Harley-Davidson's efforts were paying off handsomely in the international market and it commanded a whopping 62.3 percent of the 850cc and larger motorcycle market in the U.S. Stock prices kept rising and consumer demand was at all time highs as production struggled to meet demand. A brief strike in February, coupled with some production problems, caused a temporary shortage of product at the beginning of the selling season. One of the major contributors was the inability of the paint shop at York to keep up with production. The solution was a state-of-the-art, thirty-two million dollar robotic paint shop that soon began producing quality paint unheard of in the motorcycle and automotive industries at that time. That, and the installation of a dedicated Sportster assembly line, soon brought production back into line and new motorcycles were once again rolling out to eager dealers and customers worldwide.

A sad note in May of 1992 was the passing of William H. Davidson. Son of Company co-founder William A. Davidson and father of Willie G. Davidson, he served as vice president, president for twenty-nine years and, later, two years as chairman before retiring in 1973. While no longer active in the Motor Company he, nonetheless, remained a visible presence in the community and in motorcycling.

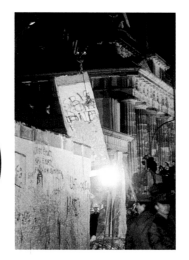

Left, Harley-Davidson's new 32 million dollar paint facility at York, PA plant.

Right, stylish screen actress Audrey Hepburn succumbed to cancer.

Above, Germans celebrate the end of the Berlin Wall and Cold War separation.

The celebration of the fiftieth anniversary of Daytona Bike Week saw all the usual attractions, but in greater abundance. There were beautiful bikes, miles of stunning beaches, more beautiful bikes, absolutely beautiful weather, more bikes, welcome sunshine, crowds of bikers and the ever-present Nancy and Willie G. Davidson.

283

# WILLIAM H. DAVIDSON

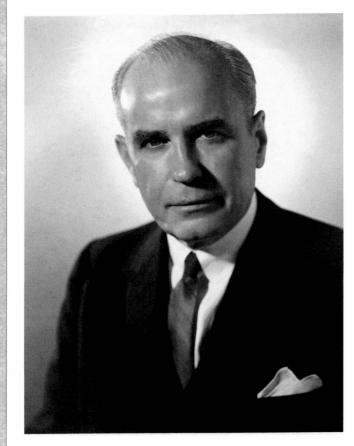

first of the superbikes. In 1971, Harley-Davidson announced the FX Super Glide which ushered in a whole new class of motorcycles, the cruisers.

Under his direction, Harley-Davidson pursued additional business opportunities other than big motorcycles. Two stroke lightweights were added to the line in 1948 and expanded in 1961 to include Italian imports. Also in the early Sixties, Harley-Davidson entered the golf car market which it dominated for several years, to be followed in the early Seventies with an entrance into the burgeoning snowmobile market. Finally, the Motor Company's manufacturing capabilities were greatly enhanced with the acquisition of the Capital Drive plant and the fiberglass facility in Tomahawk, Wisconsin.

William H. learned to ride on an opposed cylinder Sport Model. During his tenure at Harley-Davidson, he was an avid motorcyclist, often riding a sidecar rig all year long, with a lap blanket to keep him warm in the winter. As a child, William H's son, Willie G., recalled his father bringing bikes home. "It was really exciting for us as kids. He would bring these great bikes home and park them in the garage and we would go out there and look at them."

A superb rider and racing enthusiast, William H. won the grueling 500-mile Jack Pine Endurance Run in 1930 with a perfect 1000 points on known checkpoints and 997 points on the secret checks, the highest score ever reported. He could often be found in the pits or at the finish line of racing events large and small around the country, lending his personal support, encouragement and congratulations to Harley-Davidson team racers.

On May 22, 1992 William H. Davidson, son of Harley-Davidson Motor Company co-founder William A. Davidson, passed away quietly in his home just a short distance from the company he had devoted 45 years of his life to. He was 87 years old.

William H. started in 1928, like all the second generation, in a low-level job in order to "learn the ropes" of the motorcycle business from the ground up. He was elected a director of the Company in 1931 and, following the untimely death of his father in 1937, was named vice president. In 1942, he advanced to the presidency, succeeding his uncle Walter, who had served in that capacity from the beginning of the Motor Company.

William H. held the office of president for thirty-two years. Under his guidance, he saw to it that Harley-Davidson kept the U.S. military and its Allies supplied with motorcycles, spare parts and technical training for the war effort during World War II. As a result Harley-Davidson received the prestigious Army-Navy "E Award" several times for exceptional war production.

After the war, Mr. Davidson guided his company back into peacetime production with the introduction of the Panhead overhead valve V-twin engine with its advanced aluminum heads and hydraulic valve lifters. Also during his presidency, he saw the development of the 750cc Model K which eventually evolved into the Sportster, the

After serving as company president longer than any other before or since, William H. was named chairman in 1971 and retired two years later. Always interested in history, he devoted much of his last year with the Motor Company trying to identify and organize some of the Company's considerable archival materials. Always impeccably dressed, he could be seen in the halls in his tie and vest with some picture or document he had uncovered. His excitement over the discovery was contagious as he would share his new-found knowledge with fellow employees.

While not directly involved with the Motor Company any longer, he remained understandably deeply interested in its progress and development. Both sons, John and Willie G., remained as company officers. "What's new at the works?" greeted both Davidson brothers whenever they met with their father. "Then we would have to relate every little detail of what was going on back at the offices." said Willie G.

During his years with the Motor Company, William H. had been a key contributor as an officer and a director to the American Motorcycle Association and the Motorcycle, Scooter and Allied Trades Association, later to be known as the Motorcycle Industry Council.

He was also a leader in many activities outside the world of motorcycles, as well. His interests included a long time participation in Boy Scout work, culminating in him being named president of the Milwaukee County Boy Scout Council. His additional interests ranged from a directorship of the Seventh Federal Reserve Bank to such diverse activities as director and, in some cases, officer of the Better Business Bureau, United Fund, Greater Milwaukee Committee, and several planning and development commissions for the State of Wisconsin.

Following his retirement, William H. Davidson remained devoted to the business world. He worked with the business school of the University of Wisconsin-Milwaukee developing hypothetical business problems for study and then serving as a critic and advisor to those trying to solve them.

At the funeral service for William H. Davidson, many family members, friends, dealers and Harley-Davidson employees showed up to pay their respects to the man who devoted so much of his life to the Motor Company, the sport of motorcycling and the community. Perhaps the telling tribute was the many local bikers who arrived to honor the passing of one of the true gentleman of the sport and the last connection to the original founders.

Above, William H. with sons John, left and Willie G.

Always a race fan, William H. Davidson, center, was on hand at a 1973 Daytona Beach press conference honoring the Harley-Davidson road racing team.

**E**arly in 1993 Harley-Davidson management outlined a program to dramatically increase production over time to meet the ever-growing demand for the Company's motorcycles. Called Plan 2003, it would provide Harley-Davidson with the capability to build 200,000 motorcycles annually within ten years. It was quick to point out, however, that the key was to have the capability, not necessarily the intent, to produce at that level. Sales were at an all time high and no one could be sure it could be sustained, though the Company felt it should be prepared for continued growth.

It was the Ninetieth Anniversary of Harley-Davidson in 1993 and the occasion was marked by the introduction of a pair of new models and updating an existing one, the FLHT, with a new frame. The Dyna Wide Glide provided riders with the custom looks of the Softail combined with the smooth ride of a rubber-mounted drivetrain. Complete with bobtail rear fender, stepped seat and high handlebars, the Wide Glide bore a strong resemblance to its FX namesake of a decade earlier.

An equally striking motorcycle was the FLSTN Heritage Softail Nostalgia. Finished in stark black and white, its distinguishing features were natural cowhide inserts (complete with the hair), on the seat as well as on the accessory saddlebags, passenger backrest and windshield bag. Quickly dubbed the "Cow Glide" or the "Moo Glide", the Nostalgia became an instant collectors item.

Liam Neeson in 1993's Best Picture winner "Schindler's List"

Only Harley-Davidson could produce a bike with cowhide saddle bags inserts still sporting the hair. Little wonder the Nostalgia was soon dubbed the "Moo Glide."

## Harley-Davidson® MotorClothes™... *Feel The Difference*

## THE ULTIMATE DRESSER IS OFF THE WALL.

Everyone knows that your standard Harley-Davidson® is a thing of beauty. But the true Harley,® the ultimate machine, is the one that you customize. It's tailored. Personalized. An expression of yourself.

That's why your local Harley dealer has his walls full of *Genuine* Harley-Davidson accessories. Quality accessories to enhance the beauty of your ride. From luggage racks to lighted chrome rails. Air cleaners to chrome fender skirts. Classic caliper/rotor covers, custom mufflers and more. Everything the well-dressed Dresser needs.

So go ahead. Treat yourself. The ultimate Dresser is within your reach... on your Harley dealer's wall.

**HARLEY-DAVIDSON**
MOTOR CYCLES®
**AUTHORIZED DEALER**

*Where The Legend Begins.*

Call 1-800-443-2153 to find the authorized Harley-Davidson dealer nearest you.

## STOP AT HARLEY® TO START YOUR CHRISTMAS SHOPPING.

The first stop on your Christmas shopping list ought to be where the legend begins—at your local Harley dealer. You'll find special gifts for riders, non-riders and little riders, too. It's all there, from Hog® banks to Hugger jackets. V-Twin watches to earrings. Bar & Shield shirts to stars & stripes kids' jackets. Cologne to phones. Footboard and fork leg covers, oil tank trim and more to deck out your machine. Even Harley gift wrap. Get started with a stop at your Harley-Davidson® dealer today.

Call 1-800-443-2153 to find the authorized Harley-Davidson dealer nearest you.

**HARLEY-DAVIDSON**
MOTOR CYCLES®
**AUTHORIZED DEALER**

*Where Your Christmas Shopping Begins.*

"Buffy, The Vampire Slayer" fighting evil forces, every Monday on THE WB.

287

I n June, in celebration of its ninetieth year, the Harley-Davidson Motor Company hosted a huge party at Milwaukee's festival grounds on the shore of Lake Michigan. Nearly 70,000 Harley-Davidson aficionados from all over the world enjoyed the rides, the motorcycles, the music and the people who made the celebration the motorcycling event of the year. The city and the motorcyclists gained new respect for each other as bikers and non-bikers alike turned out to celebrate.

Erik Buell had been a Harley-Davidson engineer when he quit to form his own small company specializing in building sport bikes. By 1987 he was using either a 1200 Sportster motor or an XR-1000 motor to power his uniquely-styled street machines. Realizing he was on to a good idea, the Motor Company purchased a forty-nine percent interest in Buell Motor Company in order to provide the technological and financial resources needed to make Buell a force in the sport bike market. Gradually, the line began to expand and gain recognition as the might of the Motor Company assembled its forces behind the tiny manufacturer.

The Road King made its debut in the product line for 1994 to much critical acclaim. It nicely filled a niche for riders who wanted the stylish and stable platform of the FLHT but without the added weight and visual mass of Tour Pak and fairing. With its distinctive paint scheme and tasteful application of chrome and paint, the Road King rapidly became the ride of choice for many motorcyclists. Also, with the growing acceptance of the Dyna line of motorcycles, the remaining FXR models saw their last full production year.

The Road King evoked images of the Fifties.

Tom Hanks won back-to-back Oscars for his performances in "Philadelphia" and "Forrest Gump."

Part of NBC's must see TV, "ER" and "Friends."

Because the product line was growing and plans for future new models were on the drawing boards, Harley-Davidson began planning what was to become a 217,000 square foot Product Development Center on the grounds of its Capitol Drive plant on Milwaukee's far west side. Eventually named after Willie G. Davidson, the PDC would be home for all of the Motor Company's engineering, design and experimental staff members.

Always a major force on the American dirt tracks, Harley-Davidson once again proved its racing dominance by virtue of team racer Scott Parker winning an unprecedented fifth AMA Grand National Championship title, eclipsing the record held by his predecessor, Carroll Resweber, for over thirty years. In an effort toward earning a similar record in a different racing environment, Harley-Davidson rolled out a powerful 1000cc, 60-degree liquid-cooled V-twin racer to compete in the Superbike series. Despite drawing considerable attention from the fans and motorcycle press alike, the VR-1000 never quite lived up to expectations and Harley-Davidson eventually withdrew from the ultra-competitive sport at the end of the 2001 season.

The classic look of the Eighties was resurrected in a state-of-the art chassis in the 1994 Dyna Wide Glide.

The Electra Glide, born in 1965, commemorated its thirtieth anniversary with the announcement of a special edition Ultra Classic version that featured Harley-Davidson's first production fuel injection on a street bike. Handsomely detailed in Burgundy Pearl and Black, the full-dress Ultra represented the epitome of American touring comfort. A low-end version of the Electra Glide, called the Standard, also debuted in 1995, for those seeking the ride without the frills. Both versions of the Electra Glide sold well as production topped 100,000 units for the first time.

The Motor Company realized by this time that, if it was to continue to try to meet a growing demand for its motorcycles, it needed to relieve the pressure on its assembly plant in York, Pennsylvania. Even as plans were being finalized for a brand new Sportster assembly plant in Kansas City, Missouri, two new Sportster models were being introduced for 1996, the XL1200C Custom and the XL1200S Sport. The Custom created a new top-of-the-line model with a 21-inch front wheel, custom handlebar riser, bullet headlight and generous applications of chrome and wrinkle black paint. The Sport catered to a different breed of rider with its dual spark ignition, high compression heads, hot cams and gas-reservoir rear shocks. Both were welcome additions and a testimonial to the growing popularity of the entry level Harley-Davidson models.

Above, Brad Pitt showed off his acting skills in "Seven."

Pamela Anderson became a pin-up icon starring in the syndicated series "Baywatch."

The entrance to the modern Willie G. Davidson Product Development Center on the grounds of the Capitol Drive plant.

Two new Sportsters debuted in 1996, above, the stylish 1200C Custum and right, the nimble and response 1200S Sport.

Will Smith became a superstar after starring in the mega hit "Men in Black."

Madonna continued to be as breathless as usual.

291

To better serve its dealer network and its customers, Harley-Davidson broke ground for a quarter of a million square foot, sophisticated parts and accessories distribution center in a southern suburb of Milwaukee in 1996. Later that year, it also announced it was selling its Holiday Rambler Division. Never really a profitable part of the business, Holiday Rambler was generally viewed by financial analysts as a drain on company resources and long recommended its sale. Harley-Davidson once again concentrated all its resources on its core business, building quality motorcycles.

Ever-growing, Harley-Davidson purchased an existing Briggs & Stratton plant in the northern suburbs the next year for additional engine assembly. The Big Twin engine assembly line was soon moved from the Capitol Drive plant to what was to become known as the Pilgrim Road plant. In the Spring, the parts and

Fox's hit series "The X Files" became a movie, and Tom Cruise had another multi-million dollar hit with "Mission: Impossible."

"The English Patient" came away withe best pctures honors in 1996.

The latest trip down memory lane for the Harley-Davidson styling department was the retro 1997 Heritage Springer which conjured images of the 1948 Panhead.

accessories operation was moved from its Juneau Avenue site to the new Franklin Distribution Center freeing up space for the corporate Archives and, eventually, a huge dealer training facility called Harley-Davidson University.

Also in 1997, the $25million Product Development Center opened on the Capitol Drive grounds with state-of-the-art engineering, testing and laboratory facilities. It featured such amenities as a full-vehicle simulator, the most advanced in the world, especially designed for Harley-Davidson and a "mock-up" area to enhance the product development process.

Rows of newly assembled Big Twin motors lined up at the Pilgrim Road plant.

"Titanic" not only won the Oscar for best picture in 1997, it became the biggest box office hit of all time.

An earthquake rocks Los Angeles killing more than 60 people.

Israeli Prime Minister Rabin signs accord ending 27-year occupation of Gaza Strip.

CIA officer Aldrich Ames arrested on charges of selling information to Russia.

1995

O. J. Simpson is acquitted of murdering his wife.

400,000 African-American men participate in Million Man March in Washington D.C.

The United Nations celebrates its fiftieth birthday.

Terrorists release sarin gas in Tokyo subway killing 12.

1996

Russian president Boris Yeltsin re-elected with 55% of the vote.

FBI agents arrest the elusive Unabomber, Ted Kaczynski, at his Montana home.

England's Prince Charles and his wife, Diana, divorce.

1997

Dolly, the sheep, becomes the first cloned animal.

Hong Kong reverts to China after long rule by Great Britain.

Timothy McVeigh found guilty of the Oklahoma City bombing of a federal building.

On January 6, 1998, after more than a year of preparation, the first Sportster came off the assembly line at the new 330,000 square foot Kansas City plant. At a cost of $85 million, the sophisticated facility featured ergonomically-friendly production lines which raise, lower or rotate to accommodate varying types of workers and jobs. "We've been able to utilize information and ideas gleaned from our existing facilities over the years to create, from a clean sheet of paper, a collaborative working environment for motorcycle production." stated Harley-Davidson CEO Jeff Bleustein at its dedication.

Later in the year, in recognition of its growing prominence in the motorcycle world, Harley-Davidson purchased the majority of Buell, naming Erik Buell chairman and chief technical officer. Buell was becoming the fastest growing motorcycle company in the world, as a percent of sales if not in sheer volume, as riders grew to appreciate the alternative offering in the sport bike field. The model line gradually grew, both in number and sophistication, as Erik Buell applied his own unique concepts to his creations.

Harley-Davidson and the 400,000 member Harley Owners Group both celebrated birthdays in 1998 with back to back parties in Milwaukee. HOG hosted tens of thousands of its members at the Wisconsin State Fair Grounds in the days preceding the Motor Company's 95th anniversary event, once again at the lakefront, where close to 100,000 revelers assembled. A number

One of the highlights of the Ninety-fifth was the motorcycle parade down Milwaukee's Wisconsin Avenue where it was difficult to determine who was more thrilled, the motorcyclists or the spectators.

"Shakespeare In Love" won seven Oscars including one for best picture.

of special models were produced for the anniversary, all with unique paint and a cloisonné tank emblem, most notably a new model called the Road Glide. While somewhat resembling the older Tour Glide, the new FLTR sported a sleeker fairing and optional fuel injection.

It was a good year for Harley-Davidson personalities as Scott Parker dialed in his ninth AMA Grand National Championship title and fifth consecutive title, both feats never before equaled in the annals of American dirt track racing. With ninety-one wins to his credit, he was far and away the most successful dirt tracker of all times. Four other names familiar to Harley-Davidson were equally honored but in a different way. The four founders--William S. Harley, Arthur Davidson, Walter Davidson and William A. Davidson-- were inducted into the Motorcycle Hall of Fame in recognition of their contributions to the sport of motorcycling.

With a more streamlined fairing and swept-back looks, the 1998 FLTR Road Glide was an updated version of the discontinued Tour Glide.

Below, Inducted into the Hall of Fame, from left, William A. Davidson, Walter Davidson, Arthur Davidson and William S. Harley.

"The Matrix" starring Keanu Reeves changed the look of action film forever.

Above, In January 1998, the first Sportsters began rolling off the line at the new Kansas City assembly plant.

Left, 100,000 of Harley-Davidson's closest friends converged on Milwaukee to help celebrate the Motor Company's 95th birthday.

Above,
President Clinton
in the middle of
his impeachment
proceedings.

lways eager to to expand its customer base, Harley-Davidson launched three innovative programs in 1999. The first involved the formation of a new department, called Custom Vehicle Operations, specializing in low volume, high trim models targeted at custom motorcycle aficionados. Because of an existing following for the now-discontinued FXR models, the first CVO creation was a resurrected FXR with custom paint and extra chrome trim. Called the FXR2, less than a thousand were made in each of two colors. Later, FXR3 and FXR4 versions, all with even more extensive custom treatments and exotic paint, soon followed.

Also that year, the Motor Company launched the Harley-Davidson Authorized Rentals program with the purpose of exposing riders to the products and thereby creating further demand. Starting with five locations in three states, the program rapidly grew to more than 200 locations worldwide. Rental customers were offered the use of late-model Harleys as well as rain suits, luggage storage, emergency roadside assistance and insurance. Because the motorcycles are maintained to Motor Company standards, customers are assured of riding the best motorcycle rentals available.

The third program to be rolled out that year concerned itself with a topic always important to Harley-Davidson, that of motorcycle safety. Called Rider's Edge, the program taught both new and experienced motorcyclists safe riding skills. The New Rider Course, offered at select Harley-Davidson/Buell dealerships, featured both classroom and range instruction for novices taught by Motorcycle Safety Foundation certified instructors. Riding a new 2000 Buell lightweight model, students who successfully completed the course received their MSF card, which could potentially assist them in getting their motorcycle license and insurance. A second part of the program, directed at the more experienced riders, concentrated on improving a motorcyclist's group riding skills.

Rich Teerlink,
who engineered the
refinancing effort that
saved Harley-Davidson
from bankruptcy in 1985,
led the Motor Company
through the Nineties to
retire in 1999.

HOG rallies
continued to attract
the faithful during
the Nineties.

Styling Department's concept
of the Screamin' Eagle dragster.

## SCREAMIN' EAGLE PRO STOCK TEAM

For the National Hot Rod Association's 1999 racing season, Harley-Davidson
Screamin' Eagle Performance Parts teamed up with Walters/Korn Racing to
compete in the highly competitive Pro Stock drag racing series. The
Screamin' Eagle team featured riders Rob Korn and Lori Francis aboard
all-new Walters/ Korn-prepared Pro Stock drag bikes. The dragsters,
designed by Harley-Davidson's styling department, featured several
variants of Big Twin engines including the Twin Cam 88 in a massive 160
cubic inch version.

Rob Korn was the quickest Pro Stock Harley racer on the circuit upon joining
the team and holder of numerous elapsed time and top speed records and
championships in various classes. His teammate, the talented Lori Francis, was a
two-time AMRA Pro Stock champion and had captured twelve Harley drag racing records.

1998

President Bill
Clinton, following
lengthy denials,
admits to affair with
Monica Lewinsky.

Summer
temperatures
around the country
soar to record
highs as hundreds
perish.

Mark McGwire
sets a season
record of 70
homeruns, breaking
Roger Maris'
1961 mark..

1999

Two students at
Columbine High
School in Littleton,
CO go on shooting
spree killing 13
plus themselves.

To its great
embarrassment,
NASA loses two
Mars probes.

The European
Union creates a
new common
currency,
the Euro.

The 1990's, a decade of unparalleled growth and development for the
Motor Company, ended on a positive note with the unveiling of the first
all-new V-twin engine since the 1936 Knucklehead. Called the Twin Cam
88, the new motor utilized a pair of cams instead of the traditional single
cam found in previous Big Twins, similar in design to the Two Cam models
of the late Twenties. Completely redesigned inside and out, the new motor
underwent 2 1/2 million miles of testing before going into production.
Installed in the touring and Dyna product lines, the Twin Cam motor
provided increased power, performance and reliability,
plus an improved ride, by virtue of a rigid union between
engine and transmission.

As the Motor Company looked forward to starting the next
decade, it was difficult to imagine that the unprecedented
popularity and growth of Harley-Davidson and its product
line could be sustained into the 2000's. But the momentum the Harley-Davidson Motor Company had built up in
the Nineties would prove to be the impetus it needed to
launch itself full-bore into the next millenium.

# THE 2000'S

## Beginning a New Millennium

THE 2000'S

epending on what source you believed, the new Millennium either started in 2000 or the old one ended in 2000. Either way, a new era dawned that year for the Harley-Davidson Motor Company as its best-selling model line, the ever-popular Softail models, received a major boost with a stunning new model, new frames and a brand new engine.

The year before, the touring bikes and the Dyna models received the powerful 1450cc Twin Cam 88 motor while the Softail line retained the proven 80 cubic inch Evolution. The only complaint riders had with the Softail family, up to that time, was the vibration. The drivetrain on Softail motorcycle was bolted solidly to the frame, creating vibration, unlike the rubber-isolated drivetrains in the Twin Cam-powered models. All the vibration virtually vanished with the introduction of a counter-balanced version of the new motor, called the Twin Cam 88B, which combined the smoothness of the rubber-mounts with the low-slung seating position traditional to the Softail models, all nestled in a redesigned frame.

Even bigger news, however, was the unveiling of a new Softail model, called the Deuce, which mirrored contemporary customizing trends. With its shotgun dual exhausts, cut-off rear fender and stretched tanks, it projected a unique

Below, Julia Roberts, Meg Ryan and Sandra Bullock continue to be Hollywood's most bankable darlings

302

look unlike any stock Harley-Davidson model before it. Furthering its custom appearance, it also sported long, graceful forks topped by a pair of set-back handlebar risers that swept back to a sleek tank-mounted instrument panel. Finishing the radical look was a 21-inch laced wheel on the front and a 17-inch disc wheel with an extra wide tire on the rear. The Deuce quickly became one the best-received models in Harley-Davidson history.

Back in 1993, Harley-Davidson put forth Plan 2003, a ten-year plan to enable the Company to build 200,000 motorcycles at the end of the period. Some market analysts had criticized the plan as being too aggressive, arguing that the Motor Company's growth could not be sustained over such a long time. Once again, Harley-Davidson proved the skeptics wrong as it not only created the means to build that number of motorcycles, but actually did produce more than that amount in 2000 in an attempt to meet worldwide demand. Plan 2003 was not only completed three years early, but by 2003 Harley-Davidson was scheduled to build over a quarter of a million motorcycles for its world markets.

Buell rocked the sport bike world by introducing a sporty little model it called the Blast. Powered by a 492cc air-cooled, four stroke single cylinder engine, the Blast provided distinct styling with the throaty sound of a type of motorcycle commonly called a thumper. Lightweight, nimble, easy to operate and handle, and with a low seating height, the Blast was perfect for the novice rider. The Rider's Edge New Rider Course adopted the Blast as the official training bike for its programs. Soon, nearly half the new Blast motorcycles being sold were to female riders.

Willie G Davidson, hall of fame inductee.

The sleek, new Deuce

Above, Dylan McDermott, star of ABC's highly rated and award winning series "The Practice."

Left, The lightweight and nimble 2000 Buell Blast.

"The Mummy Returns" grossed over 400 million dollars world wide.

The summer of 2000 saw the Olympics being held in Sydney, Australia and Harley-Davidson motorcycles were selected to be escort vehicles for the torchbearers. Willie G Davidson, in recognition of his tremendous influence on the design of American motorcycles, was inducted into the Hall of Fame like his grandfather two years earlier. And perennial racing favorite, Scott Parker, with the most successful career in dirt track racing history, announced he was hanging up his hotshoe after the 2000 season. With nine AMA Grand National Championship titles to his credit, he had raced to heights no one had ever gone before.

Racing history was once again made by Harley-Davidson as the first female member of the factory race team took to the nation's dirt tracks. Seventeen-year-old Jennifer Snyder, wearing the factory team's leathers, signed on to campaign on the AMA and Formula USA dirt track circuits for 2001. "I'm really excited to be part of the factory team and race with Rich King as my teammate." Having finished sixth in the standings the year before, despite competing in only seven of the races, she exhibited a style and talent that caught the eye of Harley-Davidson and led to a contract. The Motor Company's faith in her abilities proved to be well-founded as she soon scored the first national win ever by a woman.

Hugh Jackman, Guy Pearce, Russell Crowe and Nicole Kidman are four Australians making a big impression in movies today.

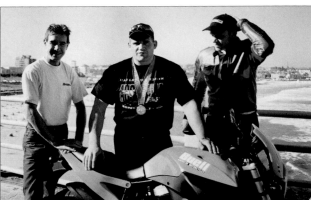

Left, Olympic Gold Medal winner Rulon Gardner and a Buell.

Below, A quartet of special Road Kings prepare to guide the Olympic flame to it's destination.

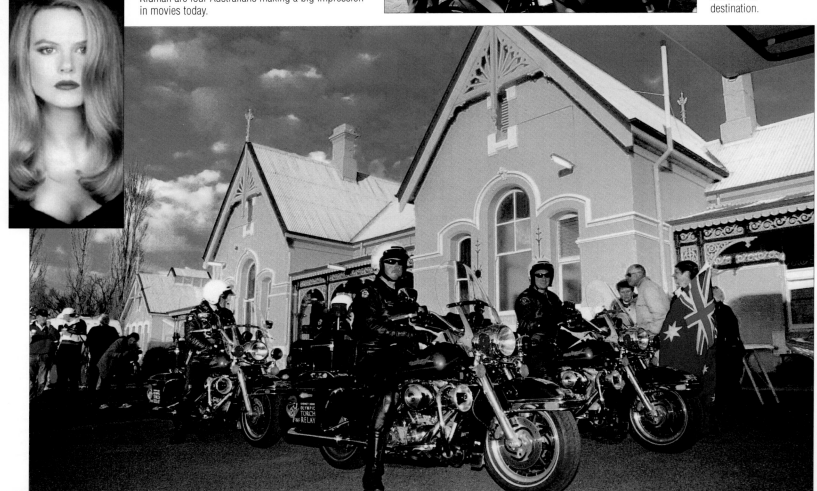

That year was one of more expansion for the Motor Company as plans were announced for additions to its Capitol Drive and Tomahawk, Wisconsin facilities, including a huge addition to the Willie G. Davidson Product Development Center. A month later, it released information on a new 350,000 square foot facility on the York, Pennsylvania plant site that would increase its area to over 1.5 million square feet of manufacturing space. Earlier, the plant had rolled its two millionth bike off the assembly line. In September, Harley-Davidson made a further announcement explaining it was moving assembly of Dyna vehicles from York to the Kansas City plant in order to better utilize the company's manufacturing resources to increase production. Over a six-month period, the Dyna assembly operation was integrated into Kansas City where they would be built alongside the Sportsters.

# THE FIRST LADY OF RACING

Late in 2001, it was announced that Harley-Davidson would boldly go where no man has ever gone before by naming a woman to its dirt track racing team. Jennifer Snyder, 17, of Grand Saline, Texas joined Rich King as the newest professional racer to wear the orange, black and white factory racing leathers. Initially signed to race in the Formula USA Pro Singles Series, Snyder also gained experience on the faster, more powerful XR-750 dirt track racer in the AMA series.

Jennifer began racing at age 11 when her father, Joe Snyder, built a track on their property so she could train and practice. "I grew up watching Scott Parker race" she said, "and I followed his career closely. We both started racing at eleven and he's been a huge influence on me."

Snyder debuted at the Formula USA opener on April 30, 2000 in stunning fashion by dominating qualifying and then, following a poor start in the final, working her way up through the pack, passing eight riders in just four laps. Battling against her teammate, King, and other top competitors, she made a daring last-lap pass in turn three to take the lead to the checkered flag. Her win marked the first time a woman had scored a national win in the history of dirt track racing.

Legendary tuner, Bill Werner, summed it up nicely with the statement, "She's the real deal." By mid-season, she was really demonstrating her skills by moving into second place in the standings, a mere six points behind the leader. Unfortunately, while battling for the lead at a race in Seattle in September, she drifted wide and crashed, suffering injuries serious enough to sideline her for the balance of the season. . Tough competitor she is, Jennifer spent the winter months getting herself back into shape for the 2002 season.

September also saw the United States and the world change forever as terrorists hijacked four jetliners and flew them into the World Trade Center, the Pentagon building and a field in Pennsylvania. The loss of life and equipment in New York alone was staggering as thousands perished, including hundreds of police and firefighters. The outpouring of grief and compassion for the victims and their families of this terrible attack was unlike anything ever experienced before as samaritans throughout the country donated time, money and needed materials to the cause.

Harley-Davidson donated the use of thirty police motorcycles and one million dollars to assist in the relief efforts in New York and Washington, D.C. The motorcycles were used to replace vehicles lost in the attack on the World Trade Center while the cash donation was made directly to the American Red Cross for use in the relief effort. "While we can never get back what has been lost" stated Harley-Davidson President Jim McCaslin, "we're hopeful that the police motorcycles will help law enforcement and Port Authority representatives move around the city with greater ease and convenience." Ten motorcycles were ridden to New York from Milwaukee by Harley-Davidson employees and local police officers with the additional twenty arriving directly from York two weeks later. Individual employees, too, donated generously to the fund at boxes locate at all the plants.

Right, The first V-Rod off the line being inspected by (clockwise from upper left) styling director Louie Netz, CEO Jeff Bleustein, Willie G. Davidson, Karl Eberle, VP of the Kansas City plant, Earl Werner, VP of engineering, and Bill Davidson, director of product development.

The H.O.G. Route 66 riding rally ended in Chicago after crossing the country.

# SCREAMIN' EAGLE PRO STOCK RACING

The Screamin' Eagle Performance Parts division of Harley-Davidson teamed up with legendary Vance & Hines Motorsports to field its first Pro Stock drag bike for the 2002 season. The efforts combined the 90 years of Harley-Davidson racing knowledge and expertise with the winningest drag racing team in National Hot Rod Association history.

The awesome-looking machine, conceptually based on the new VRSCA V-Rod street bike, was powered by a 160 cubic inch. 60-degree, air-cooled V-twin with electronic fuel injection. Designed from the ground up by Byron Hines, the powerful engine produced nearly 340 horsepower, triple that of a stock Revolution motor.

Selected to ride the potent dragster was Gary Tonglet, Jr., rookie sensation of the drag racing circuit. Tonglet, or GT as he preferred to be called, was the perfect choice to pilot the Harley-Davidson quarter mile missile.   At eighteen, the New Orleans native was the youngest Pro Stock winner ever in 2001 and the fastest through the traps. "My goal is simply to win races. " he said. "I've been running hard for two years and getting this ride with Screamin' Eagle is a dream come true."

At its very first outing, the dragster with GT aboard raced through the quarter mile traps in an encouraging 7.572 seconds and 171.51 miles per hour, the fastest a Harley-Davidson motorcycle had ever run in Pro Stock competition. While not quite fast enough to qualify, it did demonstrate the tremendous potential of the machine and give testimony to the fact that, win or lose, it was going to revolutionize Pro Stock racing and bring new attention to the sport.

Willie G. Davidson with GT.

Elijah Wood stars as Frodo in "Lord of The Rings: The Fellowship of The Rings" one of the summer's biggest hits.

The Harley-Davidson Motor Company celebrated its birthdays with ever-growing parties in Milwaukee in 1988, 1993 and 1998. With the 100th Anniversary approaching in 2003, it was rapidly becoming apparent that the event would dramatically surpass the others in impact, scope and attendance. Plans were revealed to spread the celebration out over a fourteen-month period with a huge traveling show that would encompass ten venues worldwide. Vintage motorcycles and engines, antique toys, live music, displays of new bikes, demo rides, drill teams and more were to be offered to attendees at the world's biggest motorcycling birthday party. A convoy of eighty trucks would be required to move the huge event from location to location.

Buell once again took it to the streets with the introduction of a radical, all-new model called the XB9R Firebolt. With ground-up features unlike that of any other production sport bike, the 2002 Firebolt drew critical acclaim from the motorcycle press as they predicted it would be one of the landmark motorcycles of the new millennium. The Firebolt's engine was a 984cc air-cooled, fuel-injected V-twin which redlined at 7500 rpms while delivering a massive torque-to-weight ratio. The engine was nestled in a revolutionary, all-aluminum frame, the top of which was actually the fuel tank, thereby providing a lower center of gravity. Also assisting in that regard was the location of the oil tank in the rear swingarm.

Below,
The bike for the new Millennium, the 2002 Buell XB9R Firebolt.

Always known for having superb brakes, this Buell was even more impressive with a Zero Torsional Load front brake system, which consisted of an inside-out rotor and a six-piston caliper. In layman's terms, this meant that the extra large diameter disc was mounted on the rim instead of the hub and the caliper was inside of the disc rather than in the usual position, providing for maximum braking while reducing unsprung weight. This highly-effective system was the first to appear on a standard production motorcycle. The Firebolt easily provided the power and performance of a big-bore sport bike with the size and handling of a much smaller machine.

"Spiderman" breaks all opening weekend box office records.

The Harley-Davidson product line did not suffer from lack of innovation either as the Motor Company unveiled a revolutionary new model called the V-Rod. Powered by a 60-degree, liquid-cooled 1130cc V-twin Revolution engine, the all-silver motorcycle evoked images of drag bikes with its kicked-out front forks, low, sleek profile and gracefully upswept exhausts. Producing 115 horsepower, the V-Rod was easily the most powerful production Harley-Davidson motorcycle ever.

Right,
Two Michigan legends race for the lead, Jay Springsteen #9, and Scott Parker #1.

Middle, Scott and his longtime tuner, Bill Werner, celebrate another #1 plate.

Far right,
Demonstrating the Michigan style.

# THE AMAZING SCOTT PARKER

At five feet, six inches and 155 pounds, mild-mannered Scott Parker appears anything but one of the best motorcycle racers of all times. Born David Scott Parker, though preferring to use his middle name, the Michigan native is just one of many great dirt track racers to come from that northern state, though he is unquestionably the greatest. With nine AMA Grand National Championship titles and over ninety wins to his credit, he is the unsurpassed winningest rider in AMA history.

Scott burst onto the AMA Grand National circuit in 1979 when, as the youngest rider at 17 to carry an expert license, he ushered in his rookie year with two wins. His very first win, riding an XR 750 Harley-Davidson dirt track race bike, was at the Du Quoin, Illinois mile track which put him in the record books for the first of many times as the youngest rider to ever win an AMA Grand National race.

Exemplifying the Michigan-style of dirt track racing- taking a high line through the soft cushion to win- earned Parker the attention of legendary Harley-Davidson racing boss Dick O'Brien who promptly signed the talented rider to race for the factory team in 1982. He quickly proved O'Brien's confidence was well-founded as he started his trek to the record books.

In 1985, Scott raced the fastest mile race in AMA history with a blistering 102.047 miles per hour average at the Indianapolis Mile.  Three years later, he won the first of his nine titles as AMA Grand National Champion. The next year he repeated as champion and won ten races, a new record for victories in a single season. In 1991, Parker had a banner year, winning his forty-first race and breaking the record for all-time wins held by his fellow Michigan racer, Jay Springsteen. He also won his fourth consecutive title, tying the record held by Carroll Resweber from 1958 to 1961.

Parker didn't win the championship in 1992 or 1993 but returned to the top the next year with eight wins and the number one plate. In 1997, he once again tied Resweber's record of four consecutive titles, a distinction that became somewhat moot as he easily dialed in his fifth consecutive title the next year in grand style with seven first place finishes.

In 1999, Scott Parker announced he planned to retire after the 2000 season. With 91 victories under his belt and nine AMA Grand National Championship titles to his credit, he felt it was time to step down. " I love the competition and there's a great group of guys to race with" he said, "but its time to move on." Parker planned to spend more time with his family and his hobbies and only compete a few times a season.

He finished his final year as a full-time motorcycle racer, and eighteen years on the factory team, in true Scott Parker style by winning the last race of the season at Del Mar, California by a slender .713 second margin. Always thrilling to watch, his last act as a factory team racer only disappointed one person that day, the second place finisher.

With 93 wins, he retired after the 2002 season with more than twice the total of the two second place racers, Jay Springsteen and Chris Carr, combined, a record that will last a long time and may never be broken. Opting to race only a few select events a year, Scott Parker still proved himself the man to set the pace in the new Millenium as he continued to finish on the podium.

2000

Year 2000 safely arrives despite widespread fears of a worldwide computer breakdown .

George Bush wins disputed presidential election over Al Gore.

Summer Olympics open in Sydney Australia.

2001

World Trade Center destroyed in worst terrorist attack in U.S. history.

President Bush establishes Homeland Security department.

2002

Winter Olympics debut in Salt Lake City amidst unprecedented security.

U.S. government assumes control of airport security.

Harley-Davidson Open Road Tour begins in Atlanta.

2003

Open Road Tour circles the globe and concludes in Wisconsin.

Harley-Davidson Motor Company celebrates its 100th birthday.

The motorcycle media had the opportunity to ride pre-production models at a press conference unveiling the new machine and they were unanimous in both their amazement that such a motorcycle could come from Harley-Davidson and in the feel and performance of the bike itself. In fact, one magazine editor wrote that the V-Rod was not only the best Harley-Davidson he had ever ridden but may well be the best motorcycle he had ever ridden. Nearly every major motorcycle publication in the country, and several outside the U.S., featured the V-Rod on its cover.

Because its history is such an important aspect of its culture and heritage, Harley-Davidson has had a Traveling Museum roaming the country in a 48-foot semi trailer since 1988, making thousands of stops at major events and Harley-Davidson dealerships and entertaining millions of visitors along the way. The aging trailer was retired late in 2000 and a brand new, 53-foot version hit the road early in 2002. With huge slide-outs on each side, the latest Traveling Museum offers a snapshot of Harley-Davidson and motorcycling history in a spacious, well-lighted environment with ten vintage vehicles and a variety of clothing and items of memorabilia.

Above, Halle Berry made news winning best actress Oscar for her performance in "Monster's Ball."

The spacious Traveling Museum takes the history of the Motor Company on the road to hundreds of thousands of enthusiasts every year.

Right, dirt track racer and Harley-Davidson team member Rich King slides through a corner.

2003
Softail Deuce

In the summer of 2002, the Motor Company unveiled its 100th Anniversary models. For the first time since the Fiftieth Anniversary, every single motorcycle carried an anniversary badge. The three-dimensional cloisonné logo was prominently mounted on the sides of every gas tank regardless of whether it was the anniversary two-tone or one of the striking single colors. Also that summer, the Harley-Davidson dealer network converged on Milwaukee for the annual dealer convention where the 100th celebration was officially kicked off. Following the meeting, a large group of dealers on 2003 bikes, led by factory executives, rode to the first of the ten Open Road celebrations in Atlanta.

And the party was just beginning.

2003
Dyna Super Glide Sport

2003 Road King Classic

2003
Sportster 883 Hugger

2003
VRSCA V-Rod

Above,
actress/singer Jennifer Lopez
proves you can be both a beautiful
and a strong woman at the time.

# Photo Acknowledgements

FPG International Photo Collection:
Chapter One: Page 24, Photo 4; Page 28, Photo 1; Page 34, Photos 1, 2, 5; Page 35, Photos 2, 6, 7; Page 37, Photo 2; Page 41, Photo 2.
Chapter Two: Page 49, Photos 4, 5; Page 51, Photos 3, 4; Page 52, Photo 1; Page 53, Photos 2, 3; Page 55, Photo 2; Page 58, Photo 2;
         Page 59, Photo 4; Page 62, Photos 1, 2; Page 64, Photos 1, 2; Page 66, Photo 4, Page 68, Photo 1.
Chapter Three: Page 84, Photo 1; Page 91, Photo 5; Page 96, Photo 5; Page 102, Photos 1, 4; Page 105, Photo 1; Page 106, Photo 4
Chapter Four: Page 127, Photo 2; Page 129, Photos 3, 4, 9; Page 131, Photos 6, 7, 8, 9, 10, 12.
Chapter Five: Page 137, Photo 1; Page 138, Photo 1; Page 139, Photos 2, 4; Page 145, Photos 1, 2; Page 146, Photos 2, 4;
         Page 147, Photo 1; Page 150, Photo 3; Page 156, Photos1, 3; Page 157, Photos 4, 5, 6.
Chapter Six: Page 170, Photos 2, 3; Page 174, Photo 1; Page181, Photo 5.
Chapter Seven: Page 198, Photo 1; Page 200, Photo 1; Page 202, Photo 1; Page 203, Photos 2, 3, 4; Page 210, Photo 2;
         Page 212, Photo 4; Page 215, Photos 1, 5, 6.
Chapter Eight: Page 221, Photo2; Page 225, Photo 5, Page 227, Photo 3; Page 232, Photo 1; Page 245, Photo 2.
Chapter Nine: Page 262, Photos 1, 3; Page 273, Photos 2, 3.

From the James W. Craig Collection: Chapter Three: Page 99, "Sheik Of Araby" sheet music.

Anne Marie Hunter: Chapter Eleven: Page 300 & 301, Photo 1; Page 305, Photo 1; Page 306, Photo 2.

Photos and Movie Memorabilia from the Dale E. Kuntz Collection:
Chapter Three: Page 105, Photo 3.
Chapter Four: Page 127, Photo 3; Page 128, Photo 1; Page 130, Photo 2; Page 131, Photos 2, 11.
Chapter Five: Page 140, Photo 3; Page 141, Photo 5; Page 145, Photo 4; Page 147, Photo 4; Page 152, Photos 2. 3.
Chapter Seven: Page 215, Photo 3.

Gary Nastase: Chapter 10: Page 297, Photo 3.

Andrew Rosenthal: Chapter Eleven: Page 305, Photos 3, 4; Page 307, Photos 4, 5, 6; Page 309, Photos 1, 2, 3; Page 310, Photo 6.

Photos and Movie Memorabilia from the Frank Seiy Collection:
Chapter Three: Page 86, Photo 1; Page 99, Photos 5, 7, 10; Page 102, Photo 6; Page 106, Photo 4.
Chapter Four: Page 113, Photo 4; Page 116, Photo 1; Page 117, Photo 3; Page 119, Photos 2, 4, 5, 7, 9; Page 120, Photo 6;
         Page 121, Photos 2, 4; Page 122, Photo 5; Page 126, Photo 1, Page 128, Photos 6, 7, 8.
Chapter Five: Page 136, Photo 1; Page 144, Photo 1; Page 148. Photo 1; Page 149, Photo 151, Photo 1, 2; Page 153, Photo 3;
         Page 158, Photo 2; Page 159, Photos 2, 4, 5; Page 162, Photo 1; Page 163, Photo 4.
Chapter Six: Page 168, Photo 1; Page 172, Photo 3; Page 173, Photos 3, 4; Page 175, Photos 4, 5; Page 176, Photo1; Page 178, Photo 1;
         Page 180, Photos 1, 3; Page 181, Photo 1; Page 183, Photo 5; Page 184, Photo 1; Page 186, Photo 1; Page 187 Photo 4,
Chapter Seven: Page 193, Photo 3; Page 195, Photo 4; Page 196, Photos 2, 4; Page 201, Photos 7, 10; Page 204, Photos 2, 3;
         Page 205, Photo 5; Page 206, Photo 3; Page 207, Photos 2, 5, 6; Page 209, Photos 6, 8.
Chapter Eight: Page 224, Photo 1; Page 226, Photo 3; Page 228, Photo 1; Page 229, Photo 4; Page 231, Photo 3; Page 232, Photo 4;
         Page 233, Photo 3; Page 237, Photos 4,5; Page 238, Photo 1; Page 239, Photos 4, 5, 6, 7; Page 240, Photo 3;
         Page 243, Photos 3, 5; Page 245, Photo 5.
Chapter Nine: Page 250, Photo 1; Page 252, Photo 4; Page 253, Photos 3,4; Page 254, Photo 1; Page 256, Photos 1, 3;
         Page 259, Photos 1, 2; Page 260, Photos 1, 4; Page 263, Photos 2, 4, 6; Page 264, Photos 3, 4; Page 265, Photos 1, 2;
         Page 266, Photos1, 3, 4; Page 268, Photos 1, 3; Page 270, Photos 1, 3, 5, 6, 7.
Chapter Ten: Page 279, Photos 2, 4; Page 280, Photos 1, 2; Page 281, Photos 2, 3, 4; Page 282, Photos 3, 4, 5; Page 283, Photo 2,
         Page 286, Photo 2; Page 287, Photo 4; Page 288, Photos 5, 6, 7; Page 290, Photos 2, 3; Page 291, Photos 5, 6;
         Page 292, Photos 1, 2, 3; Page 293, Photo 3; Page 294, Photo 3; Page 295, Photo 4.
Chapter Eleven: Page 302, Photos 1, 2, 3; Page 303, Photos 3, 5; Page 304, Photos 2, 3, 4, 6; Page 307, Photo 7; Page 308, Photo 3;
         Page 310, Photo 2; Page 311, Photo 6.

From the Elizabeth B. Greeley Stamps and Buttons Collection:
Chapter Five: Page 138, Photos 1, 4, 7, 8; Page 138, Photo 2; Page 145, Photo 2; Page 146, Photo 1; Page 150, Photos 3, 4;
         Page 155, Photo 5; Page 156, Photo 1; Page 157, Photo 4.
Chapter Eight: Page 226, Photo 1.
Chapter Nine: Page 252, Photo 2.

United Photography:
         Chapter Ten: Page 296, Photo 1.
         Chapter Eleven: Page 307, Photos 1, 2, 3.

Wide World Photos, Inc. Chapter Ten: Page 281, Photo 1; Page 282, Photos 1, 2; Page 283, Photo 3.

From the Bernadine and Lawerence Ybema Collection: Chapter One: Page 35, Antique Victrola.

and all Harley-Davidson related photos from the Harley-Davidson Photo Archives.